# THE BALLYHOO BONANZA

Charles Sweeny and the Idaho Mines

# THE BALLYHOO BONANZA

## CHARLES SWEENY AND THE IDAHO MINES

By *John Fahey*

UNIVERSITY OF WASHINGTON PRESS

SEATTLE AND LONDON

*To the memory of* ORNA MARTIN FAHEY, *who saw much of it happen*

# PREFACE

*C*HARLES SWEENY rose from general storekeeper to become one of the foremost mining promoters of western America. Those who lived in his time would have predicted that his name would never be forgotten in Spokane, Washington, but few citizens now remember Sweeny or recognize his name as that of a man who was influential in the city's development. Sweeny built no monuments to himself. He neither donated a park nor chiseled his name on a building. He lived in houses built by other men. Because a good many of his contemporaries feared Sweeny, there were few who might have erected monuments to his memory.

He was ambitious and shrewd. He was a boastful, aspiring Irishman who lived by avarice, bombast, contention, daring—one could progress through the whole alphabet—and by vigor and wit. Sweeny's courtship of fortune helped form Spokane and the mining regions tributary to it. He was a catalyst in the evolution of great mines from prospect holes to corporations.

I believe this is one of the few studies of a speculative mining promoter written from raw files. It therefore provides a view not available in various authorized biographies of mining entrepreneurs.

Some readers will wish for an analysis of Sweeny's character and a moral judgment of him. I believe Sweeny often acted on impulses of the moment, that the book demonstrates so, and that retrospective analysis would yield little that is not apparent from the narrative. The extant fragments of correspondence between F. Lewis Clark, Sweeny, and Weldon B. Heyburn do not sustain his enemies' portrayal of Sweeny as a calculating schemer. From the Heyburn papers, Sweeny emerges as opportunistic but somewhat naïve in his grasp of corporation law.

Sweeny's career speaks for itself. The reader probably does not need to be reminded that business ethics were different then. If Sweeny is shown to be fallible and occasionally vacillating, I think this is because he did not often pause to consider the ethics of his spurt to wealth. When he thought about such things, he doubtless fell back to memorized catechism, and concluded that he was only doing as others were doing. He lived among men whose creeds were individualistic. A man who ventured into corporate finance had better be able to look out for himself.

No reliable general history has been published of the Coeur d'Alene mining district. Sweeny's career can serve as an introduction, although this study does not consider the entire story of the mines, by any means. I have extended the chapters on labor wars and the electrification of the mines beyond close attention to Sweeny himself because these events were crucial to the development both of Sweeny's projects and of the Coeur d'Alene district as a whole.

Inevitably some repetition and convolution occur in telling Sweeny's story because the events are often complex. Sweeny tried to cover his tracks for reasons that I believe evident. Had not many of his personal letters been saved by men who wanted to sue him, Sweeny might have obliterated his path.

While gathering information on Charles Sweeny I asked aid from many persons. Without suggesting that the following roster is complete, I wish to thank these listed for their gracious help:

Herman J. Deutsch, emeritus professor of history, Washington State University, for wise counsel on historical method and guidance in treatment of specific portions of this book; Henry L. Day, chairman of the board, Day Mines, for generous assistance with the language and law of mining operations; F. M. Ethridge, superviser of libraries, Consolidated Mining and Smelting Company of Canada, for suggestions and material on the Sullivan Group and concentrating processes; Charles C. Finucane, for his interest in the study and for opening the files of the Sweeny Investment Company to me; Mrs. Elizabeth S. Gilbert, former reference librarian, Spokane Public Library, for many kindnesses over a period of many years; Kimball I. Jack, Washington Water Power Company, for information on the company and on electrical development of the mines; Mary C. Johnson, reference librarian, Spokane Public Library, for finding the elusive references that I could describe only vaguely.

I would also like to thank George T. Krempasky, United States Bureau of Mines, for suggestions on the practices and terminology of mining; Norman E. Kilgore, former manager of the library, and his staff at the *Spokesman-Review,* for the use of newspaper files that provided the general framework of the story; Richard G. Magnuson, Wallace, Idaho, whose work in the newspapers of the mining district blazed a path for me; Kenneth D. McCord, for use of Washington Water Power Company library files; William D. Roberts, for loan of the E. J. Roberts papers; Edith M. Shaw, reference librarian, Eastern Washington State College, for help in locating documents; R. Worth Vaughan, vice chairman of the board and general counsel, American Smelting and Refining Company, for permission to use the company archives in Idaho and for his own inspection of Federal minutebooks on my behalf; and the late Ralph W. Watson, veteran Spokane realtor, for his observations on real estate practice.

The maps were drawn by Carol Hamm and Lee Tallyn of the Eastern Washington State College cartographic laboratory.

Many persons helped me as representatives of libraries, archives, governments, or associations. Among these are the staffs of the auditor, Spokane County; the Gonzaga University Law School; the Oakland, California, Public Library; the Portland, Oregon, Library Association; the Northwest Mining Association; the National Archives of the United States; the New York Public Library; the Washington State Library, Olympia; the University of Idaho, Moscow; the University of Washington, Seattle; and Washington State University, Pullman.

The Spokane Posse of the Westerners listened to several chapters read in draft form and made useful suggestions. The Reverend William L. Davis, S. J., added his counsel and encouragement.

I would not have written the story of Charles Sweeny without the patience and interest of my wife, Peggy. She is mentioned last but she belongs at the top of the list.

JOHN FAHEY

# CONTENTS

# ILLUSTRATIONS

## MAPS

## PHOTOGRAPHS

# THE BALLYHOO BONANZA

Charles Sweeny and the Idaho Mines

# 1

# SOLDIER, MINER, MERCHANT CHIEF

$C$HARLES SWEENY was born in the year of the Forty-niners. He died in 1916, in the same week as James J. Hill, the western railroad builder. By lying first about his age, and next about his name, he served the Union in the Civil War and then drifted with the stream of adventure, first toward the magical lands of Mexico and next toward California. In California everyone talked about Nevada's mines, so Charles Sweeny went there. From that day, no matter what else attracted him, Sweeny returned to the mines.

He sampled sawmilling in Oregon, brokering in Portland, storekeeping in Spokane, and as a result of eavesdropping reached the Coeur d'Alene mines of northern Idaho on the heels of the first sizable incursion of gold hunters.

Sweeny wooed fortune with energy and purpose, if not always with luck, and his pursuit involved him deeply in the development of the Coeur d'Alene mines. He was a pioneer merchant in the mining country, among the first claim owners, a prospector, deputy marshal, and many other things. But above all, Charles Sweeny was a promoter, a ballyhooer whose words, it was said, could charm the birds from the trees. That he finally struck his bonanza was due to his talent as a talker.

A friend recalled that Sweeny "was not a loud talker and not a rough one. He was fluent. He scintillated—poured on the oil." Sweeny might approach the Rockefellers or the Guggenheims with diffidence—but before long he would be talking up to them, offering advice. There is a story that he once told John D. Rockefeller, Jr., to keep his mouth shut and he would demonstrate how to double Rockefeller's money. But that comes later.

Among the men who lived through the evolution of the Coeur d'Alene mines from scattered hopeful holes to modern corporations, and helped bring about the change, none were more active than Charles Sweeny. He bought the first gold-rush townsite and nineteen years later merged into one company all but two of the district's major mines. He publicized the Coeur d'Alenes. Whatever Sweeny said about the mines was news in those days. He was, in the phrase of his time, no slouch with editors, who liked to guess how many boxcars could be filled with his fortune converted to silver dollars.

Sweeny was never the most famous, never the richest. He was a catalyst in the transformation of the mines. Sweeny, Idaho, has long since disappeared. The legends of the Coeur d'Alenes venerate the names of Wardner, Kellogg, Hutton, Day, Paulsen, and the others who left towns, buildings, or fortunes. During the Coeur d'Alenes' early days, however, someone had to fan the enthusiasm that eventually made its mines great. Although Sweeny mantled the district with corporate enterprise, his chief contribution was to nurture its grand vision of its future.

His phrases long ago evaporated in the mountain air and are forgotten. But men like him were big men and necessary men once. They were all too few, those impressive promoters like Sam Hauser of Montana, Jim Wardner of Wardner, and Charles Sweeny.

Charles Sweeny was born in New York City at eleven o'clock on the night of January 20, 1849. His mother, Mary, was twenty years old, from Manchester, England, and his father, John, twenty-five, an Irishman from County Armagh who had been reared by English relatives. John Sweeny apparently was one of those immigrants who fled to the United States in the two decades before the Civil War to escape famine, religious persecution, or political oppression. Most of the Irish, who came with little more than their clothing, flocked to factories or work gangs along the new canals and railways.

Father Sweeny was a tailor by trade. Charles was the first son of the Sweenys and their second child. His sister, Sarah Ann, was eleven months older. Before Charles was three, the family moved from New York to 225 Mill Street, Paterson, New Jersey, where John set up as a merchant tailor with James A. Fleming. In the following nine years, three more Sweeny children arrived: Michael, Mary, and Bridget. Young Charlie was now twelve, attending the public school and picking up clerical jobs to help the family because his father, Charles was to say, had "a limitless capacity for going into debt."

Whether he tired of his increasing burden as the oldest son or stirred to war's tocsin, four days after his fifteenth birthday Charles Sweeny volunteered for Civil War duty with the New Jersey cavalry. With Nicholas' birth to John and Mary in 1863, there were five brothers and sisters to stay at home.

Charles had grown deep-chested and stocky, had bright blue eyes and brown hair, and was strong for his age although not tall—five feet, seven and one-half inches. The army sent him home as too young. Five days later on January 29, 1864, he went to Trenton to enlist for a three-hundred-dollar bounty in Company F, Third New Jersey Cavalry, using the name James McNulty.[1] This time they let him stay.

Company F was mustered into federal service on February 10, 1864, and during its basic training was encamped near Annapolis, Maryland, as a part of the Union force policing that restless area. Late in April the Third New Jersey was assigned to Meade's Army of the Potomac as a unit of the Third Division commanded by Major General Philip H. Sheridan. As Sheridan drove south into Virginia, the Third New Jersey was in frequent combat between May 5 and June 15, beginning with the Battle of the Wilderness, and during the actions of Spotsylvania Courthouse, North Anne, Pamunkey and Totopotomoy, Bethlehem Church, and Chancellorsville.

Private McNulty-Sweeny, assigned as a clerk, apparently took part in these engagements but early in June Sheridan directed that veteran replacements be added to the Third New Jersey's troopers, and McNulty-Sweeny was packed off on July 14 to dismount camp to learn to fight as a foot soldier. While he was gone, the Third New Jersey moved further south through the Shenandoah Valley with Sheridan, under fire during much of August.

Dismounted training completed, McNulty-Sweeny rejoined Company F at the end of August as Sheridan crushed Early's diversionary attack on Washington, D.C. On September 13, 1864, the Third New Jersey helped to surround and capture the Eighth South Carolina Infantry, consisting of 143 men and officers, in the hills near Berrysville, Virginia. In his report of this capture to General Grant, Sheridan singled out the Third New Jersey for its "gallant charge." Sheridan now held a larger command. The Third Division, of which the Third New Jersey was a part, had been placed under dashing, golden-haired Brevet Major General George M. Custer.

McNulty-Sweeny's service in the line was brief. Soon after the Confederates evacuated the Shenandoah Valley, while Union forces paused to regroup, he was ordered to remount camp, on October 31, to learn the trade of a mounted soldier. Shortly after he left, the Third New Jersey struck southward to be mentioned in dispatches a second time "for the handsome manner in which they rallied under fire" at Rude's Hill and to join in laying waste to the fertile Shenandoah. During March, 1865, the brigade participated in shattering and capturing the armies of Confederate generals Early and Ewell.

By the time McNulty-Sweeny rejoined his unit on April 30, 1865, Lee had capitulated and the last Confederate army had surrendered. On May 23, 1865, the Third New Jersey marched between the First Connecticut and the Second Ohio in a day-long victory review of the Army of the Potomac in Washington, D.C. As the federal troops began to disband, McNulty-Sweeny was assigned as a clerk to the brigade quartermaster until August 1, when he was mustered out with his company at Camp Bayard near Trenton, after seventeen months' service, still a private in grade. His service record showed that he had asked for his bounty five times and owed the sutler twenty-five dollars.

A veteran of the bitter war at the age of sixteen, Charles Sweeny returned home, vain with stories of battle. He considered himself a man. Life at 225 Mill Street seemed tame, no doubt, and perhaps he wanted to start becoming the rich man he intended to be. Within weeks, the warrior enlisted in one of the upstart companies raised among Union and Confederate veterans to fight the Emperor Maximilian in Mexico. Hundreds of former soldiers, who now missed the excitement of war or whose homes and careers had been shattered, signed as mercenaries for an adventure on Mexican soil.

Sweeny's called itself an "American Legion," as did a number of other similar casual companies. Once outfitted, Private Sweeny's American Legion embarked by ship for Acapulco on Mexico's west coast but found the harbor in control of United States marines who prevented them from landing.[2] The company therefore sailed to southern California where it disbanded. Sweeny straggled northward to San Francisco, arriving in June, 1866, to visit a cousin, Peter Donahue, one of the founders of the Union Iron Works and Brass Foundry on the old waterfront of Yerba Buena Cove.

Donahue gave Charles a bed and hired him as an apprentice bookkeeper at the iron works during the day. At night Charles went to school to study accountancy. By 1868, Sweeny had moved into his own rooms at 570 Howard Street, completed his courses, and—probably on Donahue's recommendation—found employment as a bookkeeper with a boilermaker, McAlpin, Spiers and Company.

He also clustered about him a colony of Sweenys. His parents had moved from Paterson to San Francisco with their six children (Eliza Ann had been born in April, 1864). Mary was expecting again. Charles, settled in business at nineteen, married a San Francisco girl, Maggie Swords, and she too was pregnant. In the ensuing three years, John and Mary Sweeny were to add to their brood a son and a daughter. Charles and Maggie's daughter, Lillian, was just about the age of her youngest aunt.

Nine Sweeny children and four adults living under Charles's roof, now 106 Tehama, were perhaps too much Sweeny at close range for young Maggie, for she and Charles parted, were divorced in 1871, and a few months later Maggie suddenly died. At twenty-two, Charles Sweeny was a widower with a daughter, and breadwinner for his father's family.[3]

In the next two years, however, he met two people who changed his life, one a man and the other, naturally, a girl.

The girl was Emeline Agnes O'Neil, a lass of fifteen who charmed Charles to the altar and then to jail. Sweeny married Emeline on February 12, 1873, in St. John's Church, Oakland, and escorted her home to the teeming Sweeny household. Four months later, as a consequence, he was behind bars, according to the *Territorial Enterprise:* "In Oakland, California, Charles Sweeny has been indicted by the Grand Jury for the crime of perjury. On the 12th of February, Sweeny applied to the County Clerk for a license to marry Emeline O'Neil, a minor, whose parents were averse to the suit. Charles swore her age up to the regulation standard and now pines in a dungeon for his liberty and his Emeline. He will be tried in the County Court on the 22nd instand." [4]

His new in-laws intervened and Sweeny was let off lightly.

The man he met was John W. Mackay, who, with his three partners, in 1872 had struck the bonanza of the Washoe, the Consolidated Virginia Mine. Even though riches washed over him in floodtide, Mackay usually moored himself at a poker table or boxing club in his favored harbor, San Francisco, where Sweeny made a point of meeting him. Mackay sized up Sweeny as a strong, capable young man and, as he did with many others, urged Sweeny to try the mines.

Sweeny, in 1873, just under six feet tall and weighing perhaps 185 pounds, was patently eager to improve himself. He had worked briefly in 1868 for the Marysville Mining Company in the Grass Valley district of California. Sweeny spun his enchantment of words and maybe for that Mackay, a childhood stutterer, envied him a little. Mackay must have pointed out that bookkeeping in a boiler factory offered faint promise of fortune and that a sturdy youngster with a keen head (and that protean tongue!) should be on the glittering Washoe, or as it was generally known, the Comstock. Over there men earned four dollars each eight-hour shift.

Once he captured the notion that his destiny lay with mining, Charles Sweeny never let this conviction go. Nothing would do for him but the mines.

He shut his ledgers, settled his parents in Oakland, and with Emeline headed 250 miles over the mountains to the Comstock's capital, Virginia City. A town of approximately twenty thousand, it hung high on the barren east slope of Sun Mountain (Mount Davidson) in air so clear that Sweeny could see the Humboldts a hundred and fifty miles away.

Virginia City was crowded and busy. Its conversation turned on production, overlapping claims, inaccurate surveys, lawsuits, and the biggest, newest mining machinery in the world. Miners were fatalistic: rich men might be poor tomorrow, and poor men might strike riches. In an average month, fifteen men died in mine accidents. Over the bars, the miners still mourned the forty-nine who died underground in the 1869 fire in the Yellow Jacket, Crown Point, and Kentuck. It had been the worst fire in American mining history.

Emeline Sweeny seems to have detested Virginia City from the instant she saw its steep streets and wooden, brick, and stone buildings with iron-shuttered windows. Almost inside the town, stamp mills rumbled their continuous basso. Rude homes tottered up the mountainside, unpainted and shrubless. Boisterous, dirty Virginia City was man's realm.

Charles found work in the Belcher Mine, one of the camp's consistent producers. In his words, "I worked at everything in mining—sinking shafts, running drifts, stopes—up to shift boss." The Belcher lay beside the tortuous Virginia and Truckee Railroad among the original Gold Hill discoveries. The big fire had been nearby in Gold Canyon. Just then the Belcher and Crown Point owners were pushing their crews a thousand feet underground in a contest to outproduce each other. Virginia City upbraided them for gutting the mines but the race went on: the Belcher disgorged five-hundred tons of gold and silver ore a day and 1873 was its finest year.

In later times, Sweeny declared that within a few months of his arrival in Virginia City, he again ran across John Mackay who offered him a thousand dollars to devise safe timbering at the sixteen-hundred-foot level of the Consolidated Virginia, near the floor of the great mine's lode. The bonanza mine at that depth was treacherous, hollowed in ground unstable and porous, running with streams of hot seepage water that clouded the stopes with choking steam. Powerful Root blowers could not ventilate adequately. Sweating men toiled only a few minutes out of each hour, and each man was allotted as much as ninety-five pounds of ice to chew in a shift.

The deeper mines had adopted the square-set timbering designed for the Ophir about 1860 by Philip Deidesheimer, whose reputation rested on shoring the earth successfully in his own mine at Georgetown, California. Brought to Virginia City as a timbering expert, he had copied German methods, improving his system as he studied the Ophir. Finally, with wedged, notched, interlocking timbers he had supported caverns six hundred feet long and five hundred feet high.[5]

But when the Comstock mines bored down a quarter of a mile and more, even square-sets of giant trees no longer withstood the fearsome pressure of earth above. By the time Sweeny entered the Belcher, millions of feet of timber had been wedged underground and both the Belcher and Crown Point were building bulkheads of wood and rock to keep their tunnels from crashing down.

If Charles Sweeny contributed to timbering safely the shifting depths of the Consolidated Virginia, as he claimed, he probably borrowed the bulkhead system he saw in the Belcher.

Within a few months, at any rate, he had risen at the Belcher to shift foreman. And he was there at two o'clock on the afternoon of October 30, 1874, when smoke rose from an incompleted air shaft and the steam whistle screeched that the Belcher was on fire. Fortunately the men in the mine were hoisted safely to the surface while the flames burned the six-by-twelve-foot shaft's timbers for a thousand feet downward. Then Sweeny volunteered as one of eighteen men who would go back into the mine to seal its tunnels from the fire. The volunteers, naked from their waists up, wore cotton overalls on their legs. Minutes after they began closing the bottom of the air shaft, a cave-in sucked the fire directly on them. All were painfully burned and were lifted to the surface for treatment. A second rank of volunteers went down and stopped the flames.[6]

Swathed in oiled cotton, Charles was guided home with severe burns on his face and hands. Emeline abused the Comstock as she ministered to her charred spouse, but when she leaned close to his cot with her candle, she accidentally set his bandages afire. Leaping up, Sweeny rolled himself in a blanket to smother the flames.

This was enough of the Comstock for Emeline, who insisted they leave. But San Francisco writhed in depression and anti-Chinese rioting. After serving briefly in a volunteer unit of war veterans which subdued the rioters, Sweeny set out for Oregon, perhaps enchanted by cousin Peter Donahue's reports of it. Donahue had been a partner in schemes to construct a railway connecting Puget Sound and the Columbia River.[7]

Charles and Emeline probably reached Oregon by the weekly steamer from San Francisco. Charles first took a job as a sawyer in a small lumber mill up the Willamette River from Portland, working ten hours a day for sixty dollars a month. He opened the company store before breakfast, shipped orders during his lunchtime, and in the evening sold lumber and balanced the company's accounts. Sawing held no more future than a boiler factory. When he and Emeline had saved a small stake, Sweeny quit the lumber mill to seek opportunity in Portland, taking a room at the old Occident Hotel.

Portland on the Willamette had shaded streets, and gas and running water in its homes. There were perhaps fifteen thousand inhabitants, and the town's harbor bustled with steamers bound for California and Alaska, or sailing ships carrying wheat and flour to Liverpool. Genteel Portland was comfortable, far different from the grubby hillside of Virginia City. Much of it was new, rebuilt after a fire in 1873. Charles and Emeline settled there happily. Portland was to be one of their favorite cities for the rest of their lives.

Sweeny found a post as a bookkeeper with Knapp, Burrell and Company, at 17 and 19 Front and 14 and 16 First streets, iron and steel importers, shippers, and pioneer manufacturers and distributors of farm implements and mill machinery. The firm had been established in 1859 by Martin S. Burrell and his cousins, Jabez B. and R. B. Knapp. Their partnership prospered as the Pacific Northwest entered a period of rapid growth in 1870. For some years, Knapp, Burrell and Company was the principal supplier of farm and mill machinery for Oregon and Washington.

His contacts with John Mackay and Peter Donahue had taught Sweeny the desirability of influential patrons. As an employee of Knapp, Burrell and Company, he circulated among Portland's leading men, identifying himself with them. From his vantage, Sweeny could measure Portland's commercial growth. The city had been shipping wool to eastern ports since 1862, and by 1877 exported more than 4,929,000 pounds to San Francisco alone. Knapp, Burrell and Company bought wool for New York clients and in 1865 had been entrusted with shipping 20,000 pounds for the first organization of wool producers in Oregon, the Oregon Wool Growers' Association. Oregon wheat had been transported to foreign harbors since 1868. By 1877 Portland was reducing its exports to California, striving to snare for itself the trade among western ports dominated by San Francisco.

But in August, 1878, the *Oregonian* printed a disturbing article. A number of buyers in Liverpool complained that Oregon wheat was inferior, dirty, and shriveled. Portland's direct shipments to the United Kingdom had risen from approximately 49,000 tons in 1874 to more than 112,600 tons in 1878. The stories from Liverpool, and competition with San Francisco, emphasized two of Portland's needs: unified exporting and market information. Portland had little of either.

Sweeny, like other Portland businessmen, recognized the value of rapid, accurate information from the markets of the world. A kind of clearing house for information had been established sometime in 1876 by J. R. Farish, editor of the Portland *Commercial Record,* who received reports in cipher mailed by his agents in San Francisco. He distributed whatever shipping and market news he could obtain

each week. Farish's five original subscribers were increased when he
was able to contract for London grain reports from Western Union
telegraph in 1877, and in August, 1878, for telegraphic reports from
California. Early in October, 1879, Farish organized a merchants'
exchange, a trading center for such commodities as grain, salmon,
butter, eggs, and other products from Oregon and Washington.[8] On a
blackboard in a waterfront tavern, he listed ship arrivals and sailings.
Most of the trading was done among members of his exchange.

Farish apparently did not provide the frequent and detailed market
service that Portland's commerce required, for in December, 1879,
ten men organized a new exchange, purchased Farish's business, and
set up offices in the New Market Theater Building. The new group,
incorporated as the Merchants' Exchange Association of Portland,
included John McCracken, P. Wasserman, William Wadhams, D. J.
Malarkey, M. S. Burrell, D. P. Thompson, James Steel, D. F. Leahy,
W. S. Ladd, and Charles Sweeny. Capitalized for fifty thousand
dollars, the association sold shares for fifty dollars. A good number of
subscribers represented the grain dealers and millers of the Willamette Valley where the greater part of the Pacific Northwest's ex-
portable wheat was then grown.

The purpose of the association, its officers said, was: "To acquire
and disseminate daily to stockholders and subscribers valuable
business information and the latest and most reliable market quotations from the important business centers of the world. To adjust
controversies and misunderstandings between members. To establish
at least once a year standard grades of various kinds of grain, wool,
salmon, and produce bought and sold in the markets of Portland."

Today it is difficult to say who among the incorporators actually
conceived the new Merchants' Exchange Association. Charles Sweeny,
when he grew substantial enough to be asked about his past, claimed
that he had organized it. Perhaps he did, and perhaps his gift for
convincing speech and the obvious need for an exchange drew the
other men into the association. The first officers were John
McCracken, president; Burrell, vice president; Steel, treasurer; and
Sweeny, secretary. As secretary, Sweeny maintained the office, sent
daily market reports in code to subscribers and members, sold stock
and subscriptions, kept the accounts, and, in short, managed the
exchange.

"For information regarding stock, subscriptions, etc., call on or address the secretary," ran the exchange's first advertisement. Sweeny left Knapp, Burrell and Company to hire out as a public accountant, using the Merchants' Exchange as his business address.

For a short time, the exchange prospered. Then many of its supporters defected and in 1885 it was to be presented to Dan Leahy, one of the incorporators, who with his brother, Will, was to operate it for many years. But long before its decline, Charles Sweeny resigned from the exchange and turned over his duties to Leahy, because Sweeny had an idea he thought would make him money.

He optioned open waterfront land in Portland and in Seattle and put down earnest money amounting to eighteen thousand dollars, representing his share of stock in the Merchants' Exchange and his savings. Sweeny then determined to sell his options to the most publicized American financier of his time, John D. Rockefeller, and went by ship and train to New York. His persuasiveness won him a hearing but did not convince Rockefeller that Sweeny's options were worth his price. The options expired and Sweeny, who had counted on Rockefeller's money to pay his return fare, claimed that he worked his way across the country to Portland. He could not have been wholly without funds or credit, for in 1882, he paid thirty-five hundred dollars for twenty acres of Portland city property.[9]

Sweeny was gone from Portland for the better part of a year. On his return he found work for a few months as a special solicitor for the Pacific Mutual Insurance Company. He and Emeline were again living in a hotel, the Clarendon. When his brother Nicholas, now twenty and a tailor like his father, came to Portland from Oakland, the Sweenys moved into a house on north Lincoln.

But Charles was restive. Finally in January, 1883, he summarily quit his job, took the Northern Pacific eastward, and got off at Spokane Falls in eastern Washington. He was thirty-four years old, looking for opportunity door-to-door, this time resolved to work for himself. Thirty years later Charles Sweeny told a biographer, "The night I got here, the town burned—most of it, that is. Practically all the business part of the town was in the block between Front and Main avenues on Howard Street. Fire . . . swept the row of building on the east side of Howard." [10]

Spokane Falls in 1883 had not much to burn although there were several fires that year. Its population was less than two thousand, none of its streets were graded, and in all the town there stood only two brick houses. The Northern Pacific Railroad had come through in 1881; its tracks lay six blocks south of the Spokane River, and the town was pitched on two or three streets running between the river and the tracks.

The flammable business district consisted of one- and two-story frame buildings mixed with houses cheaply built and generally unpainted, strewn along both sides of Howard Street leading south from the river, and for a few hundred feet along Front Avenue which paralleled the waterfront. Some structures bore imposing names like the Union Block and Central Block, and others the names of their owners, Browne, Glover, Burch, Rima, and French. A. M. Cannon operated a sawmill and Frederick Post an old-fashioned gristmill on the river bank. Cowpaths led to frame houses clustered near the business streets. A few rods beyond them roosted a scattering of poor shacks.

The fire sets Sweeny's arrival in Spokane Falls as the night of January 19, 1883, when flames destroyed the F. R. Moore and Company store on the southeast corner of Front and Howard. It was the coldest night of the winter, the water supply had frozen so a bucket line had to be formed to the river, and Rima's Jewelry store had to be razed to stop the conflagration. Most of Moore's goods had been dragged from the building and lay scattered in the black debris. Sweeny, walking about to look at the town, fell into conversation with Moore and concluded their talk by buying the stock for ten thousand dollars, which he did not have but promised to pay. He found a "little shack further west on the riverbank" where he set up his store. And so Charles Sweeny, wayfarer, became a merchant.

He took in a partner, Robert J. Linden, and they set about selling their fire-damaged wares, inserting an advertisement in the *Spokane Falls Review* for May 19, 1883:

☞

To Be Cleaned Out at Any Price
Having Bought this stock at 40 percent less than
any wholesale merchant could buy it, we to give our
customers the benefit thereof.
We are bound to do the business
if we don't make a cent.
Call & See Us & Satisfy Yourselves!
Sweeny, Linden & Co (successors to F. R. Moore & Co)
Dealer in General Merchandise

For his part, Moore left storekeeping for finance. He organized the First National Bank of Spokane with James N. Glover in 1882 and was examining mining claims north of the town.

Sweeny soon took sole proprietorship of the store. By June it had become Sweeny and Company, selling wholesale and retail goods. He ordered more merchandise from Portland and moved into a new building beside Ziegler's Hardware on Howard Street a few doors north of Riverside. A typical advertisement in the *Review* read: "Remember! Chas. Sweeny & Co. carry a full stock of dry goods, clothing, hats, caps, boots and shoes, crockery, glassware, carpets, wall paper and the largest stock of groceries this side of Portland." Sweeny was advertising by October: "This space reserved for Chas. Sweeny & Co.—who are so rushed with customers as to be unable to write out an advertisement."

One covey of customers attracted Sweeny's special attention. They arrived on an April day, led by a man named Endicott, "and bought a bill of $3,000 worth of goods, all put up in fifty-pound sacks—flour, bacon, picks and a great quantity of other goods." There were twenty-six in Endicott's party. As they left, Sweeny directed a half-breed who frequented his store to follow them and learn where they went, for he understood their purchases: this was the outfit of a prospecting party.

Willard O. Endicott and his company from Santa Rosa, California, came north in response to a letter from Andrew J. Prichard, who had served in the Missouri Cavalry under Endicott's father during the Civil War. Prichard had been prospecting in the Coeur d'Alene Mountains of the north Idaho panhandle since 1878, after hunting gold in New Mexico, Colorado, and Montana. As he panned streams feeding the north fork of the Coeur d'Alene River, Prichard concluded the country was rich. He fancied he would found a free-thinking religious colony in the mountains, supported by gold from the rippling creeks, so he wrote to like-minded "Liberals" that he knew or whose names he read in *The Truthseeker,* urging them to come to "a gold-bearing country that will give employment to at least 15,000 to 20,000 men. . . . I intend to reap my harvest, and should like to see my friends enjoy some of it." [11] This is the kind of appeal that brought Endicott.

On the trail, Endicott's men detected Sweeny's agent, called him into camp, threatened him if he continued to spy, and sent him back to Sweeny with little to report. Now Sweeny, himself, went fishing in northern Idaho, walking the trails and streams with his rod and creel, until he stumbled onto Endicott's party. As he suspected, they were prospecting for gold.

Sweeny's interest consequently turned toward the Coeur d'Alenes, but he continued his store in Spokane Falls, ordering new stock through Goldsmith and Loewenberg of Portland, and acquiring the goods of H. J. Brown and Company of Spokane Falls when Brown's junior partner, E. J. Swartz, said the Brown firm had gone to the wall. Brown happened to be out of town when his merchandise was transferred to Sweeny and Company very early one Saturday morning. When he returned, he denied that he was bankrupt and cried collusion, but Sweeny kept the goods and Swartz went to work for Sweeny.[12]

By December, 1883, Sweeny and Company expanded to the center of town, taking part of the ground floor of the Union Block at Howard and Front. On the other corners stood the California House (Spokane Falls' leading hotel), Glover and Gilliam's livery stable, and Glover's and Moore's First National Bank. Gove and Bean, grocers, were also situated in the Union, and the *Spokane Falls Review* published upstairs. Sweeny and Company maintained its earlier location on Howard, too, as a second store trading in crockery, glassware, carpets, wallpaper, and similar goods.

Although Charles Sweeny was considered sharp by his fellow merchants, he prospered and he could charm them with his fancies. He led in planning a water distribution system by organizing the Spokane Falls Water Company with Moore, the man whose store he had bought. After contracting for $24,500 worth of equipment from Lockport, New York, the company could not pay for it and thirty men (including Moore but not Sweeny) contributed $200 each to the Spokane Falls Waterworks Association, acquired the franchise, met the company's obligations, and later turned over the system to the city.[13] Sweeny's heart was neither in water distribution nor in store-keeping—it had fled to the mines. When J. H. Curtis of Coeur d'Alene City promoted a twenty-one-mile wagon road to connect the decaying Mullan Road to the gold country, Sweeny gave $100 of the $470 raised in Spokane Falls toward the project. But Curtis' road was never built.

Suddenly a gold rush overran the area, and roads were to come

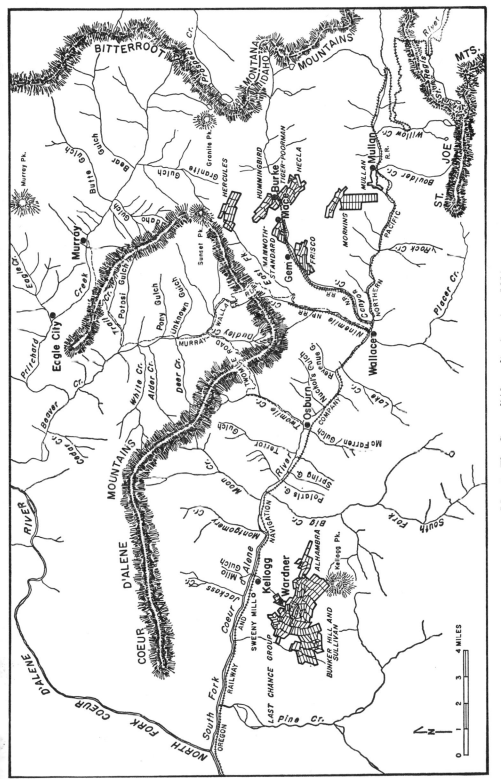

MAP 1. The Coeur d'Alene district, circa 1910

after the stampede rather than before it. In the winter of 1883–84 the rush billowed over the inland country, despite snowfalls that drifted twenty feet deep in the valleys and clogged the mountain trails. The hillsides were thickly forested, steep, and sliced by abrupt canyons.

Prichard had been prospecting that winter with three partners. He snowshoed out for supplies in January, 1884, and mailed more letters to his Liberals. Most of the true believers were farmers from western territories who contented themselves with tacking location notices on trees and returning home to wait for spring and wealth. Prichard himself filed eighty-acre claims for his son, Jesse, and three friends. As they started for the Coeur d'Alenes, the Liberals had whispered, "Gold!" Newspapers talked of it. Railroads promoted it. Swells of prospectors broke across the mountains, some dragging supplies on sleds behind them, others struggling under heavy packs.

By the early months of 1884, a raw lumber and tent town called Eagle City had taken root where no town stood the previous fall. At the confluence of Eagle and Prichard creeks, it huddled within walking distance of the streams most prospectors were working. As many as eight hundred men emerged from the forests each night to eat and sleep in Eagle before resuming their search for gold in the morning.

Spokane Falls' merchants, who provided food and equipment at fancy prices for many of the gold seekers, were not fondly regarded. At Osborne's saloon, wrote a newspaper correspondent, a man could "get whisky . . . for twenty-five cents that will make him lie worse than a Spokane outfitter."

Sweeny's own dash into this country was typical, because western men of that day considered themselves informed about mining and everyone had prospected at some time. Tenderfeet heard talk of nights on the trail and nuggets in pans until they fancied themselves veteran prospectors. A new rumor of gold could clear a western town in minutes as every man scrambled for the hills, and when the clerk ran down the street, his employer often locked up to join the charge. Sweeny's time on the Comstock had qualified him, in his mind, as an expert miner. Moreover, he could visualize the profit to be made near the mines by a merchant. In May, 1884, Sweeny bought most of the townsite of Eagle City for six thousand dollars from Sam H. Hayes, a Rathdrum dealer in wines, liquors, and cigars, who had staked his eighteen-acre town as a placer claim on January 25 of the same year.[14] Hayes's ground lay next to Prichard's own claim. There were perhaps one hundred and fifty structures in Eagle City and, with the exception of individual lots Hayes had previously sold, Sweeny became landlord of nearly all. No plat existed. The lots were described by visible boundaries: the foot of a hill, a blazed cedar stump, or a squared pine tree.

Sweeny opened a general store in Eagle City, Sweeny and Company, and turned over his Spokane Falls stores to Bernhard (Ben) Loewenberg, who had been a storeman and prospector in north central Idaho since the Oro Fino rush of 1861. The Spokane Falls stores became Sweeny and Loewenberg, doing "the heaviest business of any house between St. Paul and Portland," bragged the *Weekly Eagle*.

"Quick sales and small profits," advertised Charles Sweeny. "Successor to Sam H. Hayes, the Leading Merchant of Eagle City and Murrayville, carries a stock of goods worth $25,000, embracing a full line of clothing, groceries, underwear, blankets, provisions, wall paper, hardware and tinware, hats and caps, boots, shoes, miners' tools, miners' supplies, tobaccos and cigars, also a full line of the ☞ Best Rubber Goods, and a large assorted stock of ladies' wear." One might wonder about the ladies' wear advertised because the damsels of the camp generally wore men's clothing and were hardened to their rough life.

Eagle City consisted of rude board and canvas structures strung for about two miles along its two streets, Eagle and Prichard, which met at right angles in the town's center. "Houses and tents appear like magic where yesterday there were only snowdrifts or tamaracks," marveled the *Coeur d'Alene Nugget*. "New signs, painted on canvas, peep up in the most unexpected places and give legends . . . 'Tin Shop,' 'Jeweler,' 'Dance House.' " The *Nugget's* editor thought that three thousand people must have found their way into the mining country by March, 1884, of whom "a large proportion are business men. They are men of means, of energy, of intelligence. . . . There are hundreds of laborers here." There were then, he guessed, nearly a thousand claims on the records.[15]

The new claimants ignored the boundaries staked by Prichard, who objected that his locations had been "laid over" until June 1, 1884, and that the new locators were usurpers. Prichard brought a ten-thousand-dollar suit against Charles Sweeny, Wyatt and John Earp, tourists from Arizona, Henry White, and others—he amended his complaint several times—to test ownership of a triangular piece of property in Eagle City. Sweeny, with the Earp brothers, apparently undertook to resolve Prichard's claims on behalf of the whole camp. A jury awarded Prichard a technical victory, allowing that he might be right, but refused him damages, costs, or return of the property.[16] Prichard filed other lawsuits that dragged on; he went to his grave insisting that the United States Supreme Court would vindicate him, alluding to hidden mineral he alone could find.

In the early months of 1884, before purchasing Hayes's claim, Sweeny had been buying Eagle City land from others. His purchases were described in the deeds by their relationship to other property. From William T. Stoll and Frank E. Geraghty, for example, Sweeny bought a wedge-shaped lot "twenty-eight feet northeast from the storeroom and saloon occupied by S. E. Child and Son, thence northeast along Eagle Street twenty-four and three-quarters feet." From F. M. Washburn, to mention another, Sweeny obtained a lot "situated on Eagle Street . . . next to Taylor's Store northerly and opposite the Nevada Chop House."

Among those to whom Sweeny sold property were Wyatt and James C. Earp, who paid $132 for the site of their saloon, the White Elephant, in the New Theater Building, a tent behind the Eagle City Bank. In his later years, Charles Sweeny liked to recall that he once stopped a gunfight between the Earp brothers and Bill Buzzard, and then had the temerity to award Buzzard the town lot they had been fighting over.

All told, Sweeny invested perhaps seventy-five hundred dollars cash and nobody knows how much gilded persuasion in Eagle City during the first five months of 1884, when it teemed with prospectors bent on exploiting the hills and merchants bent on exploiting the prospectors. From the day Sam Hayes unloaded his townsite and nine other mining claims on him, the indomitable Sweeny bought, sold, and traded ground—sometimes at a profit, sometimes at a loss —in his determination to put his hands on the one bonanza he knew the Coeur d'Alenes must yield.

The prospectors, however, began moving upstream from Eagle City, and although Sweeny continued to buy and sell claims in its vicinity until well into 1887 when the town disappeared, he sold most of his claims, his store and stock, his town lots, and his buildings by the end of September, 1884, seven months after buying the townsite from Hayes. Bernhard Loewenberg, Sweeny's erstwhile partner in Spokane Falls and Eagle City, acquired the bulk of his Idaho holdings for ten thousand dollars on September 15, 1884, buying Sweeny's Spokane Falls store at the same time, to be reopened after inventory with Herman Loewenberg as Loewenberg Brothers, "again in the field with the largest stock of general merchandise in the entire Northwest." One week later, Sweeny sold his father-in-law, Jeremiah T. O'Neil, everything else he owned in Eagle City for thirteen thousand dollars.[17]

Now Sweeny moved to Murrayville, soon to be called simply Murray, whence most of Eagle City's population had decamped when new strikes drew them deeper into the mountains, too far to hike to Eagle City for bed and board. Sweeny continued buying and selling mining claims. During 1884 and early 1885, he bought the Discovery and a scrap here and another there of what were known as the Dawson Bar claims on Beaver Creek, including water rights, tools, pipe, and equipment left at the location. After spending twelve thousand dollars on the Dawson Bar, Sweeny began to sell: five-eighths of his combined Discovery and Dawson Bar claims to five Portland investors who each bought one-eighth for fifteen hundred dollars. The remaining three-eighths of the Dawson Bar, Sweeny sold as three-sixteenths each to Gustav Kutschan, Portland, for one thousand dollars, and father-in-law O'Neil for four thousand dollars. He kept three-eighths of the Discovery.

Sweeny apparently thought that he would manage mining properties for Portland buyers, but none of his claims so far proved worth operating. He continued to turn them over, briefly owning part or all of more than a dozen claims near Murray, including two town lots in Beaver City which faded faster than Eagle, and the ground where James F. Wardner conducted his store in Murray. Of Sweeny's claims, three were to prove eventful if not productive: the Fanny, half owned by James Steel of Portland, the Crown Point, and the Ella.

Sweeny acquired a one-quarter interest in the Fanny for ten thousand dollars. The deed referred to "the Fanny mining claim in the Beaver district in Shoshone or Kootenai county, Idaho (the exact county not known)." Half of this quarter Sweeny sold to Horace L.

Cutter and Frank R. Moore of Spokane Falls, the same Moore who had sold Sweeny his burned merchandise and joined him in organizing the water supply company—and with whom Sweeny was to form a mining partnership that would influence the district's development.

In the Crown Point and Ella, Sweeny re-entered partnership with Robert Linden, who had been in his Spokane Falls store. This time Sweeny and Linden worked together for nearly two years. In that period, Sweeny was to become acknowledged a power in the Coeur d'Alenes.

Sweeny's early years in the Coeur d'Alene region were summarized on May 30, 1886, by the *Spokane Falls Review* as "varied and not at all times as happily fortunate as to be encouraging. He has handled placer claims and quartz ledges in and around Murray with indifferent success." This was true, but Charles Sweeny's luck was about to change.

Together with Linden, Sweeny moved south from Murray over the mountains that separated the north from the south fork of the Coeur d'Alene River. Along the streams feeding the slender south fork lay the claims that were to supply the district's great wealth. Here was Milo Gulch where the Bunker Hill, the Sullivan, and their neighbors had been claimed in 1885. With Steward Fuller, Sweeny and Linden bought the Republican Fraction, astride the vein the Bunker Hill tapped, paying John M. Burke one thousand dollars for two-thirds, and George B. McAuley five hundred dollars for his third of the Fraction.

Sweeny also joined other men, among them Jim Wardner, in buying and selling locations. With varying associates, he bought the Hercules (not the claim to be made famous by the Day family) and the Louisa, and located the Virginia, himself, in April, 1886. All were within a short distance of the Bunker Hill and, consequently, easily resold, although Sweeny and Linden kept one-sixth of the Virginia, the Republican Fraction, and lesser claims like the Gladstone and Henry Clay. Both were disappointed that Portland investors failed to sustain them, despite the purchase of the Bunker Hill and Sullivan by Simeon G. Reed of Portland.

To add a moneyed man to their partnership, Sweeny and Linden sold Frank Moore one-twelfth of the Republican Fraction, and cut in Moore's banking partner, Glover, for eleven-thirty-sixths of the claim in August, 1887. After Linden suddenly died, Sweeny drew closer to Moore and an acid-tongued Montanan, Anton M. Esler, builder of the district's first concentrator for the Helena Concentrating Company. Esler had some money from sale of the concentrator to Reed and he also had a reputation for support from Samuel T. Hauser, governor of Montana Territory.

By this time in 1887, two major districts had been delineated among the south fork mines, the Yreka, which included roughly the claims clustered about Wardner and Milo Gulch, and to the east, the Lalande, embracing the claims near Canyon Creek where the Tiger, the first notable silver-lead discovery of the Coeur d'Alenes, had been staked in 1885.

With Moore and Esler, Sweeny now commenced a strategy he had seen on the Comstock—encircling major claims. On Canyon Creek, they picked up the Bengal Fraction and shares in the Gray Wolf and Ajax, lying on the hillside above the Tiger. They acquired the Sherman, next to the Union, and then sold one-tenth of it to an astute miner and investor, John A. Finch, for one thousand dollars. Finch and his partner, Amasa B. Campbell, had come to Spokane Falls from Youngstown, Ohio, and had sold a good many shares of stock in their enterprises to Youngstown investors.

In the Yreka district, the Bunker Hill and the Sullivan were beyond Sweeny's grasp, but their great vein rambled through the hills. The direction of the vein had not been accurately determined, and other claims ribboned along its supposed course like the tail of a kite—the Tyler, the Last Chance, the Stemwinder, various fractional claims, and others. (Fractions were bits of odd-shaped ground left over when claims were staked. Prospectors sprang hungrily on these peelings from bigger claims in the hope of selling the fraction at a high price; if the vein should rise in the fraction, it might prove more valuable than the original claim.)

The Republican Fraction and the Virginia comprised the first substantial foothold for Sweeny, Moore, and Esler in the Yreka district, or as it was popularly known, the Wardner district. Next, they took into their group a young engineer, W. Clayton Miller, to obtain his one-tenth of the Last Chance Fraction, and bought the other nine-tenths from its various owners.

Through John Burke, who had bonded the Last Chance claim itself, they bought the Last Chance for fifteen thousand dollars and brought Burke into their company.[18] This Last Chance claim roosted high on the hill above the town of Wardner. Everyone expected it to be one of the important mines of the Coeur d'Alenes, and it was to be the hub of Sweeny's future assault on the mining region.

Buy and encircle was to be his pattern. By the end of 1891, when he had been active in the Idaho mines for seven years, Sweeny had been partner or agent for no less than thirty men from Salt Lake, San Francisco, and Portland. By himself or with others he had controlled as many as sixty mining claims, some sold within days, some held for years. He was not unwary of a quick profit, as in the case of the Homestake, which he bought in a morning for fifteen hundred dollars and sold in the afternoon for two thousand.

# II

## "AT THE MERCY
## OF F. LEWIS CLARK"

*O*N the thirteenth day of April, 1886, Charles Sweeny, with Steward Fuller and Robert Linden, contracted to buy the Emma and Last Chance lode claims near the Bunker Hill. The Emma and Last Chance were on the right-hand side of Milo Creek going upstream, between the Tyler and Stemwinder locations. Linden was no richer than Sweeny. Fuller had some money; he had transferred his wholesale liquor business to Eagle City from Missoula, Montana, to be on the ground while he sought mining investments. John M. Burke, agent for the men who discovered the Emma and Last Chance, handled the sale to Sweeny and his partners, and shared an interest with them in the claims. The attorney who drew their contract and witnessed their signatures was Weldon B. Heyburn, a florid, round little man about five feet, six inches tall, weighing perhaps 250 pounds.

None of this group could foresee that the names on the deed, those of men and mines, were to reverberate through the Coeur d'Alenes for the next twenty years in struggles for ore and for survival.

Because the Emma and the Last Chance lay on the same side of Milo Gulch as the fabled Bunker Hill, they were regarded as potential treasures. There was, even then, no question of the Bunker Hill's abundant future. Early in the district's short span, richer ore from the Bunker Hill was used to salt that of the Sullivan to maintain a consistent quality while Jim Wardner worked the two from open cuts into the hillside.

So rapidly was the Milo area growing by April, 1886, that only six days after Sweeny and the others signed for the Last Chance properties, a regular stage began running from Kingston to the town of Wardner (originally called Kentucky) over a widened trail. Previously only horses, mules, and human beings in single file could travel the route; even after the trail had been improved, timber continued to scratch wagons lurching along its narrow ruts.

At Wardner, Anton Esler's concentrator chewed ore at the end of the trail, and new frame structures rose in the town. One newcomer counted 166 houses completed or abuilding and wrote the *Spokane Falls Review:* "The town seems to have sprung up like magic. Business houses open the instant the roof is on the building. Houses building for occupation by the owner or rental purposes. Blocks on the main street held from $250 to $1,000." Half a mile below Wardner on the south fork of the Coeur d'Alene River, a Kentucky company raised its tiny experimental smelter to process the gray carbonate ore taken from the Sierra Nevada claim at the southwest end of the Tyler.

This was the burgeoning country where Charles Sweeny, resolved to find his bonanza, bought into the Emma and the Last Chance. Four men staked the Last Chance in September, 1885; the Bunker Hill was located only days before. One of the Last Chance discoverers, Sam P. Divine, said later that he and his partners were camped on Jackass Prairie, two or three miles north of Milo Gulch, when Mike Carlin arrived with the news that he had seen the Bunker Hill stakes.[1] Everyone had heard of the Bunker Hill, so the next morning the group followed Carlin there and began to claim open ground remaining around the stakes. Other prospectors' parties also beat through the brushy, steep slopes, calling back and forth to each other good-naturedly.

Divine posted a location he named the Stemwinder. The other men chose a claim next to it where they uncovered a mineralized outcrop, which they called the Last Chance, one of the names found in every northwest mining camp. This was September 17. On the twentieth, Divine claimed the Tyler, leaving room between its lines and his Stemwinder for the Last Chance. He found one of his partners' stakes in his ground and demanded its removal. While Divine and the others worked, a widening circle of claims rippled over the hills from the Bunker Hill, and perhaps the men truly thought that this was their last opportunity near the Bunker Hill—their Last Chance. Its location notice listed as discoverers John Flaherty, Carlin, Divine, and John (Yellow Dog) Smith. Burke, an experienced manager, joined them a few days later as agent and promoter.

The Last Chance claim was a 600- by 1,500-foot rectangle, the usual dimensions of a lode claim, lodged 1,200 feet northwest of the Bunker Hill. After recording it, the four prospectors went off to search for another chance on another hill, leaving Burke in charge, and did nothing more with it.

Unwittingly they left behind them the genesis of legal controversy, for as strange as it may seem, no one then perceived the true direction of the Bunker Hill's vein. Engineers and geologists eventually were to show that the Bunker Hill, Last Chance, Tyler, Sierra Nevada, and others all worked the same ore. Geologists named its host rock the Revett formation, an area approximately one thousand by six thousand feet where mineral had been deposited in pockets by percolation ages before. For many years after 1886, however, few men understood the formation's complex structure.

Staking the Last Chance on the same ore as the Bunker Hill was sheerest accident, even though that is what its locators had intended to do. Con Sullivan tried to guess the direction of the Bunker Hill vein when he staked his Sullivan; like the finders of the Last Chance, Sullivan reckoned the lode ran opposite from its actual direction.

Once they owned the Last Chance, Sweeny, Fuller, Linden, and Burke tunneled into their ground and stockpiled some ore, but none of them had money enough to develop the claim into a mine. Fuller soon left the partnership and Linden died. Sweeny, consequently, persuaded three Portland men to form a stock company, the Emma and Last Chance Consolidated Mining Company, with an authorized capital of one million dollars. The company accomplished little until the man whose store Sweeny had bought, the Spokane Falls banker, Frank Moore, joined it and bought out the Portland stockholders. Moore began to form other companies to raise money by stock sales to exploit the Last Chance and other claims.

To consolidate claims he bought in the Canyon Creek district, Moore organized the Coeur d'Alene Mining and Concentrating Company on November 25, 1887, bringing into it his crony, Fred H. Mason of Holley, Mason, Marks and Company, dealers in retail and wholesale hardware, a Spokane Falls attorney named Kennedy J.

Stout, and the Youngstown partners, Finch and Campbell. Capitalized for $2,500,000, the company controlled shares of the Union, Cleveland, Bengal Tiger Fraction, Sherman, Union Fraction, Tiger Fraction, Gray Wolf, and Ajax, adjoining the Tiger, and what the newspapers called "the wonderful Custer group" on the hill above Canyon Creek.[2] These were not mines. They were names dignified by peeled trees at their corners and, at their outcrops, rain-dimmed location notices rattling in the mountain winds.

Moore's Wardner interests, principally the Last Chance, Emma, and the Republican Fraction, passed through successive companies as he sought funds to develop them. The first was the Emma and Last Chance, as mentioned, and the second, the Spokane Concentrating Company, organized August 14, 1888, with the intention of operating a smelter that was erected in fifty days during June and July by Esler and his assistant, R. K. Neill. In addition to Moore, Esler, and Sweeny, this company numbered two prominent and wealthy Spokane Falls contractors and druggists, John W. Chapman and Cyrus R. Burns. Chapman and Burns had bought into Moore and Sweeny's Emma and Last Chance company the preceding March, displacing Bernard Goldsmith of Portland and John Burke, who was succeeded by Esler as manager.

Undeterred by frequent changes in the names of their companies, Sweeny and Burke tunneled 250 feet into the hillside during 1887, struck pockets of galena from four to eight feet wide, and started a second adit 130 feet down the hill, expecting again to intercept a vein in approximately 500 feet. When Burke resigned, some four thousand tons of silver-lead ore from the upper adit lay on their dump awaiting concentration. Esler built the company a concentrator, at the head of Wardner's Main Street, with a daily capacity of ninety tons, more or less, depending on the quality of the ore. When an 1,800-foot aerial tramway, swinging one-ton buckets, rattled from the upper tunnel to wooden bins at the concentrator, the Last Chance joined the producing mines of the south fork.

The Spokane Concentrating Company's mill rose on a site owned by Sweeny, Esler, and Moore, who sold their land to their company for fifteen thousand dollars including water rights to Springs A and B in Milo Gulch, some town property in Wardner, and their shares in the nearby Belcher and Midas lode claims.[3] It was not unusual for the stockholders of one company to sell themselves property as stockholders of another because one company's stock was likely to be valueless and another's worth something, if only a few cents a share.

But within a year, the Spokane Concentrating Company's mill and its shares of mines were resold for seventy thousand to another firm, the Last Chance Mining Company, organized September 26, 1889, with four familiar faces—Moore, Sweeny, Burns, and Chapman—and a new one, C. Herbert Moore, a Spokane stockholder in Holley, Mason, Marks and Company. Herbert Moore replaced Esler among the directors. Esler left to form the Helena and San Francisco Mining Company to operate the Gem and Frisco mines on Canyon Creek with financing from Montana and California men.

During the next six months events moved faster. Sweeny (who succeeded Esler as manager) contracted to furnish seven thousand tons of concentrates to the Omaha and Denver Smelting and Refining Company from the Last Chance mill. This was the company's first major sale of its product. Next, Burke, Frank Moore, and Sweeny bought the Empire State claim near the Last Chance for forty thousand, expanding their hold on the hill overlooking Wardner. In the same half year the business district of Wardner burned nearly to the ground. Its citizens partially smothered the fire by throwing snow on the flames, quelling it at last by blowing up the Grand Hotel in the fire's path. Wardner quickly rebuilt, encouraged by the outlook of its mines. Most of the workings of the big mines could be seen by a man who stood in the middle of Wardner's principal street and looked up to the hills.

Rich as it proposed to be, Wardner offered no haven of gentility. It was flung together with the materials at hand. A lady described it as "most unattractive, situated between high mountains which shut out the sun most of the day, and with space for only one street. There were miners with pack animals and four-mule teams lumbering up the narrow street, hauling ore to be shipped; capitalists with new corduroy suits and shiny high boots; gamblers, and women of easy virtue, and many families of substantial citizens." [4]

Wardner was, as she said, narrow, crowded, unpainted, its buildings strung along the canyon floor for two and a half miles with hardly a level lot in town. A few homes rose on an excavated tier above the winding street. But the mines looked impressive if the town did not, and the town existed for them. The editor of the *Wallace Press* panegyrized the "Last Chance, Emma, and the Republic, a most magnificent group of mines owned by the Last Chance Mining Company . . . today producing more ore than any mine in the vicinity of Wardner. It concentrates ore of high grade. Were the capacity of the mill equal to the output of the mine, the present output would be trebled." [5] These glowing words missed the truth, which was that the Last Chance mill's machinery was inadequate, the mine's pockets of ore sparse, and its compressor plant (to drive air drills) large enough for only three drills, requiring most of its hard ore to be broken tediously by hand. Frank Moore's personal finances worried the company; rather than meet his obligations, he was to renew notes with Burns and Chapman in 1891, 1892, 1893, and through his estate in 1896.[6] To outside observers the Last Chance seemed prosperous, however, and after two years of reorganization, recapitalization, and development, 1891 seemed to dawn propitious for it and for Charles Sweeny.

The second, or lower, adit of the Last Chance struck ore, as expected, about five hundred feet into the hill, assaying 80 to 85 percent lead and 15 to 20 percent sulphur with good silver values, the company reported.[7] "The ore bodies are so big," insisted an editor, "it would be hard to describe them." But this ore proved to be merely pockets, like the mine's other strikes. In the first six months of 1891 the Last Chance produced 545 tons of concentrates and 149 tons of carbonate in the average month, a good but not exceptional showing.

As he had in Eagle City, Sweeny bought. The Russ House, a hotel on Main between Third and Fourth streets in Wardner, he acquired from Burke for thirty-five hundred dollars, renamed it the Central, and delegated its management to Al Page, a one-time prospector who ran a restaurant. When Wardner incorporated and absorbed the hamlet of Kellogg in April, 1891, Sweeny and Page were elected town trustees with Alec Monk, A. E. Carlson (the Wardner manager for Holley, Mason, Marks and Company), and Henry Drought of Drought and Lamb, commission merchants. Charles Sweeny also concocted the grand scheme of digging the longest tunnel in the whole Coeur d'Alene mining district to intersect the Last Chance vein eight hundred feet deep in the earth. W. F. Martin, a mine and tunnel contractor, was hired to bore a seven-by-eleven-foot adit three thousand feet long, starting four hundred feet uphill from the concentrator. The Coeur d'Alenes' first big burrow, this came to be known as the Sweeny Tunnel. The long adit held special importance for Sweeny because the other Last Chance tunnels, so glittering at first, had run into a wall of rock, prompting talk that the Last Chance had dug out all its ore. Martin put twenty men to work May 1, 1891, driving into the spring-green hillside in view of the idlers on Main Street, and Sweeny's fortunes again seemed ready to blossom with the flowers that colored the slopes of northern Idaho.

But reaping did not follow mere sowing. On August 9, 1891, the owners of the Tyler mine renewed a feud with the Last Chance that dated as far back as April, 1887, when the Last Chance had won a lawsuit over a triangular piece of ground that both companies had claimed. The court had sliced 1.474 acres from the Tyler's bounds which overlapped the Last Chance lines. The owners of the mines became antagonists, and in the four years after the court's ruling, their bitterness pervaded even their crews underground. When Tyler men followed the foot wall of their vein downward into Last Chance ground in 1891, Last Chance miners listened in the earth to the Tyler digging closer and closer. When the Tyler broke through, there occurred a brief subterranean fight with fists and shovels in the fluttering light of miners' candles.

To add to their enmity, on March 7, 1891, Sweeny, the two Moores, Mason, and Hew G. MacDonald (secretary of the Last Chance Mining Company) organized the Idaho Mining Company with the intention of securing additional ground—which the Tyler also claimed— west of the Last Chance boundaries. Despite Tyler protests, Last Chance crews dug toward the ore in this disputed section. Confronted with Last Chance expansion above and below ground, the Tyler resorted to law, charging that the Last Chance had followed the vein beyond its rightful limits.[8]

The district court at Boise enjoined the Last Chance from taking ore outside its vertical boundaries after September 4, 1891. The mine's production stopped, its tramway was stilled, its concentrator shut down, and 120 miners were laid off. So began "one of the most noted mining cases, an exciting feature of Idaho's courts," an editor later remarked, a historic legal battle involving bigger issues than a local squabble over some spongy vein matter. Before this case was closed the United States Supreme Court was to deal four times with its problems of apexes, extralateral rights, prior location, trespass, and boundaries, and would comment on the inadequacy of mining

laws and the erratic course of ore deposits. No matter how finical
the law, mine owners understood that the Tyler–Last Chance decision would set precedents for scores of other disputed claims, and
they followed the case with avid interest.

As was Sweeny's custom, the Last Chance retained the portly
Heyburn, a serious, lettered man in days when attorneys often learned
their law reading in a barrister's office and practiced with agile and
sonorous oratory spiced with quotations from literary classics and
the Bible. Because a good trial was generally the best show in town,
lawyers regarded themselves not only as sentinels of culture on the
frontier but as superior showmen; they comprised a hard-drinking,
envied, influential, witty estate.

The Sweeny Tunnel construction continued, unaffected by the
injunction. The court appointed Frank R. Culbertson its agent and
allowed him to operate the Last Chance inside its bounds after
October 10. When the judge announced this concession, Sweeny
telegraphed Wardner from Boise, "Resume work on Last Chance
mine. . . . Injunction removed." However, the judge required the
Last Chance company to post a $17,000 bond before processing or
selling its production, a heavy financial burden in view of the
$560,000 spent developing the mine, most of the thousands borrowed
from Frank Moore's First National Bank of Spokane.[9] (The "Falls"
had been dropped from Spokane's name early in 1891.)

Moore, who as president of the Washington Water Power Company
in Spokane now preferred to be addressed as F. Rockwood Moore,
had invested his bank's deposits heavily in the power company, in
Spokane real estate, and in the Last Chance Mine, which had offices
in the bank building. He was also deeply in debt to the banking house
of J. A. Prickett and Son of Edwardsville, Illinois. Banks commonly
speculated in this manner: the Spokane National, for example, was
the principal stockholder in the Morning Mine in the Coeur d'Alenes.

The Sweeny Tunnel alone cost the First National seventy-five
thousand dollars before it apparently ran onto pay dirt 2,200 feet into
the hill in May, 1892, and "put a million dollars worth of ore in
sight," wrote a correspondent to the *Spokane Review.* "The tunnel
has been in course of construction for more than a year and the
results have been awaited with a great deal of interest. . . . Mr.
Sweeny is not in town. When he returns a reception will probably be

given him." Despite its troubles, the Last Chance company began to consider a three-hundred-ton concentrator.

Wardner's excitement was short-lived. The Last Chance plans were shelved. Although the Last Chance had won in 1891 in the district court, the Tyler appealed to the Ninth Circuit Court in San Francisco, which overturned the Boise decision and ordered a new trial. This time, in February, 1893, the Tyler won its claim of trespass, based on the contention that when its miners ran into a Last Chance tunnel, the Last Chance was digging in mineral owned by the Tyler.[10] As a result, the restraining order was reinstated on March 14, 1893, and the Last Chance shut down again after its brief reopening.

Wardner, in consequence, virtually closed. The Last Chance miners boarded in private homes and traded with town merchants because the mining firm operated no company boarding houses or stores. The region's other mines, embattled by miners' unions, worked sporadically, while across the United States spread the Panic of 1893, depressing the prices of metals, throwing thousands out of work, and closing business houses.

In Spokane the nation's financial distress precipitated a run on old Anthony M. Cannon's bank. His assets, tied up in coal mines, a proposed coking plant, and one of several schemes for a portage railway on the Columbia River, could not be liquidated. The Cannon Bank failed early in June, setting off a series of closures, among them the chief support of the Last Chance, Moore's First National and its associated Spokane Savings Bank.[11] Seven of Spokane's ten banks went to the wall in that bleak summer of 1893.

When it became obvious that the First National would not survive, word had quietly spread. As a result, observed its receiver later, "on the last day something like $40,000 was checked out by individual stockholders in the bank or by men who were intimate personal friends of some of the directors."

Now the Last Chance Mine was closed by court order, its future doubtful, and its creditor, the First National Bank, suspended. "The bank's heaviest debtors were the very people who might, in different times, have been able to discover funds to reopen," remarked a judge who listed the bank's obligations.[12] On November 20, 1893, a slim, sharp-featured, purposive man named F. Lewis Clark was appointed the bank's receiver. Born June 21, 1861, in Bangor, Maine, educated

there and at Harvard, the only son of a banker, Clark had come to
Spokane in 1885. Quickly prominent, he entered partnership in the
construction and flour milling firm of Clark and Curtis, and spent his
leisure hours on horseback riding through the piney forests around
the town, studying the terrain to deduce where future roads must run
and homes rise, so that within a few years, Clark closed shrewd
purchases of large tracts northeast and east of Spokane. One quarter-
section he bought for $960 was to sell for a reputed million dollars
for a Northern Pacific Railway shop site.

As bank receiver, Clark found a tangle of debts knotted through
Moore's various companies, involving his home, his real estate, and
unpaid loans dating as far back as 1883. The Last Chance owed the
First National more than $145,000; Moore personally owed the bank
$77,091; the Last Chance had been permitted overdrafts totaling
$19,032.22. The mine was mortgaged to the bank, the bank's share
of the mine stock amounting to eighteen twenty-fifths. Moore's obligations were secured by a blanket mortgage on his real estate and by
hypothecating to the bank his interest in the Washington Water
Power Company.[13] But Moore's real estate had been covered earlier
by mortgages and Clark learned, he wrote the comptroller, that "in
many instances, the first lien is for more than the property is worth.
Nearly all of the Washington Water Power Company stock pledged
by Mr. Moore is also previously pledged for more than it is now
worth. The claim this bank has on it is subject to a prior lien." With
Moore's failure, the Prickett bank of Edwardsville, Illinois, also
collapsed.

Certain that a lucky stroke would rescue him, Moore had pledged
and repledged his property and stock as security for loans on top of
loans. The First National had been paying the legal and operating
expenses of the Last Chance without enough income from ore sales
to recover these costs. The greater share of Moore's securities held
by the bank were worthless on the market. At the moment, only
the Washington Water Power stock flickered some feeble comfort to
the bank's creditors because the electric company was being reorganized by a committee of eastern bond-holders.

As for the Last Chance, there seemed two possibilities: the bank's
creditors—the "trust," Clark called them—could sell the mine as it
was, taking whatever money the sale might bring, or they could try
to find money to continue fighting the Tyler in court and to operate

the mine in the hope it would eventually make good its arrears. On April 2, 1894, the Last Chance lost an appeal of the 1893 decision in favor of the Tyler in the Ninth Circuit Court of Appeals, and pushed on to the U.S. Supreme Court on a writ of certiori, that is, a request that the case be reviewed. Receiver Clark continued to pay the mine's legal costs, while public sympathy generally sided with the Last Chance, for it was whispered that the Standard Oil Company was backing the Tyler and had spent upward of $100,000 in court.[14] "As the Tyler stands now, it is the cheapest property ever developed in the northwest," commented the *Spokesman-Review*, "as the work the Tyler people performed was nominal, while the Last Chance expended upwards of half a million dollars before the big ore body was struck."

Despite the mine's clouded title to its ore, Clark authorized one George S. Terry to offer the Last Chance to New York buyers. After several months, Terry reported that the mine could not be sold due to news of union unrest in the Coeur d'Alene district. For a short time, Clark thought the Tyler might bid for the Last Chance but nothing came of this.

There seemed little to do but wait. In the midst of waiting, Charles Sweeny was flat broke, in debt twenty-five thousand dollars to the suspended First National for two promissory notes, apparently for real estate on Havermale Island in the Spokane River.[15]

The Coeur d'Alene labor war and the Panic of 1893 spread apace. Men idled in the streets of mining towns, stores were boarded, houses gaped empty. Standing in Wardner, Sweeny could look up at the Last Chance works on the hillside, its tram and mill silent, its tunnels empty. Now he faced the task of raising money to feed his family. His solution, ironically, rose from the spread of the depression across the United States. Jacob S. Coxey of Massillon, Ohio, advocated a national road improvement program to create jobs, organizing the Good Roads Army of the Commonweal to march on Washington, D.C. All over the West, unemployed men began forming companies to join Coxey's army. It was something to do.

A man named James Dolphin, derisively called "Doctor," drifted into Spokane that April, announced he would recruit a local Coxey company, and opened his rolls in a Main Avenue saloon after learning that Populist Party leaders planned to break up his intended street meeting. Within half an hour, Dolphin signed up ninety men, and three days later, with four hundred enlistments, took the old hay-market at Sprague and Bernard for his campsite, and set up barracks, tents, field kitchen, and mess. Over the Commonweal headquarters floated the American flag and a banner reading, "Going to Washington to see Grover." [16]

By the end of April, the *Spokesman-Review* estimated 512 Commonweal members in the Spokane company, uniformed in castoff clothing, who "spend the day sunning themselves and lingering around the barracks, discussing finances, the condition of the country and politics." Dolphin held inspection at 8 A.M. and a parade at 7:30 P.M., and his squeaky voice frequently piped in the regular evening round of speeches. Many citizens sympathized with the company and donated food and some clothing to its members, who canvased the town daily.

As the days passed, however, Dolphin was not able to arrange transportation to the national capital. He had promised his men that they would ride trains east, as many Commonwealers were reported doing in other parts of the West. When newspaper items from Butte, Montana, and Puyallup, Washington, said that trains had been commandeered by Coxeyites there, the movement lost some of its popular support. At North Yakima, a deputy marshal was shot attempting to eject a Commonwealer from a train. Commonwealers were arrested in several western cities and sentenced for trespassing or theft. Pressed by authorities, those in Seattle and Tacoma began drifting on foot toward Spokane, walking in groups up to seventy-five. The Spokane company, after moving its camp to ground near the Great Northern yards at Hillyard, disintegrated. Some of its members straggled eastward into northern Idaho and Montana. Samuel Vinson, the U.S. Deputy Marshal in Spokane, hired additional deputies to keep the Seattle and Tacoma Commonwealers moving, and the unemployed army shuffled good-naturedly eastward.

Newspapers that previously had printed droll comments on Coxey's army now cried alarm at the disorganized bands wandering over the countryside, but the vagrants generally proved orderly.

Charles Sweeny, who needed the money, signed on as a deputy United States marshal on May 8, 1894. Joseph A. Pinkham, the marshal for Idaho, considered himself "fortunate in securing the services of Mr. Sweeny," who was "thoroughly competent to take charge of the large force of deputies." [17] At ten dollars a day, Sweeny was placed in command of all the temporary five-dollar-a-day marshals in northern Idaho; he was directed to protect railroad property and to keep the Commonwealers moving.

Sweeny was now forty-five years old, barrel-chested, strong from hard physical work, confident, and well-knit, and nearly six feet tall. He already was marked as a man of action against labor; in 1892, he had personally escorted strike-breakers into the mining camps, using armed guards.

As the Coxey encampments in Spokane, Seattle, and Tacoma broke, Sweeny's fifty-five deputies dealt with a steady file of drifters along the railway tracks near Idaho towns. The Great Northern Railway was halted by an American Railway Union strike for higher wages, but the Northern Pacific ran, and many railroad employees let the Commonwealers board trains whenever they could. Townspeople in Rathdrum and Bonner's Ferry put up the stragglers for a night.

On May 17, Pinkham wired Washington, D.C., that a troop of more than 400 Coxeyites had swarmed into northern Idaho, and called for a company of regular Army infantry—about 125 men—to support his marshals. The soldiers were directed to Sandpoint where they also served under Deputy Sweeny. Just outside Sandpoint, at Ramsey Station, Commonwealers tried to overrun a freight carrying Sweeny when it slowed to climb a grade, but his men beat off the boarding party. Dolphin himself evaded Sweeny's attempt to intercept him by abandoning two handcars he and his companions were riding near Sandpoint to cross the area on foot.

Soldiers and marshals forced Coxeyites from trains, jailing them if they refused to depart. One Commonwealer cut the rubber airhose to the brakes of a Northern Pacific train at Wallace. The *Spokesman-Review* now printed a column of Commonwealers' movements headed, "The Move-on People," and quoted the *Rathdrum Post:* "Citizens are getting a bit weary of furnishing hobos and bums with grub. . . . The novelty has worn off." Indeed the novelty had tarnished. Marshals sternly prodded the motley corps out of northern Idaho. Soldiers chased Coxeyites from the Coeur d'Alene mining district where most of the mines continued to operate by grace of a two-year-old restraining order issued against the unions.

Even though Coxey himself reached Washington, D.C., he was summarily arrested in April for trespassing and his army dispersed. The movement lost force everywhere; by the middle of June, 1894, the Commonwealers were gone from Idaho. Charles Sweeny turned in his badge, pocketed six hundred dollars in pay, and looked for another job.

Of Sweeny's performance, Judge James H. Beatty, federal district judge for Idaho, wrote the Attorney General, "I state that . . . Mr. Sweeny had entire charge in the North while the Marshal was engaged in South Idaho; that Mr. S. is a man of more than usual ability; that he managed the business well; that he had much hardship, often making long trips by handcar and otherwise, when trains were not running, and I considered his services far more valuable than an ordinary deputy." [18] Judge Beatty was explaining his approval of ten dollars a day for Sweeny when the other temporary deputies were paid half that amount.

Sweeny had not asked for ten dollars "until after the services were rendered," explained Pinkham in his own letter, and he, too, described Sweeny's work in glowing words: "His successful management is best demonstrated by the fact that, during the movement of the 'Commonwealers' numbering several thousand men, over the lines of the Northern Pacific Railroad within the State of Idaho, by his superior tact, the destruction of property was prevented, serious conflicts were avoided, and with but few arrests being made. His wise judgment resulted, no doubt, in the saving of a large sum of money to the government. The arrest of any considerable number of these men . . . would easily have cost for Marshals' fees alone, for their transportation to Court for trial, a sum equal to the total expenses of the deputies under his charge." [19]

Meanwhile, the year that had passed since the failure of the First National Bank in Spokane brought only slight economic recovery. F. Lewis Clark, the receiver, told the comptroller that for the first time in the history of the area, cereal crops were ruined by wet weather, forestalling an expected upturn in farm income. Grain prices fell again after everyone thought they had reached their lowest in 1894. Clark estimated that building rental collections would not pay the cost of maintenance. "Owing to the enormous mortgage debt at high rates of interest which rests as a burden upon nearly everyone and nearly every piece of property here [Spokane] right now, it becomes a matter of gravest consideration whether recovery can come soon enough to leave to this trust [the bank's creditors] an equity over and above the present incumbrances on property owned by it," he wrote.[20]

Dutch investors were lending money to Spokane men and taking mortgages on their property, so that within a few months much of downtown Spokane would be pledged to the Northwestern and Hypotheekbank and the German Savings and Loan Association of San Francisco. The Amsterdam directors of the Hypotheekbank opened a permanent office in Spokane.

Rossland, British Columbia, seemed to be recovering from the panic on the promise of its gold and copper mines, and many of the Coeur d'Alene old-timers headed there. Three Rossland mines, the LeRoi, War Eagle, and Josie, all controlled by Spokane investors who had mortgaged themselves to the Dutch, produced marketable ore in 1894. On February 1, 1895, the War Eagle paid its first dividend of thirty-two thousand dollars. The announcement of this disbursement brought fresh hordes of prospectors into the camp. No matter how bleak the depression elsewhere, Rossland sparkled with expectation. Charles Sweeny joined the throng bound for bald Red Mountain, overlooking Rossland. In later days he told the story that he found two twenty-dollar gold pieces in his pocket. One he gave to Emeline, who had moved their family from Wardner to Coeur d'Alene City, and the other he used to see him north to Rossland.

Although occasionally he talked of abandoning Idaho, Sweeny was still deeply involved in the Coeur d'Alenes. He was approached by a well-to-do wholesale wine and liquor dealer, Jeremiah J. O'Connor of Elmira, New York, to handle O'Connor's one-sixth interest in the Cariboo claim near the Last Chance at Wardner. O'Connor let it be understood that he could be persuaded to invest in any likely prospects Sweeny turned up.

And in April, 1895, the United States Supreme Court, on the finding that Idaho's district court had failed to "give proper effect to a former judgment establishing priority of the Last Chance claim," directed a new trial in Idaho between the Last Chance and the Tyler.[21] Sweeny did not have enough money to send Heyburn a congratulatory telegram when he heard of the ruling, a victory of sorts for the Last Chance. "This decision means a great deal to the depositors of the First National Bank and the Spokane Savings Bank," exulted the *Spokesman-Review*. "The mine and its owners owed a great deal to these banks. . . . A favorable decision would give the banks a big asset."

At the new Boise trial to contest disputed ground, the Last Chance won a verdict in its favor and costs amounting to $14,298, although the court disallowed $6,287 of the bill submitted.

The injunction that had prevented the Last Chance company from operating outside its lines was lifted, at last, on June 28, 1895, and on the strength of $16,435 profit in the preceding January under Culbertson's management as court agent, Receiver Clark persuaded an employee of the mine, John Presley, to spend $2,000 repairing the workings and to operate the Last Chance under a lease that gave the company a royalty of not less than twelve dollars a ton. The lease was to be temporary until all suits were settled, for naturally the Tyler had appealed.

The Coeur d'Alene mining district, at the moment, continued to flounder in financial quagmire and union warfare. The most powerful company in the district, the Bunker Hill, had only recently reopened after six months' idleness from union conflict. Nonetheless, after its success in the Boise court, the Last Chance again looked potentially valuable. Sweeny returned to Wardner to oversee its reopening under Presley's lease. By early August forty to fifty men were working one shift in the mine and mill, at the same wages the Bunker Hill paid, $3.00 for underground miners, and $2.50 a day for carmen and shovelers—rates bitterly contested as too low by the unions.

Clark was elected to the board of the Last Chance Mining Company and appointed its manager. Cyrus Happy, a major shareholder and representative of the Prickett family of Edwardsville (Moore's substantial creditor), was also put on the company's board with Moore, Sweeny, and John Chapman. Clark and Sweeny were the strong men of this directorate. Moore was bedridden with a stomach disorder that had troubled him for nearly a year, his youthful, clean-shaven face sunken with pain.

Eager to free his home from debt, Moore now proposed a new way to secure his obligations. He offered the receiver, Clark, 440,000 of the 500,000 shares of stock issued by the Shoshone Mining Company in return for a reduction in his interest rate and the release of mortgages on the Last Chance and Moore's real estate. In addition, Moore offered to turn in 100,000 shares of Last Chance capital stock to

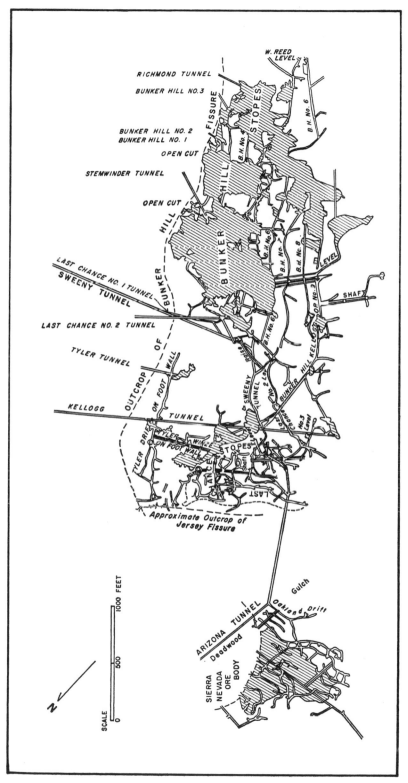

MAP 2. Simplified diagram of the underground workings of the Last
Chance and the Bunker Hill and Sullivan

secure his personal debts at $1.50 a share.[22] Moore's proposal was prompted partly by his concern for his three-story native stone home on Seventh Avenue, among Spokane's finest; it may have been urged on him by Clark to forestall the foreclosure advocated by several of the bank's creditors. Clark was able to defer steps against Moore by the Shoshone stock plan.

The Shoshone claim was unusual, for its boundaries were based on a discovery of mineral 1,200 feet underground in August, 1895, during development of the Last Chance Mine. Heyburn explained, "There was a place where a vein within the Last Chance claim passed outside the plane of its rights. . . . There was a body of ore, a ledge, . . . and the locator went upon that ledge . . . and made the location of the Shoshone claim." Unlike prospectors who poked over the surface of the earth to post their claims on exposed mineral, the owners of the Last Chance found ore underground, followed it upward, and then staked the surface based on what they had found underneath.[23]

As a consequence, another of Moore's companies was formed, the Shoshone Mining Company, on March, 20, 1896, by the same men who were directors of the Last Chance Mining Company, with the addition of several others who were figureheads. A part of the ground that the Shoshone now claimed had been staked twice previously as a mineral claim. One day in 1886, Jacob Johns and Philip Kirby had posted a claim there and called it the Edith, and on the next day had enlarged the Edith and renamed it the Kirby.

Thus when the underground locators of the Shoshone extended their vertical boundaries from inside the earth upward to its surface— in reverse of the customary procedure for staking ground—they came out partly in the Kirby. When the Shoshone company applied for its patent in the land office at Coeur d'Alene City on August 21, 1895, the Kirby's owners, Royal F. Rutter and F. W. Bradley (manager of the Bunker Hill and Sullivan), contested it, and sued in the district court to protect their boundaries. The suit was complicated by the Shoshone's assertion that it also owned mineral rights in the Wardner (Ibex) claim, which overlapped most of the Kirby ground not described in the Shoshone's surface location.[24]

Bradley and Rutter purchased the Kirby after the Shoshone had been surveyed, and they claimed the Kirby's area on the basis of a resurvey. There was some justice, therefore, in the assertion by the

Shoshone's owners that Bradley and Rutter merely hoped to block the Shoshone for the benefit of the Bunker Hill and Sullivan.

This was the intricate background of the Shoshone, whose stock the ailing Frank Moore offered as security for his debts. Receiver Clark favored Moore's proposal because, by using the Shoshone stock to refinance the Last Chance, he might be able to get the mine in shape to work it. Therefore, Clark, Moore, Sweeny, Fred B. Grinnell (receiver for the Spokane Savings Bank), and Happy (whose office was right upstairs from Clark's in the First National Bank building), conceived a stock pool to give them control of the Last Chance Mining Company's directorate and operations. They felt a centralized control necessary to restoring the mine. Their pool agreement was signed on November 5, 1895, and thereafter was known as the "November agreement" among those persons close to the affairs of the First National and the Last Chance—affairs that daily seemed more complex.[25]

Using the Shoshone stock as collateral, and pooling their shares of Last Chance stock to master the voting power in the Last Chance company, the members of the November pool proposed to issue gold bonds backed by a mortgage on the Last Chance Mine. By selling these bonds bearing 6 percent interest, they hoped to raise four hundred thousand dollars to pay the debts of the mining company and restore the mine to production on a scale that would assure profit.

The November agreement was written largely by Happy, upon whom Clark often relied for legal advice during his term as receiver, and the agreement was also, Clark acknowledged, "dictated partly by me, somewhat hurriedly in order to obtain the signature of Mr. Sweeny, there being some provisions in the agreement he was reluctant to accede to." [26]

The November agreement and the mortgage on the Last Chance Mine were curious documents. They were loosely drawn, perhaps due to haste, and they were written at different times so that the mortgage did not contain provisions to support the pooling. H. M. Stephens, one of the Spokane attorneys who represented the comptroller of the currency, pointed out the deficiencies of the mortgage. In his opinion the success of the enterprise depended wholly on the performance of Clark rather than on written contracts. "I cannot satisfactorily explain Mr. Stephens' sudden hostile attitude," Clark grumbled to the comptroller. "He acts as if he thought that he had just discovered that the Receiver was to be at the mercy of F. Lewis Clark, and that it was a nefarious plan on the part of said F. Lewis Clark." [27]

Stephens' principal objection—to a provision that was to play an important role in the subsequent acquisition of the Last Chance by Charles Sweeny—was that the documents were "not sufficiently definite as to the capacity in which you [Clark] hold the stock." The mortgage did not provide funds for operating the mine, failed to repeat the dividend provisions of the November agreement, required that three months had to elapse before the company's foreclosure after any notice of such an action (a condition omitted from the November agreement), and stipulated that no foreclosure could be accomplished without consent of a majority of the bond holders.

Despite the attorney's objections, however, the agreements and various amendments were signed. Sweeny wrote his name reluctantly, for he had talked earnestly with Moore at the sick man's bedside and doubtless believed that control of the Last Chance was about to pass to him alone as heir to their partnership.

On November 21, 1895, Frank Rockwood Moore died at his home at the age of forty-three, leaving his widow, Sarah Frances (Fanny), who was to survive him forty-six years. Nothing was achieved by the time of his death to relieve the burden of debt that was to fall to his widow except a contract which stated that his stock in his companies could not be sold without her consent. Moore willed Fanny all his possessions in a brief handwritten testament.

To protect himself and Mrs. Moore, Sweeny now arranged a supplemental contract to the stock pooling of the November agreement. Under the terms of this supplement, Clark, the widow, and Sweeny stipulated that Clark "should hold and vote the pooled stock" and that the officers of the Last Chance Mining Company should remain in office as long as Clark held the stock. These clauses were inserted at Sweeny's insistence. The officers thus perpetuated were Sweeny as manager, Clark as treasurer, and the pliable Happy, who succeeded Moore as president.[28]

With the execution of this supplemental agreement on the last day of 1895, Clark's caustic summation materialized: the receiver of the First National Bank was, indeed, at the mercy of the private citizen, F. Lewis Clark.

# III

# AFFAIRS
# OF A MOST PECULIAR NATURE

*T*HE three years that followed the death of Frank Rockwood Moore brought Charles Sweeny to the threshold of his fortune from mining. Sweeny was not willing to return to prospecting—to rejoin the nomads of the West who found claims, sold them, and went off to find others. He had been in Grass Valley when the district exploited vein mining methods brought from Nevada, and he had been on the Comstock where a few resolute men grew rich by thrusting deeper and buying better machines while the mob indulged its fruitless speculations in claims and stock.

With the benefit of experience that miners gained in Nevada, California, Colorado, and Montana, the Coeur d'Alene matured rapidly. It had its quota of frenzy, too, but Patrick Clark and his Butte cronies were veteran mining promoters, and the Bunker Hill company gave its management to able men like Victor Clement, hand-picked by John Hays Hammond, the famous mining engineer.

The Coeur d'Alene launched quickly on a course of stable development; it had railroads to smelters within twenty-four months of its gold rush. Its major deficiency was its umbrageous labor force. It is true that the Coeur d'Alene discovery occurred comparatively late among western mining excitements and, consequently, met with some wariness from eastern capitalists, but it attracted substantial investors from California, Oregon, and Montana.

Sweeny enjoyed no personal acquaintance with eastern business houses as did, for one, Sam Hauser; he had probably exhausted the

credulity of his Portland friends, and his association with Frank
Moore closed doors that might otherwise have been open. But Sweeny
knew men who had started with little more than he—Mackay, Burrell,
cousin Peter Donahue—and who had prospered by their diligence
and by shrewd analysis of their positions.

Sweeny's chief asset was the Last Chance Mine, to which, as bank
receiver and voter of the mine company's stock, F. Lewis Clark held
the key. If the mine itself was of doubtful value, it represented an
established foothold, strategically located, useful for raising money. In
the three years after Moore's death, therefore, Sweeny edged closer
to Clark, held onto the Last Chance, and began to look for money.
For capital, Sweeny saw two possibilities: promoting other mines,
and cultivating men like Jeremiah O'Connor who were ready to spend.
He pursued both.

Sweeny jauntily exploited their mutual Irish ancestry and Catholic
faith in his letters to O'Connor, and, in his first after Moore's demise,
seemed sad but confident: "My dear friend and partner has been laid
away in his long home and I feel very badly about it. . . . He was
the very best disposition and had the best control of himself of any
man I ever met. . . . Everything was fixed up in a very satisfactory
and agreeable manner during his last illness, and the business goes
along just about the same as though nothing had happened." [1]

The earnest face Sweeny presented O'Connor was not the face the
bank's dissident creditors believed they saw. To them Sweeny and
Clark seemed at first to be working quietly in collusion, and soon after
as unabashed partners. Together Clark and Sweeny stalked new
capital for mining companies in British Columbia, for new companies
in Idaho, and for the Last Chance; together they bought Spokane
city real estate. And together Clark and Sweeny refused to discuss
the Last Chance Mine with anyone in Spokane, save to complain that
prices of silver and lead had fallen so low that the mine could not
dig a profit. Cyrus Happy fretted that "after Mr. Moore's death,
nothing more could be ascertained as to the proceeds of the mine."

In fact the Last Chance had deteriorated during its inactivity under
the Tyler's injunction, and John Presley's two thousand dollars hardly
started the refurbishing needed. During the winter of 1895–96, Clark
spent twenty thousand dollars repairing the mill to increase it to a
capacity of two hundred tons a day, run by water power supplemented
by steam. Even so, Clark acknowledged that the machinery for mine

and mill was not adequate; he said a small three-drill compressor at the mine furnished air enough for only one drill when two compressor-driven hoists were used. Culbertson, who had managed mill and mine, believed that eight or ten drills were needed for efficient operation, and vouched, "Some of the ore in the mine is extremely hard and to break it with hand drills is very slow and expensive."

Clark confided of the Last Chance to O'Connor, "The hoist was broken down, the tram was rotten and the cable rusty and useless. The mine seemed almost gutted, tools gone. . . . Parts of the timbering had fallen in, etc., etc. The reason for all this was partly that Sweeny and Moore during the litigation, had been obliged to put irresponsible leasers in the mine." To another director he wrote, "The Last Chance Mining Company in all its operation has not made money." After an inspection of the works, Clayton Miller reported "a net loss per ton of concentrates of something more than one dollar per ton" for July and August, 1896, while Clark urged Presley to produce six hundred tons of concentrates a month as the minimum required for profit, noting that the output had fallen to fifteen tons shortly before.[2]

Despite the mine's air of desolation, it produced ore worth eighty thousand dollars in 1896. Clark spent this to restore the property, using thirty thousand for development and repair and fifty thousand to settle preferred claims, clear titles, buy some additional ground, and pay the ubiquitous attorneys. By the beginning of 1897, the Last Chance was in a position to resume profitable operation with no debt except the mortgage against it.[3]

There was one deterrent. The development—consisting of new stopes to investigate likely areas—exposed no worthwhile ore inside the boundaries of the Last Chance itself, but did uncover ore in the Shoshone and Ibex claims. Both lay in disputed ground. The Shoshone, located underground, conflicted with the Kirby, and the Ibex overlapped both the Kirby and the Wardner. As Culbertson explained, "The underground locations were made by running cross-cuts from the lower workings of the Last Chance out beyond their sidelines. And as a portion of the Last Chance vein dips into both the Shoshone and Ibex claims . . . the ground covered by these two locations is of great value to the Last Chance company."[4]

Just how essential the Shoshone and Ibex were to the Last Chance Clark revealed in his letter accompanying a map of the workings that he sent the comptroller. "I have indicated on this map the lower tunnel," he wrote. "I have also indicated the dip of the vein which shows that the ore chutes dip away from the extra-lateral rights of the Last Chance claim. . . . The Emma and Last Chance claims by themselves are not a property comprehensive enough to be attractive to mining people." Nevertheless, Clark believed, "There is enough ore in the Last Chance claim to pay out the debt of the Last Chance company." [5]

Since bad publicity or loss of lawful title to its best ores could destroy the Last Chance and, with it, the hope of the First National Bank's creditors for some return of their money, Clark and Sweeny refused to talk about the mine. Clark did tell the major stockholders the true situation—but these stockholders were Sweeny, Fred Grinnell, and Happy. The smaller creditors were purposely kept in the dark, lest one prove too talkative. "While I should like to explain matters fully to all the depositors," Clark told the comptroller, "yet circumstances are such in regard to the Last Chance mine that we cannot with prudence make public the true condition of the mine."

These smaller, circumscribed creditors concluded that Clark must be hiding the value of the mine because he had found it rich beyond anticipation. For the next ten years, this discontented coterie viewed the actions of Clark and Sweeny, partners in real estate and other mines, as strokes in an audacious plot to steal the Last Chance for themselves alone. This group fed its lack of information with conjecture that was freely published by the newspapers. One of the smaller creditors, a lawyer and real estate man, Arthur J. Shaw, was to allege some years later that Clark was fifty thousand dollars in debt and that Sweeny owned "no property whatever" until the two gained control of the Last Chance, when, suddenly, they had money. Thirteen years after the failure of the First National Bank, this group continued to fasten a stigma of fraud on Clark and Sweeny. Jules Prickett, overseeing his father's interests in Spokane, sued Clark and Sweeny, convinced that they had used secret information about the Last Chance "to benefit themselves" and had operated the mine to incur losses deliberately until they had achieved undisputed dominion over it. [6]

Viewed in this obdurate light, Clark's relations as bank receiver with Sweeny, one of the two major shareholders in the bank's largest asset, reflect some curious beams. For one, both men seemed well off despite stories they spread of their hard luck.

Clark and Sweeny had sources of money other than the Last Chance, however, both in New York and in Canada. Apparently they also obtained loans from the Exchange National Bank in Spokane. Clark was, after all, the only son of a wealthy father. Sweeny applied, about this time, to patent a 39.13-acre gold-silver-copper claim at Rossland, called the Red Mountain. It was next to the Pilgrim, which lay immediately north of the War Eagle, one of Rossland's beneficent producers. A stock company that included Clark and Sweeny was formed in July, 1896, to exploit the Red Mountain.

Portland, Seattle, and Spokane men bought shares in the venture, called the Rossland Red Mountain Gold Mining Company, and Sweeny tried to sell its dollar stock to easterners. He offered a bloc to O'Connor "with the understanding that you will help us place a quantity . . . at Elmira or elsewhere in New York at fifteen cents a share." O'Connor was widely acquainted among the Democrats, the Irish, and the Roman Catholics of New York state, and held sizable real estate tracts in Seattle and Montana. He hesitated, but others bought, and by 1897 the company had enough money to be one of the few on Red Mountain that accomplished some exploration, hoping by its activity to attract a favorable price from London investors who were taking Rossland mine stocks even though the district had been notoriously promoted in England.[7]

Sweeny also formed the five-hundred-thousand-dollar Silverene Gold Mining Company in October, 1895, to promote a gold-silver property in the Rossland area. His stock, printed at one dollar par value, rose in 1896 to eleven cents a share, its highest. The Silverene was one of dozens of Rossland companies with extravagant capitalization selling penny shares. Sweeny sold a bloc of Silverene in November, 1896, netting twenty thousand dollars for himself. In later years this sale was to seem to him a turning point in his career, and he was to say, "When I got that money, I actually bit it to see if it was real!" The Silverene, adjacent to the Colonna which was owned by Montreal people, shortly afterward was reported without funds by the *Rossland Miner*.[8]

While Sweeny was busy in Rossland, the creditors of the insolvent First National Bank of Spokane, swallowing their misgivings, approved refunding the Last Chance through the issue of gold bonds recommended by the late F. Rockwood Moore. The bonds would pay off a mortgage dated March 6, 1893, held by the Spokane and Eastern Trust Company, amounting to $327,993.32, representing the debt incurred to develop and operate the mine to that time.

The Last Chance issued 940 gold bonds in varying amounts, from $10 to $1,000 at par, coming to a total par value of $400,000. The bonds were secured by assigning all of the real and personal property of the mining company to the Spokane and Eastern—this included the Last Chance, Emma, and Republican Fraction lode claims, and the Emma and Last Chance millsite at Wardner. The mining company also turned over to the Spokane and Eastern the late Moore's 440,000 shares of Shoshone stock, to be sold only if the contract were defaulted. Dated January 2, 1896, the gold bonds bore 6 percent interest, and were marked redeemable in gold coin on or before January 2, 1902. Of the $400,000 worth of bonds, the First National "trust" received $176,000, the Spokane Savings Bank $40,000, the Prickett family $70,000, Sweeny $15,000, Happy $20,000, the Last Chance Mining Company $15,000, and various lesser creditors the remaining $54,000.[9]

The First National's creditors believed that the gold bonds would restore the Last Chance to a condition which would allow them to sell it and that, after three years, they might liquidate the defunct bank's biggest asset. Under Clark's receivership, no dividends of any kind had been paid.

Despite approving the bond issue, the dissident creditors continued to oppose almost anything else the receiver proposed. F. Lewis Clark confessed that creditors of the bank, some of them persuaded to deposit in the First National by Sweeny, "have been critical of Sweeny's connection with the Last Chance." Sweeny, who received three hundred dollars a month as manager of the mine, frequently threatened to quit but Clark wheedled him into staying on.

It was to prevent the Last Chance from slipping from them that the bank's creditors had adopted their November stock pool. Under it, enough stock was turned over to the receiver to assure his control of the mine. Moore contributed 180,424 shares of his capital stock, Sweeny an identical amount, Happy his own 21,500 shares plus 39,892 belonging to the Pricketts, and Clark 490 shares. Grinnell added 13,111 held by the Spokane Savings Bank and Clark afterward

Charles Sweeny, about 1908, President of Federal Mining and Smelting Company

The Charles Sweeny family, about 1898. Left to right: Mrs. Charles Sweeny (Emeline), Fran
Rockwood, Mary Gertrude (later Mrs. Francis J. Finucane), J. Sarsfield, Charles (the olde
son), Mrs. Clarence Edwards (Lillian), Robert, Charles Sweeney, and Emeline (later Mr
Clifford Lee Corbin). (Fort Wright College Historical Museum, courtesy of Mrs. Charles
Finucane)

Eagle City after it had been abandoned. (Barnard-Stockbridge collection, University of Idaho

contributed 53,997 more shares that he obtained from Sarah Frances Moore in return for releasing her from certain obligations of her husband's estate.[10] In Clark's hands, as a result, were 489,838 of the 500,000 shares of stock issued by the Last Chance Mining Company.

Unknown to the bank's creditors there also existed that supplemental contract among Clark, Sweeny, and Sarah Frances Moore, stipulating that Clark hold and vote the pooled stock. And there was, as well, Clark's receipt for stock written to the late Frank Moore, stating that Clark was "entitled to hold and vote [the stock] during the life of the mortgage to be issued."

Clark regarded himself as custodian of the stock as an individual citizen, as an associate of Moore and Sweeny, and not as receiver of the bank, because "otherwise creditors of the Last Chance Mining Company and F. Rockwood Moore would fear that the deposit of the pooled stock with a Receiver might possibly give rise to complications; and . . . then we would be uncertain whether I could vote that stock or whether the people for whom I held it in trust should vote the stock." [11]

This precise distinction between F. Lewis Clark as receiver and F. Lewis Clark as citizen, elucidated for the comptroller, never penetrated the minds of the bank's unhappy creditors. But in Clark's view, and in his agreement with Sweeny and the Widow Moore, the separation was plain: Clark held the stock as a trusted individual on behalf of its owners, and only incidentally did he happen to represent, too, their creditors. Clark's two roles daily seemed less distinct because, as the comptroller's agent, A. D. Lynch, later remarked, "The . . . Receiver of the bank is now an active and open participant in the management of the affairs of the Last Chance Mining Company."

Clark, the businessman, maintained offices with Charles Sweeny in the Hypotheekbank Building.

None of the hopes of the bank's creditors for revival of the Last Chance Mine by gold bonds were to be realized. A little more than a year after the bonds had been issued, Clark petitioned the comptroller for permission to sell the Last Chance securities at fifty cents on the dollar, urging as his reason the precarious position of the mine; he recommended that an option be given to Sweeny. The creditors demanded that before any sale, some impartial person investigate the Last Chance to establish its value. Clark chose E. B. Braden of Braden Brothers, Helena, Montana, northwest representative of the American Smelting and Refining Company.

After his inspection of the Last Chance, Braden's letter transmitting his report contained a paragraph that said, "Personally, I would not touch the proposition with a ten-foot pole and I can only regret that the bank is involved in it to such an extent." [12]

Braden's report said, "Under the circumstances, management has been fairly good," and advised the bank to sell the Last Chance for fifty cents or even twenty-five cents on the dollar. Clark excused some of Braden's pessimism by explaining that Braden had visited the mine shortly after a section of the lower works collapsed.

Braden pointed out that the Last Chance company had searched sixteen months without finding worthwhile ore, saying, "In the lower workings there is practically no ore in sight. Occasionally there is a little stringer, but nowhere did I see what I could consider as pay ore." The Last Chance ore consisted only of pockets, and Braden concluded, "As to the present outlook of the mine . . . I must say that I consider it extremely poor." He valued the mine at no more than $75,000. Between November, 1895, and February, 1897, the Last Chance had sold concentrates, carbonates, and crude galena worth approximately $249,000, he observed, while the costs of operation amounted to $282,000. "Taking everything into consideration as I view it . . . I would strongly advise the disposal of the bank's interest at as early a date as possible by obtaining fifty cents on the dollar . . . and I would consider the bank to be very lucky and the depositors would have no cause for criticism."

Some of the creditors doubted Braden and insisted on another inquiry, wrangling about who would do it until Frank Culbertson's name was advanced. Although he had worked with Sweeny, Culbertson proved satisfactory to the entire creditors' committee.

Culbertson therefore examined the familiar Last Chance, giving his opinion that both mine and mill were poorly equipped and the ore expensive to take out. His report mentioned several lawsuits contesting the Last Chance's title to ore bodies, particularly to the Shoshone and Ibex claims, and said, "Were it not for this litigation and with the title of these two claims assured . . . I should estimate the value of the Last Chance company's properties at not less than $400,000." But considering the lawsuits and inadequate machinery,

Culbertson recommended that "the creditors of the First National Bank . . . accept seventy-five cents on the dollar." [13]

With his report, Culbertson enclosed a letter from G. Scott Anderson of Wallace, Idaho, a surveyor hired by Culbertson, who explained that the Last Chance stope no. 3 "has overreached its south boundary limit and into the territory of the Kirby lode claim." The Kirby now belonged to the Bunker Hill and Sullivan. Culbertson's opinion was that "were the Bunker Hill and Sullivan fully cognizant of the amount of ore now being extracted from this disputed ground, an injunction would probably follow restraining the Last Chance from taking out any of this ore until . . . ownership of this ground has been finally determined."

Clearly the future of the Last Chance depended on mining ore outside its vertical limits. Neither the Shoshone nor the Ibex, however, was a property of the Last Chance company; both claims, with the Summit, belonged to the Shoshone Mining Company. On March 26, 1894, the Shoshone company had entered a lease with the Last Chance for joint use of its lower [Sweeny] tunnel because, as Clark explained, certain officers of the Last Chance, acting as individuals, had filed on Last Chance discoveries underground, claiming the new locations in the name of the Shoshone, a separate company that did not own a tunnel.

Moreover, after the death of Moore, Clark and Sweeny had formed yet another company to buy up the Shoshone's claims and those adjacent to the Last Chance but not owned by it. Sweeny suggested to Jeremiah O'Connor that he join this newest enterprise, pointing out, "Now is the time to pick up the property while the depression is at its worst," and proposing that they name the new firm the Chemung Mining Company.[14] (Elmira is the seat of Chemung County, New York.)

In Sweeny's chatty letters to O'Connor, the Last Chance sounded promising; his optimism would have puzzled the First National's creditors, had they read his observations. In one letter, Sweeny fondly mentioned the "old reliable Last Chance," and in another claimed, "We have operated this property for seven years and every year's work makes it better and puts more ore reserves in sight." And: "This mine nets $10,000 a month now at the very lowest figures for silver and lead ever heard of." At approximately the time in January, 1897, that the First National Bank's creditors were demanding an unbiased inspection of the Last Chance, and Braden and Culbertson were successively engaged for this examination, Sweeny, Clark, and O'Connor were discussing their possible purchase of the Last Chance by their Chemung Mining Company.

The Chemung was formed as a Washington corporation on August 5, 1896, to buy and operate mines in the United States and British Columbia, capitalized at $2,500,000 with 500,000 shares at five dollars par, and listing as trustees Clark, Sweeny, O'Connor, Willis E. Goodspeed, who was Clark and Sweeny's bookkeeper, and Miller, their mining engineer. The Chemung owned all or parts of the Skookum, Butte, Good Luck, Jersey Fraction, Skookum Fraction, Palmer Fraction, and Cariboo lodes, all near the Last Chance. Kennedy Hanley, a prospector, received 100,000 shares of Chemung stock for his interests in the locations, principally the Skookum.[15] And Clark wrote O'Connor, "The main Bunker Hill–Last Chance lodes run through these claims."

During the last six months of 1896, Charles and Emeline Sweeny left their new home in Spokane to travel throughout the eastern United States and Canada, contacting prospective investors interested in Idaho and British Columbia mines. They ranged as far south as New Orleans, north to Toronto, spent a good deal of time in New York City, days in Elmira as guests of the O'Connors, and in Paterson with Sweeny's relatives. In December Sweeny wrote O'Connor from Toronto, "I feel confident by Spring I can place not only Chemung but entire Last Chance here if we want to."

By this time, O'Connor and his parish priest, Father Michael J. O'Dwyer, pastor of St. Mary's at Elmira, were stockholders in the Rossland Red Mountain, and Sweeny and Clark were advancing the market price of its stock by manipulation to thirty or thirty-five cents a share, "which will establish a basis for the sale of it in Canada." They purchased three thousand more shares themselves to inflate the price.[16] Clark and Sweeny organized still another, the Northwestern States and Kootenay Mining and Investment Company, to absorb the Native Silver Bell, Trapper, and Hunter claims in the Slocan district of British Columbia, and Sweeny offered O'Connor one-third of the stock if he would meet one-third of its expenses. They had high hopes—a sample carload of ore returned $3,904. 39.[17]

These Canadian hazards remained subordinate, however, to the Coeur d'Alene district claims near the Last Chance. To Clark and

Sweeny, the Last Chance was most important because they needed its Sweeny Tunnel, its connected workings, its mill, and its equipment to operate their Chemung properties.

Once the Last Chance had been refunded with sale of the gold bond issue, and some indication of its real value disclosed by Braden's and Culbertson's reports, competitive buyers appeared: Marcus Daly, the Butte copper baron, who shrugged off the Idaho mine when Clark refused to let him look inside it, and the more obdurate managers of the Bunker Hill and Sullivan, to whom Clark also denied an inspection "on the ground that the Last Chance Mining Company was not interested in any way in the sale of the securities held by the First National Bank, and that it was merely a matter for creditors of the bank."

The Bunker Hill may have been gesturing simply to vex Sweeny. Its overture prodded Sweeny to pay from his own pocket the interest due in April, 1897, on the gold bonds. He told the *Spokesman-Review,* "I own a large majority of the stock . . . and do not want the default of interest on the bonds to prejudice my stock." Sweeny and his family then owned 180,424 shares of the Last Chance, but the Bunker Hill, intimating it would pay a high price for the mine, continued its demands to inspect the workings, so that Sweeny hurried to enlarge his holdings. He feared that the Bunker Hill might buy a majority of the stock, and asserted that the Bunker Hill had tried to purchase stock for ten cents a share and bonds for sixty-five cents on the dollar from creditors of the First National Bank.[18] "I had to buy a great many bonds at seventy-five cents on the dollar in order to get the stock. . . . I have been paying as high as seventy-five cents for bonds cash, and fifteen to twenty-five cents for stock," he told O'Connor, but despite the relatively high prices, Sweeny quickly increased his bloc to approximately 300,000 shares, three-fifths of the total issued.

Sweeny maintained that he bought his stock from eastern holders. It is interesting to speculate, however, that his own shares, added to those 39,892 belonging to the Pricketts, the 21,500 owned by Happy, the 53,997 held by Clark for the release of debts against Moore's widow, and Clark's own 490, amount to 296,303 shares. Events of the next weeks indicate that Sweeny's stock control came directly out of the pool.

With his three-fifths, Sweeny—with Clark beside him—believed himself invulnerably in command of the mine because, he wrote O'Connor, "We don't believe that any purchaser sufficiently strong to buy the bonds of the company would think of purchasing unless he got control of the stock, for the reason that the control of the stock controls the corporation . . . and the parties owning could . . . possibly absorb the profits for five years, by which time the present ore reserves within the limits of the property would be entirely used up and an empty shell would be all that would be left to the bond-holders. . . . Hence we have not much fear of anyone buying the bonds unless they have a contract for purchase of the stock. Such a contract could only be made with us." [19]

In addition to whatever stock Sweeny bought, he demanded and received the return of his stock in the pool, held by F. Lewis Clark under the November agreement. Before handing back Sweeny's paper, Clark consulted his personal attorney, Henry M. Hoyt, who gave his opinion that the November agreement was invalid and that Clark had no choice but to turn back Sweeny's stock on demand.[20] This return of Sweeny's stock was consistent with Clark's assertion that he held the shares as a trusted friend, not as receiver of the First National Bank, and it gave Sweeny physical possession of the majority of the stock of the Last Chance Mining Company. He could now out-vote the stock pool, if indeed it existed still—the pool formed previously to assure creditors of the bank that through their receiver they governed affairs of the company.

After restoring Sweeny's stock to its owner, Clark forwarded the comptroller an offer from Sweeny to buy the Last Chance at fifty cents on the dollar for the bonds and five cents a share for the stock. "I am glad to be able to submit a definite offer from someone at last," he wrote. "I have been approached by several persons concerning the Last Chance mine, but up to this writing, the only other offer that seems to me to come from a legitimate purchaser was the one from Mr. Bradley. I think Mr. Bradley of the Bunker Hill & Sullivan Mining Company wants the Last Chance securities and it is just a question with him how cheap he can get them." Clark added, "Sweeny has recently bought enough of the stock . . . to give him control." [21]

Charles Sweeny was the last man the vociferous dissenters among the bank's creditors wanted to sell to. They considered Clark's return of Sweeny's stock as nothing less than high-handed treachery, although Hoyt attended a creditors' meeting to corroborate his opinion that the pool had not been binding. The newspapers printed the creditors' accusations. Sweeny scoffed to O'Connor, "It has stirred up a great deal of public talk, as it naturally would in a small town like this, where everybody thinks a thing of this description is public property and a subject for talk." "At all times," the attorney Frank Post later was to remember, Clark and Sweeny "were dealt with at arms' length and all of their conduct was viewed with suspicion."

Three of the dissidents, Judge Norman Buck, William S. Norman, and Shaw—Shaw had some political influence, for he had received presidential appointments as receiver of public monies at Lewiston, Idaho, and later as postmaster at Spokane—wrote directly to the comptroller, James H. Eckles, charging that Clark had surrendered the stock but lied to the creditors about it. They imputed that, by breaking the pool, Clark had obstructed any equitable sale of the Last Chance Mine because Clark and Sweeny had become the only possible buyers as a result of their stock majority. These accusations were among the most moderate directed toward Clark; others were neither so reasoned nor so calm.

The creditors were not pleased to discover that Cyrus Happy, sometime earlier, had sold his own shares to Sweeny for five cents each, and contracted to sell the stock belonging to the Pricketts and to the Spokane Savings Bank at the price offered by Sweeny. "The mine is always in litigation," Happy said in excusing himself. "I am sick of this continual waiting and waiting. I don't care if the offer does come from Lewis Clark and Charles Sweeny. Let's take it at once and get our money." [22]

Criticism of Clark's return of Sweeny's stock, and his partnership with Sweeny in a bid to buy the Last Chance, culminated in Clark's resignation as receiver. In leaving the post, he dismissed his critics as "lawyers who know nothing of mining." A. D. Lynch, the examiner from Denver, appointed receiver of the First National Bank on May 7, 1897, came to Spokane to see what was happening. He confirmed immediately that Charles Sweeny refused to turn back the stock Clark had given him from the pool.

"The affairs [of the First National Bank] are of a most peculiar character, in that there is almost daily a change of conditions," Lynch's plaintive report to Comptroller Eckles recited. "One of the embarrassments is that the late Receiver of the Bank is now an active

and open participant in the management of the affairs of the Last
Chance Mining Company, and while he has in a number of instances
endeavored to have Mr. Sweeny more nearly meet the views of the
creditors, he has been unsuccessful. There have been interviews,
meetings, and propositions in succession such as to make the conditions almost kaleidescopic." [23]

Some years later, when the question of Clark's performance arose
again, Lynch would recall that he "found . . . that the accounts of
the Receivership had been correctly kept, but I also found that there
was much dissatisfaction and criticism on the part of the stockholders
and creditors as to Mr. Clark's methods of administering the affairs of
the trust." In the matter of the pool, Lynch would remember, Sweeny
acted on Heyburn's advice and "refused to give the stock to me or to
Mr. Clark." [24]

One of Lynch's measures was to form straightway a committee of
larger creditors which included councilman J. M. Comstock, representing the City of Spokane's $34,000 deposit; Grinnell, receiver of
the Spokane Savings Bank, $47,000; B. S. Prescott, city water de-
partment, $11,355; Frank T. Post, attorney for the American Ex-
change National Bank of New York, $41,000; and Arthur Shaw,
$8,500. This committee consulted with Lynch daily, met frequently
with Clark, and talked among themselves, determining at last to sell
the Last Chance, as Clark had. They advertised for sealed bids; none
were submitted. One creditor, an attorney named Samuel R. Stern
who had deposited not more than $300 in the bank, asked for thirty
days to find a buyer but conceded at the end of his month that he had
failed. On the advice of Frank Post, Lynch went personally to see
F. W. Bradley of the Bunker Hill and Sullivan, but he "could not
induce Mr. Bradley . . . to make any offer whatever." The majority
of the committee wanted to sell the mine, sell the bonds, and close
the trust, even though "Mr. Sweeny was the only bidder and refused
to increase his offer."

It finally was evident that Clark and Sweeny simply had waited
until the mine was theirs at their price. Sweeny had written O'Connor,
shortly after he acquired three-fifths of the stock, "It is just a question
now of paying interest on the bonds, managing the property, accumu-
lating the money and like Micawber 'waiting for something to turn
up,' and we are in the finest possible position that we could possibly
be in to wait." [25]

Eventually—in July, 1897—the creditors' committee approved the sale of the Last Chance bonds. "This suggestion met with almost unanimous approval; but two dissenting, and then not active opposers," Lynch noted. He and Post went to Washington, D.C., to discuss the proposed sale personally with Comptroller Eckles, who authorized the transaction. The sale was also approved by the Spokane County Superior Court, "for the best price obtainable." Lynch believed the mine worth less than the value of the bonds and urged closing the trust with all haste.[26]

With Eckles' sanction, on January 19, 1898, Judge Leander H. Prather signed an order in Spokane County Superior Court authorizing the receivers of the First National and Spokane Savings banks to accept Clark's and Sweeny's proposition. The First National then held Last Chance bonds valued at $181,420 par and 83,997 shares of stock, for which Clark and Sweeny offered $99,781. The Spokane Savings held bonds valued at $43,780 par, and 13,111 shares of stock which went for $24,079.[27]

Clark handed over fifty thousand dollars as first payment and agreed to pay the balance within six months. He and Sweeny thus obtained the Last Chance bonds for less than 55 percent of their face value. The bonds and stock (there was no payment for stock) were deposited in escrow at the Exchange National Bank in Spokane for the two partners, to be released to them on payment of the balance of their contract with the receivers.[28]

"The Last Chance mine, whose ownership is acquired by Clark and Sweeny by this action . . . is working 140 men and its mill is handling 200 tons of ore daily," observed the *Spokesman-Review*.

Although Clark and Sweeny extended their contract, the final payment was delivered hurriedly in November, 1898, because the Bunker Hill and Sullivan had filed an injunction to stop the Last Chance from using the Sweeny Tunnel, and possession was important to answer the challenge. Clark offered to pay up early for a consideration and the comptroller approved a discount of $1,000 on the final installment—so the bonds and stock belonging to the two defunct banks finally cost Clark and Sweeny $122,860 plus interest of not more than $100.

Clark and Sweeny, by this time, were overt partners not only in mining but in extensive purchases of Spokane city property.

Before the Last Chance passed wholly into their possession with approval of the court, the two sought new financing for their group of claims surrounding the Last Chance. They pressed O'Connor to advance them money for a new $34,000 compressor, never bought, to pay a $50,000 note against Last Chance bonds, and to buy $5,000 worth of Rossland Red Mountain Gold Mining at ten cents a share— all capital for their Wardner claims. They induced O'Connor to advance $10,000 for one year in August, 1896, by forming a new company, F. Lewis Clark and Company, in which O'Connor, Clark, and Sweeny were to share in equal thirds their three-fifths of the Chemung stock.[29] Their contract for this new company provided that the vote of any two members bound the third, and in May, 1897, Clark and Sweeny voted to dissolve the firm, without rendering an account of its condition. Then, without further exchange of funds, they organized O'Connor and Company which was to be "broader in scope." Within a month they threw up this company, too, without a reckoning satisfactory to O'Connor. O'Connor's compensation from these two contracts appears to have amounted to his listing as president of the Last Chance Mining Company in the *Spokane City Directory* for 1897–98. Clark and Sweeny continued to deal as individuals in mining claims that did not belong to either short-lived company.

O'Connor relied on Clark and Sweeny until they refused him a balance sheet for O'Connor and Company, then severed his association with them. Six years later, convinced Clark and Sweeny had profited $1,500,000 from the Chemung properties, O'Connor was to file suit for the $500,000 he believed his share. He was at litigation for eight more years until his plea was finally dismissed on May 4, 1912, when O'Connor, invalided from a fall in 1906 in a New York subway, neglected to file yet another replication to one of Sweeny's amended answers in a weary round of legal instruments.

Clark and Sweeny seem to have anticipated O'Connor's defection, for late in November, 1897, they convenanted with a Toronto hardware dealer, Alfred D. Benjamin, to form a company that would acquire the bonds and stock of both the Chemung and Last Chance, agreeing that the three would share equally in this new company. Benjamin put in $30,000. Clark and Sweeny, whose investment was valued at $100,000, received $5,000 a month and Benjamin $2,500 from the proceeds of the Last Chance until their loans to the new company were repaid. In addition, Benjamin, a pillar of the Jewish community in Toronto, became eastern financial agent of the Last Chance for two years at a retainer of $6,000 annually.[30] Moreover, Benjamin bought a one-third interest in other Clark and Sweeny mining promotions, shares in the Last Chance, the Chemung, the Native Silver Bell, and Rossland Red Mountain. For this one-third, Benjamin advanced $15,000 and paid another $60,000 during the ensuing year, 1898. A stockholder in the Rossland Red Mountain sued the partners on the ground that they had sold pooled stock without authorization, but lost his case.

Benjamin stipulated that Bruce Clendening of Toronto enter the new firm, eventually to become its treasurer, with the understanding that Clendening report directly to Benjamin. He also ordered James Parkes, an attorney who owned small mining interests in the Coeur d'Alene, to spy on Clark and Sweeny. Parkes had introduced Benjamin to the partners. Consequently, although he signed a proxy on December 2, 1897, allowing Sweeny to vote his Last Chance stock, Benjamin proved more cautious than O'Connor—but then, Benjamin did not respond to the Irish blarney that Sweeny lavished on O'Connor while O'Connor put his money into mines a continent distant.

In 1897, Benjamin was forty-nine years old (two years younger than Sweeny), a native of Melbourne, Australia, whose father took his family to London to live when Alfred was six. At twenty-seven, Alfred, accompanied by a younger brother, Frank, emigrated to Canada, settling first in Montreal in 1875 and then moving to Toronto. Both entered the wholesale hardware firm of M. and L. Samuel; when the Samuels and Benjamins became partners, the firm's name was changed to M. and L. Samuel, Benjamin and Company.

Shortly after Benjamin joined Clark and Sweeny, his uneasiness seems to have been heightened by a decline in production at the Last Chance, which, Clark assured him, would not have happened if Sweeny had not been ill in New York. On his return to Idaho in May, Sweeny laid off seventy-five miners and reduced the mill force to one shift, confident that "as soon as the property gets to running full time, it will soon catch up on the loss." "Mining, of all business ventures," Clark counseled the wary Benjamin in a letter written May 21, 1898, "requires courage and patience and will reward those who possess those great qualities." These words may not have reassured Benjamin, whose Toronto friends were warning him that he dealt with sharpers.

At Benjamin's request, Parkes inquired into the reputations of

Clark and Sweeny. "I am pleased to assure you that the result of my enquiries does not justify or tend to confirm the [adverse] report," Parkes advised Benjamin. "I found Mr. Sweeny's general repute of Spokane and neighborhood [sic] to be that of a hard-headed, shrewd, sharp, business man, but no charge of dishonor or dishonesty was ever hinted at. It must, however, be kept in mind that the standard of business morality in that new country is not as high as in the East." Parkes believed Sweeny worth fifty thousand to seventy-five thousand dollars aside from his Last Chance stock, and reported that Clark was "a gentleman of high education and good repute." Since the latter held real estate bound to increase in value, Parkes "would not like to place an estimate of Mr. Clark's personal worth, but he promises to be a very much wealthier man than his partner, Mr. Sweeny." [31]

Clark and Sweeny, heeding Heyburn, concluded that a new company would be necessary in order to use the Sweeny Tunnel without paying any share of profits from their ore to the Last Chance or Chemung companies. "In view of the fact that the Last Chance bonds and stock to a considerable amount are still outstanding, we could see no good reason why the bonds and shares should reap the profit," Clark expounded to Benjamin, "when . . . the ore does not belong to the Chance property but to the three of us jointly."

Consequently, to keep any profits among themselves, they bought Kennedy Hanley's 100,000 shares of Chemung and his one-eighth interest in the Skookum for $2,000 cash and a promise to pay him $18,000 more. Hanley also had held one-third of the Skookum, which he had purchased for $750 in 1896 from the estate of David McKelvey after outbidding Clark and Sweeny by $50, but they charged fraud and, in the name of the Chemung Mining Company, forced him to turn the one-third over to the company by court order. In his turn, Hanley was to cry fraud within a few months with the charge that Sweeny had switched deeds on him. Clark went to New York where the new firm was formed, the Empire State–Idaho Mining and Developing Company, with officers different from those of the Last Chance and Chemung companies. The president of the New York Guaranty and Indemnity Company, Edwin Packard, was president and—except for Packard and a broker, George Cox, Jr.— the directors gave their written assurances that they would resign when it suited the convenience of the firm's organizers. Packard had met Sweeny during a pleasure trip to the Coeur d'Alenes in 1890, kept in touch, and purchased stock in Sweeny's Idaho and British Columbia companies.[32]

The Empire State–Idaho was capitalized for 75,000 shares at $10 par, and began business with a paid-in capital of $375,000.[33] Of the 37,500 shares issued to organize the company, 37,410 were held by the New York barrister, James Dunne. Six other New York residents owned 15 shares each: Packard, Cox, J. Edward Weld, Herbert W. Grindahl, William S. Dennett, and Richard M. Hurd. Dunne's huge majority of stock was due to his trusteeship of thirteen-twenty-fourths of the Skookum lode on behalf of Clark and Sweeny. At its first meeting on May 31, 1898, the new company's directorate voted its entire $375,000 capital stock to purchase this share of the Skookum, from which the Empire State–Idaho expected to extract most of its paying ore.

The new company then undertook a public offering of its stock to raise money, selling through Cox and his partner, Thomas Callender, members of the New York Produce and Cotton exchanges, "who put it in very conservative hands, only their friends." It was agreed that as soon as the Empire State–Idaho had paid two monthly dividends, Packard was to sell twenty-five thousand shares at $9.00, the revenue to discharge the outstanding notes held by Sweeny, Clark, and Benjamin on the Last Chance, and to buy bonds and shares of the Last Chance. The Empire State–Idaho now leased the Sweeny Tunnel and Last Chance mill and tram for one year at $1,000 a month. There were high hopes for a productive vein in the Skookum that Sweeny described as ten to thirty-seven feet wide and worth $75 a gross ton, compared to Last Chance ore at $54 to $56. Conflicting estimates of this Skookum ore emerged. Clendening reported in May, 1898, that it was "not as good as hoped," and that Sweeny was considering defaulting the Last Chance bonds, while John Presley and Sweeny together wrote Benjamin that the ore was rich and the company ought to clear $18,000 a month on it.

The Empire State–Idaho extended its holdings: in May it purchased the Likely lode for $1,000 and the Cuba Fraction for $750 near its other properties clustered around the Last Chance ground; in September, the directors paid F. Lewis Clark $250,000 for a majority of the bonds of the Last Chance Mining Company which, Clark remarked, had "a peculiar value owing to the language of the mortgage and the relation of the Last Chance to your company's properties." The Last

Chance bonds covered the Last Chance, Emma, Puritan, Republican, Sampson, and millsite claims as well as a lien on the stock of the Shoshone Mining Company which owned the Shoshone, Ibex, and Summit locations.[34]

With this purchase, the Empire State–Idaho swept into its fold virtually every important lode property in the Wardner area not controlled by the Bunker Hill and Sullivan. In barely five months, the Empire State–Idaho had blossomed dominant in the Coeur d'Alene district. Its principal stockholders, Clark and Sweeny, negotiated also for new gold claims in the rugged Buffalo Hump area of north central Idaho where a frantic rush of prospectors plowed through snowdrifts twenty feet deep.

Benjamin was not in the Buffalo Hump venture, although some of his Toronto associates were. He needed money, and apparently grew restive in his connection with two fast-moving western promoters. Clark tried to allay Benjamin's obvious apprehension: "I want to call your attention, my dear friend, to the fulfillment of my promise on this property that it would pay $90,000 a year. . . . I hope you have been successful with your other operations as you have been with the so-called sharpers from the West, as I understand some of our Toronto friends have been pleased to call us." [35]

Benjamin sold, despite efforts to hold him, and his stock went to Clark and Sweeny, who paid $18,162 for his 12,166 shares, including 4,055 acquired when the Empire State–Idaho increased its capitalization to $1,000,000 in September, 1898.[36]

To all intent, therefore, A. D. Benjamin was out of the Empire State–Idaho, and out with rancor, for his attorney, Parkes, found collecting his $5,000 fee difficult. Benjamin had ordered Parkes to close him out with Clark and Sweeny. On completing his task, Parkes commented, "So far as the Last Chance or Empire State venture is concerned, into which I advised you, you cannot have made less than $100,000." Benjamin would have been out of the company shortly, notwithstanding, for before the end of January, 1900, he was dead.

Through Parkes the Empire States–Idaho found a substantial Toronto investor, H. S. Strathy, manager of the Traders' Bank of Toronto, who bought thirty-two thousand shares for $716,000 in the summer of 1899—an average of $22 a share.[37]

Seven months before Benjamin's death, Packard, as president of the Empire State–Idaho, reported to his stockholders, "The result of the business in the first year of existence of this company . . . is most satisfactory." Net receipts from the sale of ore had amounted to $482,988 and net profits for eleven and one-half months to $270,000. The company had paid dividends of $125,638.[38]

The company had obviously prospered. But there were ominous undertones: the Bunker Hill and Sullivan threatened an injunction to prevent removal of ore from disputed ground near its Stemwinder claim, south of the Emma and Last Chance; Kennedy Hanley maintained he had been cheated of his share in the Skookum by Clark and Sweeny; Rutter and Bradley had their case in the courts to resolve title to Kirby ore bodies claimed by the Shoshone; and Sweeny and Clark found themselves increasingly at odds in their partnership.

Shortly after the end of 1899 their partnership broke apart, and they agreed that Clark should acquire their real estate and Sweeny their mining properties. Clark resigned as treasurer of the Empire State–Idaho Mining and Developing Company on May 3, 1900, and was succeeded by the late Benjamin's watchdog, Bruce Clendening.[39] Sweeny moved his offices to the Exchange National Bank Building. He and Clark were linked, thereafter, mainly by lawsuits brought jointly against them.

On his break with Clark, Charles Sweeny attained single eminence among the mining men of the Coeur d'Alenes. The *New York Tribune* interviewed him, calling Sweeny "one of the greatest mine owners and mine operators of the West." He stood virtually alone at the head of two thriving companies, the Empire State–Idaho and the Buffalo Hump.

Times in the Coeur d'Alenes were improving despite limitations imposed by smelters on the production they would accept from each company. Late in 1898 Sweeny attempted a bold stroke—a contract for lead from the Empire State–Idaho at four cents net for "as long as they liked" with the Omaha and Grant smelting company. The smelterers declined. The average price of lead had not risen above 3.70 for ten years. Had Sweeny achieved his proposed contract, his mines would have enjoyed a stable market for years, perhaps for as long as they produced.

By the end of 1899, however, the reorganized American Smelting and Refining Company controlled practically 90 percent of the lead output of the United States and could set quotas for production and smelting as well as dictate prices to its suppliers. With lead plentiful, American was, by January, 1900, advising mining companies, including the Empire State–Idaho, of lowered prices and a need for curtailing production.[40]

Even with limited output, at the end of its fiscal year in July, 1900, the Empire State–Idaho reported dividends paid in the preceding twelve months amounting to $206,879, and dividends paid during the twenty-five months of its existence totaling $524,917. In addition to the Skookum, the company was extracting mineral from the Cuba Fraction, San Carlos, Likely, and Jersey Fraction.

The Empire State–Idaho continued to consolidate and enlarge, buying from Clark and Sweeny the Last Chance bonds previously held by the American Exchange National Bank of New York (which Clark and Sweeny had obtained in March, 1898, for $6,000 cash). From the Buffalo Hump Mining Company, the Empire State–Idaho acquired the Tiger-Poorman properties in the Coeur d'Alene district in 1901 for $2,100,000 worth of new stock voted at a special meeting on January 14, 1901, to increase the company's capitalization from $1,000,000 to $6,000,000.[41]

The Tiger-Poorman included the Ella and Missing Link claims, over which one of the district's historic lawsuits was to rage when Patsy Clark and his allies charged that Sweeny had found a half-million dollars worth of ore but had hidden the fact until he could buy the claims for four thousand dollars.

Although the Tiger-Poorman—on Canyon Creek rather than in the Wardner district—was considered worked out by its sellers, the Consolidated Tiger and Poorman Mining Company, the Buffalo Hump Mining Company spent four hundred thousand dollars to enlarge the mills, develop new reserves, and discover new ore bodies that added half a dozen years to the mines' life.

The Empire State–Idaho, furthermore, excavated the Arizona Tunnel during 1900 from the Viola Mine's portal to provide a second ingress to the Skookum in the Wardner district, which until then could be reached only through the Sweeny Tunnel.

The Empire State–Idaho was profitable enough, in fact, that two million dollars of the increased stock voted in January, 1901, was "distributed or divided among the present stockholders as a distribution of its surplus property value" to give each owner two shares of new stock for one of his old. "The stock of the Empire State–Idaho company is selling in New York for a premium of about 115 percent and passes as a gilt-edged collateral on Wall Street," stated the *Spokesman-Review.*

The company was able, in the summer of 1901, to build and partially equip a new $55,274 mill at Sweeny, on the railroad half a mile below Kellogg, Idaho, to handle four hundred tons of ore daily, and to discuss seriously a plan to erect its own smelter at Spokane in partnership with James J. Hill of the Great Northern Railway. The smelter project was abandoned after inquiry showed insufficient available ores from other mining companies. And the Empire State–Idaho now numbered important men among its directors, including Colgate Hoyt, once a close friend of John D. Rockefeller, Sr.

Edward J. Roberts, general manager of the Empire State–Idaho, wrote in his annual report April 30, 1901, to the stockholders:

I would call your attention to the fact that at the present time, your company is the largest lead producer in the United States, if not in the world, having a shipping capacity of over 4,000 tons of concentrates per month, or say, yearly shipments of about 50,000 tons. This is equal to twenty-five percent of the entire output of the Coeur d'Alene lead district, which section of the country is recognized as producing at least fifty percent of the lead output of the United States. In other words, your company is able to furnish about one-eighth of the entire lead output of the United States, and is in a position to secure the best market prices for our product.[42]

Despite a certain exaggeration in Roberts' estimate of Coeur d'Alene lead production, it was true that the Empire State–Idaho had attained leadership. It was also true that as chairman of its board, Charles Sweeny seemed to have risen to the status he had sought so long. Now he was rich and, within his environs, famous.

# IV

## DISSENT AND DYNAMITE

$C$HARLES SWEENY'S formation of the Empire State–Idaho Mining and Developing Company coincided with the climax of a violent struggle between labor and management in the Coeur d'Alenes. Until the issues between them were resolved, development of the district flagged.

In those bitter nineties even the affluent Bunker Hill and Sullivan threatened to abandon the region rather than work under labor's sway. Time after time investors refused to put money into Coeur d'Alene mines while the labor unrest continued. During his attempts to sell the Last Chance Mine, F. Lewis Clark pointed out to the comptroller that capital could not be lured to a district continuously at war with its workers.

From the day of their discovery, the Coeur d'Alene lode mines required skilled underground workmen. Many of the first miners came from Colorado, Montana, and California, intending to prospect, but after their own claims proved valueless, some stayed to work the mines of the fortunate and aggressive. Owner and laborer lived side by side as easy comrades for a brief period when the camp was new.

Their concord quickly dispelled, however, as absentee owners bought the better mines. The first major sale was that of the Bunker Hill and Sullivan in March and April, 1887, to Simeon Gannett Reed of Portland, Oregon, for approximately $731,765. With the appointment of the aristocratic Victor M. Clement as general manager of the Bunker Hill properties, the company in October, 1887, reduced its wage scale for underground employees from $3.50 a day to $3.00 and $2.50, depending on the company's estimate of the skill and danger involved in particular jobs. The miners struck for restoration of the previous rate and, because workers were not plentiful, the company changed the scale to $3.50 and $3.00. Still alarmed by the arbitrary wage reduction, the Wardner miners organized the Wardner Miners' Union on November 3, 1887, the first union in the Coeur d'Alene district.[1]

This signaled the start of a twelve-year contest between management and labor. Management united to resist labor, then tried to break the unions, sought nonunion workers outside the district, and finally joined in an appeal to the courts and to force—thus following the historic course of management in its early confrontation with workers' organizations. The unions, with advice from Butte's more experienced labor leaders, used threats—and, finally, violence. Eventually the strife deteriorated into an undisguised display of superior force. And in this, management held the trump: the injunction, enforced by federal troops. In the years from 1887 to 1899, the district was to fall twice under martial law. Disputes about the justice of this labor war have echoed as long as survivors of those malevolent days have lived.

Unionism as the undesirable baggage of immigrant workers had been a theme of eastern newspapers sympathetic to management as early as the 1830's. After the Civil War, most of the nation's editors abandoned the thesis that unionism itself constituted a criminal conspiracy from abroad, and attacked, instead, the legality of union methods. But in Idaho, management's newspapers hurled "anarchism" at the unions, and the union's journals flung back the taunt that the mines belonged to the maligned "trusts."

As a consequence, the twelve years between the formation of the Wardner union and the destruction of all the district's unions presents a microcosm of primitive labor-management relations in which both sides were remarkable for their naïveté. Curiously, the mine owners generally were men of wide acquaintance who saw the progress of personnel techniques in other industries, while the miners corresponded with Samuel Gompers, who represented the most advanced thought among the craft organizations of the time. No one on either side of the Coeur d'Alene contention seemed to consider applying the lessons from other industries, perhaps because—as labor continually asserted—so many of the imported workers were immigrants from agricultural regions of Europe, whose acquaintance with unionism was sketchy, and filtered by religion and emotion.[2]

At the beginning of the conflict in 1887, Charles Sweeny was spending his time with John Burke tunneling into the hillside in the Emma and Last Chance claims. Beyond applauding any deterrent to the Bunker Hill company, Sweeny apparently took little notice of the incipient labor movement. Whenever trouble developed between the Bunker Hill and its men, the workers walked out the road from Wardner as far as the Last Chance and, standing on Last Chance property through which the Bunker Hill road ran, catcalled the Bunker Hill. Throughout the years of labor conflict in the Coeur d'Alenes, the Bunker Hill and Sullivan provided a focus for miners' grievances, and the Last Chance stood as a convenient outpost for union men deployed against the Bunker Hill.

By 1891, when the Last Chance had become a producing mine and the Tyler had enjoined it, four miners' unions existed in the Coeur d'Alenes, named for the towns where they met: the Wardner; those at Burke and Gem organized in October, 1890; and the Mullan, dating from November, 1890. On January 1, 1891, each union chose two delegates to a central executive committee, as the unions attempted to unify. By various estimates their total membership was between 1,600 and 2,200 men, the Wardner unit the largest with approximately 800 members. The 1890 census of Shoshone County discovered only 5,382 white persons; Wallace, the most populous town, counted 878 of them.

The unions were not founded after cataclysmic onslaughts, but following pocket skirmishes like the 1887 wage cut by the Bunker Hill or the strike in May, 1890, occasioned by poor food in the Tiger-Poorman boarding house—a quarrel resolved in five days. The year 1891, when the union central executive committee began significant operation, the *Wallace Press* characterized as quiet, peaceful, and full of progress. It was July when the central committee, rather than a local union, notified the Granite and Custer managers that all underground workers ("candlebearers") must receive $3.50 daily. When the companies ignored this ultimatum, two hundred workers left their jobs until the pay issue was settled.

Although the issue of wages seems clear enough, as a consequence of political, religious, and economic ferment the formative activities of the Coeur d'Alene unions were diffused by other discords. It was then, and remains today, perplexing to define the specific causes for any dispute involving workingmen in the Coeur d'Alenes during the last decade of the nineteenth century.

The Knights of Labor, who enjoyed their greatest influence in Idaho during the early nineties and frequently were accused of directing the Wardner union, lobbied in both national and state legislative bodies because many union men believed political action necessary to improve their condition. The owners lobbied directly as individuals, and gained political strength by running for office. John A. Finch, an owner, was elected an Idaho state senator in 1890 when Shoshone County went Republican. The effectiveness of political action, however, was dissipated by party instability. Within four years of Finch's election, all of Idaho and much of the West was split on the issue of bimetallism. There were Silver Republicans, Silver Democrats, Gold Republicans, Populist–Silver Democrats, and so on.

The American Protective Association, the anti-Catholic movement born in 1887 in Iowa, also exercised some influence in Idaho through the regular Republican Party. A Catholic missionary in 1891 found "the APA's at this time . . . working hard in northern Idaho." At the height of the labor war, Charles Sweeny complained to his erstwhile benefactor, Jeremiah O'Connor, "The APA's are making it hard for me and the Catholics." [3]

Other political and economic events shaped the expanding struggle. A series of local bank failures and news of a near panic in Wall Street presaged the financial collapse of 1893. The Spokane National and associated banks at Wallace and Murray suspended in December, 1890.

The compressed air drill, which the miners called the "buzzy" and "the widow maker," was introduced to Coeur d'Alene mines during 1890 and 1891, and rude electrical plants rose by 1891, the district's first dynamo located at the Last Chance. [4] With a machine, one man could do the work of several hand drillers. With machines and electricity, the mines' operating efficiency improved, although general mechanization lay years ahead.

The Bunker Hill and Sullivan, with 350 to 400 employees, was the largest employer in the Coeur d'Alenes—and its mines among the easiest to work. Along Canyon Creek, near Burke, the mines were wet, constantly pumped, and the men wore gum (rubber) clothing they supplied themselves. At Wardner the mines were dry and required no special clothing, a fact often mentioned by the Bunker Hill management in its colloquies with labor. The management also noted that its boarding house rates had been reduced from seven to six dollars a week when wages were lowered.

The Bunker Hill employees disputed with their management, however, over one dollar a month withheld from each man's wage to pay the company doctor. The workers ignored the fact, if they knew it, that withholding the dollar was customary in Rocky Mountain mines. The Wardner union proposed to build a union hospital, the company protested that nonunion men would not benefit from it, and finally Clement allowed his employees to vote on various medical plans on August 6, 1891.[5] When the candlebearers discovered their union plan was not on the ballot, only two bothered to vote. Clement nonetheless declared that his tabulation favored a company hospital, and added haughtily that employees who did not approve of having a dollar withheld were "not only at liberty, but requested to call at the company's office for their time." His notice was tacked up at the mine entrance, the traditional bulletin board. When the night shift read Clement's notice, all but four walked out. The Wardner union met, declared a strike against the company, and urged all workmen, union members or not, to join them. In addition to demanding its own hospital, the union insisted that the $3.50 wage be restored to all underground workers.

Sweeny's Last Chance continued to operate, unaffected by the Bunker Hill's dispute. Most of the Last Chance men were union members who stood beside the strikers on Last Chance property to jeer the handful of men walking to work along the road toward the Bunker Hill portal.

After fifteen days the Bunker Hill's absentee stockholders capitulated, agreed to reinstate the $3.50 daily scale, to withhold for the company doctor only after an individual employee assented, and to rehire without discriminating against union men. As the company had discovered, it was cheaper to keep the mine running without profit than to incur the expense of reorganizing its crew.[6] Wardner's narrow street rang with celebration when the agreement was announced, women and children beamed, merchants shook miners' hands, and the unions at Burke, Gem, and Mullan jubilated, too.

Had the miners detected the ominous events in other mines of the West—layoffs, lockouts, closures due to high operating costs, and political pressures—or interpreted correctly the resolution of the Bunker Hill's owners, their return to the stopes would have been less confident. From this day, there was to be no turning back until the superior force of management had destroyed unionism in the mines.

Before acceding to the union, the directors of the Bunker Hill secretly ordered Clement to eliminate gradually the organized workers and replace them with nonunion employees. Clement stationed a hiring agent in Spokane and the company actively sought immigrant mine workers in California, Colorado, and Michigan, so that within three years the union would charge that the company "has been persistent in bringing Italians" to the Coeur d'Alene district.[7]

Meanwhile, during the winter months of 1891, the Northern Pacific and Union Pacific railroads increased their ore-hauling rates on a schedule that averaged $2 more a ton and would cost the Coeur d'Alene mines collectively perhaps $20,000 more each year. The Anaconda company in Montana asserted it could not profit under higher railway rates, shut down, and put sixteen hundred men out of work. Other Montana companies did the same. This news from Montana failed to impress Idaho's unions. When the mine owners of the Coeur d'Alenes decried the twin adversities of $3.50 wages and freight rate increases, the district's unions regarded the owners' threats to close their mines as a local imbroglio. They did not detect the pattern of management's increasing unity against labor in Rocky Mountain mining districts.

In the Coeur d'Alenes, the mine owners had organized themselves into what the *Wallace Press*'s editor, Adam Aulbach, believed to be the first owners' union in the United States. A preliminary organizational meeting of "all the producing mines" on November 21, 1889, resulted in a draft of proposed by-laws for the approval of each company's owners. Clement, who represented the Bunker Hill at this meeting, explained to Reed that "the objective is mutual benefit and protection. We will act in a body if necessary when dealing with smelter and railroads for incoming and outgoing freights. Will also endeavor to regulate many abuses in the labor question." The principal managers formally accepted the bylaws and formed the Mine Owners Association at Wallace on February 16, 1891, as E. J. Roberts later explained, "for the purpose of mutual benefit and protection, . . . the settlement of labor conditions, the maintenance of the secret service bureau, and the adjustment of claims for damages resulting from several concentrating mills contaminating the Coeur d'Alene River with wash and tailings." [8] Although the MOA functioned without written charter or incorporation, it was empowered to tax the companies according to their tonnage and to bargain in their behalf.

It was the Mine Owners Association, therefore, that assailed the railways and ordered the mines of the Coeur d'Alene district shut down on January 19, 1892, in protest against higher ore-hauling rates.[9] The closure affected nearly sixteen hundred mine employees. Next, the owners met on February 25 in Spokane, agreeing to meet every two weeks thereafter, and appointed delegates to treat with the railroads at St. Paul and Omaha. Charles Sweeny was among the MOA representatives, with Clement, Esler of the Helena and Frisco, Patrick Clark of the Poorman, S. S. Glidden of the Tiger, John Finch and Amasa Campbell of the Gem and Union, C. D. Porter of the Custer, and George McAuley of the Stemwinder and Sierra Nevada.

After two months without shipments, the railroads yielded, restored their former rates, and the owners announced that the mines would reopen on April 1. Having won their demand for lower railroad rates, the owners determined to reduce wages, too, so as they published the date for reopening, they declared, "Believing earnestly that the advance of the wages of carmen and shovelers, which was forced upon the mine owners during the last year, was unjust and unreasonable," wages again would be $3.00 for candlebearers for each ten-hour day. This declaration was signed by the MOA, demonstrating that within three and one-half years, labor relations in the district had evolved from employer talking to his individual employee, to company speaking to its organized workmen, and finally to united management negotiating with unions directed by a central organization.

The unions' central committee rejected the proposed wage reduction. Mass meetings at Wardner, Burke, Gem, Mullan, and Wallace indicated that merchants and townspeople generally supported the unions, as well they might, as less money for miners meant less money for merchants.

The owners' deadline, April 1, passed without one mine reopening. When A. M. Esler growled that "a million lies" had been circulated in the press by "certain flannel mouths," several of the talkative owners, concluding Esler meant them, drew a little apart. The unions, too, bickered within ranks: the Wardner union was miffed that, after it had stood against the Bunker Hill, the other unions voted to erect the new hospital at Wallace rather than at Wardner. As an added abrasive, the United States Marshal for Idaho, Joseph Pinkham, prowled the district serving nearly two hundred warrants obtained from Federal Judge James H. Beatty by the Bunker Hill and Sullivan to quiet union men who allegedly encouraged others not to work.

With tempers edgy on both sides, the Miner Owners Association announced, "We have decided . . . to allow our mines to remain idle until June first, by which time we hope to have made such arrangements as will enable us to resume business." [10] The association added that "certain and speedy means" would assure reopening. Esler and McAuley both said publicly that the MOA would never hire another union man. Such statements could only mean that the owners intended to import crews and that the primary issue now was recognition of organized labor. Union strength washed at low ebb, if enthusiasm did not. During the wintry months that the mines had been closed, the labor force in the Coeur d'Alenes dwindled to perhaps eight hundred men. Retail trade withered; many businesses boarded up; houses stood vacant along the narrow streets of towns gripped in canyon jaws; idle men gossiped on the boardwalks.

Each contending side now sought help, the mine owners from the government, the union from Butte's strong and militant unions. With ready sympathy, the Butte Miners' Union lent the Coeur d'Alene central committee five thousand dollars to underwrite its campaign against the companies, taking as collateral a ten-year lien without interest on the frame union halls. Butte's union also voted to assess each of its six thousand members five dollars a month to help their Idaho brethren as long as necessary. Infiltration from Montana brought experienced, aggressive labor leadership to the Idaho mountains, some of it tinged with socialism. These Montanans were the men Charles A. Siringo, a detective, later typified as "vicious, heartless," and of whom Mrs. Victor (Flora) Clement was to aver, "The men of the inner circle . . . who had been imported from outside the Coeur d'Alene district, were of a different breed" from the area's citizens. [11] The mine owners generally referred to the unions' advisers as "anarchists."

By May 1 the mine owners had succeeded in recruiting, through a hiring agent, a contingent of seventy-eight workers from the Iron Mountain district of Michigan with promises of $3.50 a day. The editor of *Iron Ore*, the newspaper at Ishpeming, warned the recruits that they were to be strikebreakers in the West. Most who ignored the editor's admonition were recent arrivals from Finland, Denmark, Poland, Austria, and Sweden, the least stable element among Michigan's miners, those who might be expected to move on. Each paid his own transportation, or agreed to repay money advanced for it, amounting to $33.00 from Duluth to remote Idaho.[12]

When this scab patrol entrained, Charles Sweeny "assumed on the part of the mine owners the position of guarding or superintending them," he later testified.[13] Why was Sweeny chosen? Was it because his mine was enjoined and he had little to do, or because he talked boldly, or was a war veteran inured to armed conflict if it came, or because he was the principal manager at troublesome Wardner, except for the Bunker Hill which some owners believed the core of the strife? Whatever the reason, Sweeny's bellicose behavior as weeks passed suggest that he enjoyed his job.

Sweeny expected the union to resist imported labor "to the extent of open force and violence" and believed that Thomas O'Brien, president of the central executive committee, had received several cases of Winchester rifles. Company detectives warned that certain union elements would not shirk violence. Campbell and Finch received a threatening letter that said, "We are seventeen strong and the miners' union is too slow for us."

For its part, the union assumed the owners would apply force through the courts and militia. The union could not doubt from past events that the state government would support the owners.[14] The central committee charged that the Mine Owners Association shut the mines "to throw the onus of stoppage and stagnation in business upon the Miners' Unions," as O'Brien phrased it, and that when the union rejected lower wages offered in May, the MOA had begun "sedulously to work against" the unions. There was not a strike but a "lockout," declared O'Brien, quoting Amasa B. Campbell of Campbell and Finch to that effect.

If there had been doubt that union recognition or, indeed, union survival, was at issue, it was dispelled on April 22, 1892, when Campbell and Finch's Consolidated Mining and Concentrating Company and their Badger, Union, and Standard mines discharged their crews for belonging to unions. The Mine Owners Association, determined to reopen before June 1 with nonunion labor, consigned the Michigan imports to the Union Mine, protected by armed guards.

Sweeny engaged Joel Warren, a former chief of police in Spokane and in 1892 a deputy sheriff in Kootenai County, Idaho, to hire guards.[15] Warren produced fifty-three men from Idaho towns at three dollars a day. His guards traveled by special car hitched to a Northern Pacific freight train from Spokane to Rathdrum, Idaho, to stay overnight, where Sweeny joined them, bringing aboard several cases of Winchester and Marlin rifles labeled with his name. As the train proceeded to Helena, Montana, to meet the Michigan scabs, Sweeny and Warren handed out guns and blue arm- and hatbands as identification.

While they were riding westward, the Michigan miners were warned again by union men at trackside that they were to be strikebreakers. Four or five deserted the train at Helena; the others were locked in their cars by Sweeny's guards and the train started for Idaho, rerouted to avoid Missoula where the union prepared a major effort to stop the convoy. After a switch found open at Mullan, Idaho, had been closed, the scabs rode to Burke, arriving May 14, 1892, where a noisy crowd jostled on the station platform but parted to let the Michigan miners and their keepers through. Led by the resolute Sweeny, fluttering a blue ribbon from his hat, his company of fifty-four guards and seventy-four "first-class miners" marched the thousand feet up the wooded hillside to the Union Mine.[16]

When Warren ventured into town, he was arrested on the charge of impersonating a deputy marshal, and was released on a one-thousand-dollar bond posted by Sweeny and McAuley. While Warren was jailed, however, McAuley asked the union's secretary what might happen, was assured Warren would not be harmed, and then invited the union men around him to Cameron's saloon where they toasted a peaceful solution to their differences. McAuley, Sweeny, and the other mine owners knew many union men personally, did not fear them, and maintained an amicable if strained relationship. For a time the union guaranteed that mine owners would not be physically attacked.

Sweeny often conferred with union groups, and would have relished Flora Clement's melodramatic account written some years later: "Victor told me Charlie Sweeny had volunteered to go up to Burke to have a conference with the miners. It was like putting his head in the lion's mouth, since it was nothing for a man to be 'bumped off' without warning. He came back safe and sound, however, and was looked upon as more or less of a hero."[17]

Once the Union Mine reopened, Sweeny asserted that many Colorado and California miners applied for jobs in the Coeur d'Alenes. "I personally have guaranteed them employment and the [mine owners] association will see that they get it," he said. The owners preferred to rehire a former employee, he added, and "all we require is that he sever his connection with the union and leave us to manage our business in our own way, and not try to run the mine for us." [18]

Trains bearing scabs continued to reach the district. One carried 365 men for the Bunker Hill and Sullivan, recruited in California by John Hays Hammond, and most of them United States citizens, observed the *Coeur d'Alene Miner*. The *Wallace Press* counted six scabs at the Sierra Nevada, twenty-one at Sweeny's Last Chance, and others at the Gem, Frisco, and Union mines, a total of 403 nonunion men working. The workers ran a vocal gauntlet of union men each day. A number of scabs went over to the union side, joining the others dependent on a central depot in Wallace where four hundred dollars' worth of food and clothing was distributed daily to strikers' families.

On June 1, when the Mine Owners Association estimated it had eight hundred imported workmen employed, its spokesmen telegraphed Idaho Governor Norman B. Willey that "a state of lawlessness exists," urging that he exert the force available to him when "civil law is inadequate," and setting forth various alleged beatings and threats to nonunion men. Willey replied with a personal tour of the district, followed by his proclamation of June 8, 1892, importuning that unlawful congregations, combinations, and interference cease, and threatening martial law.

Shortly before, when a rumor spread that martial law had already been invoked, the recording secretary of the Butte union, Gabriel M. ("One Eyed") Dallas, accused Sweeny of spreading the tale and gave him a message to deliver to all the mine owners: "We withdraw our protection from you, and hereafter you must look out for yourselves." [19]

With several mines working, although none had attained normal production with imported labor, the Tiger-Poorman company, to restore its income, determined to reopen on June 13, and to pay $3.50 to all workers, asking no questions about union membership. The wage rate was consistent with that formerly paid in shaft and wet mines, and the Tiger-Poorman was both. The central committee hailed this erosion of the owners' unity as a union victory—bands marched, and as a huge bonfire crowned one hill above Wallace, exuberant miners set off dynamite on another. After the mine owners met at the Carter House, a grim Sweeny asserted, "The rest of the association will stand like a rock. We have signed an agreement to stay by one another and there will be no more breaks." [20]

The Fourth of July, traditionally a day for union parades, patriotic speeches, picnics, and sports, passed in an atmosphere of tension. Esler hoisted an American flag on a broomstick at his home to observe his efforts toward importing labor, sent four kegs of beer to his men at the Frisco Mine, and helped them drink it, offering the toast, "Here's to the health and prosperity of non-union miners."

Governor Willey, frightened by the mine owners' constant warnings as phrased by Heyburn, had written President Harrison asking for four companies of federal troops to prevent an armed outbreak, and Harrison, replying on the Fourth, declined. Willey's report from the Idaho National Guard showed it lacked "effective order or discipline," and might muster no more than two hundred men.

Within five days open conflict erupted, as Willey had feared. The *Coeur d'Alene Barbarian,* a monthly newspaper published by R. E. Brown with bias for the owners, had been printing information the union considered secret. One of the *Barbarian*'s sources was the Pinkerton detective Siringo who, under the assumed name of Leon C. Allison, acted as recording secretary for the Gem Miners' Union. For seven months his reports of union plans, posted to St. Paul, typewritten there, and mailed to John Finch, provided the principal information about union activities for the owners. Finch leaked tidbits to the *Barbarian.*

Recognizing that there was one spy, if not several, within their ranks, the union organized its own secret detective system to expose informers and defectors. This secret union detective bureau was also charged with ejecting unsympathetic workers from the district, often going to this task masked and armed. Siringo was uncloaked on Saturday, July 9, and the news of his activities rippled angrily through the mining towns. Ten stands of National Guard rifles were stolen that day. Armed men began converging in Gem. Women and children left town as the sullen crowd increased. Siringo escaped capture by crawling under a board sidewalk until he could slip through the brush into the hills.

Three hundred feet above the town, a cordwood barricade protected the Gem Mine's guards and workmen, forbidden to leave their enclosure. Since the tension seemed to ease toward evening, the Idaho inspector general, James F. Curtis, who was visiting the district, assumed the crisis past and took a train from Wallace to Boise on Sunday.

At five o'clock on Monday morning, July 11, however, union men began firing toward the Gem and then at the Frisco, aiming above the barricades simply to frighten out the scabs, but when mine guards returned their shots, both union and company marksmen sought human targets. Bullets shattered windows and splintered frame buildings in Gem.

At approximately eight-thirty, union men slid dynamite down the penstock (an inclined sluice for water) at the idle old Frisco mill to blow it up. The Frisco crew surrendered, and after a short negotiation the Gem workmen and guards capitulated. They were escorted to Wallace and given twenty-four hours to leave the district. Three had been killed in the fighting, a detective and two nonunion men.

The union was not done, however, for that evening approximately four hundred armed members rode hand- and flatcars on the railway to Wardner where they discovered unguarded the concentrators of the Bunker Hill and Sullivan, the Sierra Nevada, and Sweeny's Last Chance. They occupied the plants, placed dynamite beneath that of the Bunker Hill, posted sentinels on Last Chance property to protect its union workmen, and dispatched a committee to tell the mine owners their mills had been captured.

Confronted in this manner, the owners acceded to a demand that they pay off their scabs and tell them to leave the Coeur d'Alenes within forty-eight hours. Attorney Heyburn, meanwhile, telegraphed Governor Willey what had happened. Willey ordered out the Guard, 196 men in six companies, and wired President Harrison for federal troops. The War Department directed nearby military posts to put down what Washington clearly believed an insurrection.

The first troops to reach the district—they found it quiet—were three companies of blue-clad Negro infantrymen from Fort Missoula, Montana. Other soldiers routed from the west stopped when Victor Clement wired frantically that troops must not tie up trains until his nonunion employees had escaped the district. About three hundred scabs were evacuated on a Union Pacific train guarded by union men. An army officer who saw the herd of escapees at Tekoa, Washington, concluded that most were foreigners, cursing, wailing, "a class not calculated to excite much sympathy either by their appearance or actions." [21]

The governor proclaimed martial law in Shoshone County on July 13, troops continued to flow in with foot patrols preceding trains to inspect trestles for explosives (finding none), and by July 15 there were fifteen hundred soldiers encamped in the narrow canyons of the Coeur d'Alene district. Company B, Fourth Infantry, brought back the scabs from Tekoa with them.

The soldiers could not have found a more orderly population, for the union miners had returned to their jobs or homes. To hear some tell it, the events of July 11 had resulted from antagonism between the *Barbarian* and Adam Aulbach's caustic *Wallace Press* which supported the unions, while others blamed inflammatory letters and telegrams sent the governor by Heyburn.

State deputies, accompanied by soldiers, arrested between three and four hundred men from various towns, confining them in warehouses or an enclosure at Wallace called a "bullpen," on diverse charges that included conspiracy, destruction of property, and even murder. The mines reopened with nonunion men protected by companies from the Fourth, Fourteenth, Twenty-second, and Twenty-fifth infantries commanded by General W. P. Carlin.

Both sides behaved well. The Negro troops were well disciplined, cheerful, and efficient, an officer observed, although "extremely objectionable to the lawless element." By August the area seemed docile to the military commanders, but Heyburn insisted that the troops stay on.

Residents who feared a renewal of violence after the troops left petitioned for a permanent military post in the Coeur d'Alenes, and because a post would afford good business for the merchants, the jealous towns fell contending among themselves which should have it. Willey, however, showed no interest, and the proposal waned. Even Heyburn's eloquence could not hold the soldiers indefinitely; by mid-September they began breaking camp. The last unit departed November 15, and martial law terminated November 19, 1892.

The battle between owners and union thereafter deteriorated into an uneasy truce, for the unions returned to intimidation and the owners to coercion by judge and politician. Before the last soldiers had decamped, indeed, someone posted a notice at the Gem's portal:

"Look out, scabs! Before this month is over 1,500 pounds of Giant powder will be exploded and all in this mine will be sent to hell. If we cannot work this mine, no one shall." A number of union men wrote James Curtis, who had been elected Idaho's secretary of state, their whimsical requests to locate guns or other property lost while they were in the bullpen. Curtis replied politely but restored none of the articles.

A large number of prisoners' cases were considered by a grand jury that convened at Coeur d'Alene on August 23, 1892. Indictments were returned there against perhaps one hundred and fifty men, and others were brought to trial May 28, 1893, in Boise, but in both jurisdictions only thirteen union men were convicted of contempt of court (for disregarding injunctions) and four of criminal conspiracy. Released, the remaining bullpen prisoners found their belongings and scattered in all directions. The conspiracy convictions were reversed by the United States Supreme Court because the defendants had been convicted of crimes against the State of Idaho in a federal court which lacked jurisdiction.[22]

One of the union leaders, a Butte attorney named Peter Breen who had helped frame Montana's mining laws, recovered his ten-thousand-dollar cash bail, said to have been provided by Marcus Daly. By the end of March, 1894, all those convicted were free. In addition, Victor M. Clement was gone, succeeded as manager of the Bunker Hill and Sullivan by F. W. Bradley on March 20, 1893.

Sweeny joined Bradley, and McAuley of the Sierra Nevada, in announcing that employees of Wardner area mines might board and buy supplies where they chose. There would be no company stores or boarding houses, and, significantly, the owners would not protect anyone on their payrolls. The Mine Owners Association loosed its requirement in many towns of the district that unmarried workmen must trade and live in company stores and houses, a restriction that had been widely resented.

Union warfare was by no means Sweeny's sole pursuit, although labor relations took a good deal of attention. The Tyler closed the Last Chance by injunction for a second time in March, 1893, and Sweeny's personal resources neared exhaustion. He cooperated with other owners, nevertheless, in urgent meetings in Spokane with the traffic managers of the Northern Pacific and Union Pacific railways to demand reduced ore-shipping rates, asking a decrease of as much as

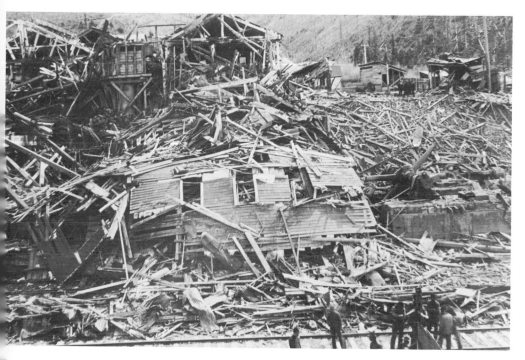

Wreckage of the Bunker Hill mill, 1899, after dynamiting by union members. (Barnard-Stockbridge collection, University of Idaho)

Wallace, 1899, with United States troops encamped on the bank of the south fork of the Coeur
d'Alene River during the period of martial law which followed destruction of the Bunker Hill
mill. (Barnard-Stockbridge collection, University of Idaho)

Last Chance mill, mine, and buildings, about 1900. Several Wardner residences can be seen to the left beyond the mill. (Barnard-Stockbridge collection, University of Idaho)

Miners riding the Last Chance tram to Wardner, below, about 1900. Down the gulch behind the hills lie Kellogg, the river, the railroads, and the mills. (Barnard-Stockbridge collection, University of Idaho)

four dollars a ton to Omaha and Denver. The arguments over rates duplicated those of one year earlier when the owners blamed high shipping costs and high wages for their mines' inactivity.

While the Last Chance was enjoined and the mine owners embroiled with the railroads, the First National Bank of Spokane failed. Sweeny was deeper in financial mire than ever. When asked the state of his health, he would answer—as he did for the rest of his life—with a phrase that became his slogan, "There's nothing wrong with me that money won't cure!"

The year 1893 was memorable in the Coeur d'Alenes both for financial panic and for ebullient renewal of union confidence. A number of union men released from the bullpen attended the five-day convention, May 15–19, in Butte where the Coeur d'Alene joined the Montana unions in forming the socialist-bent Western Federation of Miners. This alliance ended whatever influence the Knights of Labor had enjoyed in the Coeur d'Alenes. The new federation was to direct a series of violent strikes throughout the West, and to extend revolutionary industrialism beyond the mining industry. For the Coeur d'Alene unions, the WFM represented national leadership and propaganda to combat the owners' recruitment from other mining districts. After Charles Sweeny's armed convoy of 1892, one of the federation's stated aims was abolition by law of private armed guards.[23]

"We have given the mine owners a fight to the finish," Breen crowed, "and if they are not satisfied we can give them some more." The Gem and Frisco discharged, without demurring, twenty-three nonunion men identified by a union committee. The union's secret detective bureau frightened out a number of scabs, one tied to a handcar turned loose on a hill, and others hauled from their beds at night. July 11, the anniversary of the Frisco and Gem surrenders, displaced July 4 as a day of union parades, speeches, and fireworks.[24]

Even resurgent unionism could not dispel the facts that most of the mills closed periodically, many men were laid off, and the mine owners, who won another $2 reduction overall in freight rates, declared they could not continue to pay wages of $3.50 without incurring operating losses.

The unions were never surer of their strength. They supported the Populists, who in 1894 won all but two elective offices in Shoshone County, and they seated the president of the central executive com-

mittee, Edward Boyce, in the state senate. Evidently satisfied their
dominance could not be challenged, about forty union men, masked
and with their coats turned inside out, on July 3, 1894, shot and
killed John Kneebone, an employee of the Gem who had been a
witness against the union in 1892. Then the forty attempted to evict
the Gem's superintendent, R. K. Neill, its foreman, and two others.

A grand jury sat more than a week deliberating Kneebone's
murder. They found no one who would identify his killers, and reported in part: "We . . . suspend our labors . . . deploring the
spirit of our citizens, which, either through a reign of terror . . . or
through sympathy with crimes of this character, prevents the bringing
of these murderers to justice." Four days after the Kneebone killing,
a charge of high explosive, rolled under the Bunker Hill and Sullivan
electric powerhouse, damaged the building. When two hundred and
fifty miners and fifty millhands struck for higher pay on November 23,
1894, the directors of the Bunker Hill and Sullivan ordered the mine
and mill closed.

As a consequence Wardner was virtually without a payroll after
seventeen months of turmoil—the Bunker Hill closed by terrorism
and wage demands, the Last Chance by injunction (its manager,
Charles Sweeny, had recently been rounding up Coxeyites and now
prospected in British Columbia), and the Sierra Nevada pressed by
a union demand to discharge one John Perry as an APA. Heyburn,
a stockholder, shrugged, "Under present conditions, property in the
Coeur d'Alenes is worth nothing, anyway. If necessary, let the
property go." The Sierra Nevada refused to fire Perry.

To the east of Wardner the Canyon Creek mines, however, had
returned to work in August, 1894, paying $3.50 a day, rehiring union
men, and saying, "Long existing differences are hereby buried for
all time." Sam M. Roberts, president of the Western Federation of
Miners, referred in a union circular to the "amicable settlement"
between a majority of the Coeur d'Alene mine owners and the union,
although the Bunker Hill, "controlled by the Standard Oil Trust,"
held out.[25] Roberts labeled Wardner a "scab" town, urging every
western labor organization to warn men away from the Coeur d'Alenes.
Such was union supremacy for the moment that C. R. Corning, the
Bunker Hill and Sullivan consulting engineer, declared he would not
recommend resuming operations until the district's citizens assured
him of their support.

Early in 1895 businessmen of Wardner circulated a petition—doubtless inspired by the Bunker Hill—pledging their "moral support" and endorsing wages of $3.00 and $2.50 a day for mine employees, with the understanding that the company would advance pay to $3.50 and $3.00 when the combined value of one hundred pounds of lead and two and one-half ounces of silver reached $6.00 on the New York market.[26] Henry Drought headed a mass meeting of Wardner and Kellogg merchants where 170 signatures were obtained. The union stigmatized the petition as an "APA trick," proclaiming, "Here is the true motive of the APA organization—destroy organized labor." Although union men were by no means uniformly Catholics, they were predominantly Populists. The American Protective Association, allied with the Republican Party, drew little distinction between papist and Populist. Of the petition, a union pamphleteer wrote, "The APA's signed unanimously, and in return for this favor the [mine owners'] association agreed to employ only such men as that organization should recommend." [27] The company boycotted those merchants who did not sign its petition; the union, those who did.

Even though lead and silver prices had not recovered from 1893, with the petition as assurance of citizen support the Bunker Hill and Sullivan prepared to reopen, applying first to Federal Judge Beatty to enjoin union men, under his restraining order of 1892, from entering the company's property or interfering with its operation. This accorded with the usual management practice between 1880 and 1930 when industries applied for, and were granted, injunctions both to prevent possible damage to property and to assure a justifiable expectation of profit. By mid-June the mine was working again, using inexperienced labor, with ten or twelve armed guards patrolling its flume and mill.

On June 28 the Tyler injunction was lifted from the Last Chance and suddenly Charles Sweeny was back on the scene, busy, secretive, and purposeful. By the fall of 1895 perhaps five hundred men were working in the Wardner mines, the Last Chance's mill running at capacity with three teams of horses hauling its output to the railway in constant rotation. Sweeny paid generally the same wages as the Bunker Hill, but his was considered a union mine. The union apparently forgave him for importing Michigan workers at gunpoint, and condoned his wage scale because he hired union members. Union antipathy centered, as usual, on the Bunker Hill and Sullivan.

The general return of good times improved the New York combined prices for lead and silver very little, for lead continued to fall during 1896. Silver, on the other hand, achieved its highest average prices in 1896 for the entire period 1893–1913.[28] Under a wary truce with the unions, the mine owners returned to their customary occupations—to suing one another, to exploration, development, and merger. With relatively stable employee relations, lower rail rates, and better equipment, the mines again profited.

Behind the improved economy lurked the owners' certain knowledge that some day, the union must be broken. Terrorism continued, deplored by citizen and union officer alike. On May 10, 1896, another dynamiting and an arsonist's fire damaged the Bunker Hill's mill machinery.

Although the influence of the APA in the mines broke, as it did everywhere, against the political shoals of 1896, neither labor nor management won a clearly superior position in the elections in Shoshone County. The 1896 Republicans shattered into factions—Heyburn led the gold wing's rump convention—allowing a coalition of Populists and Silver Democrats to win many offices, and to cast, as well, a strong vote for Frank Steunenberg, who became governor.

After the election, labor, which took credit for Steunenberg's majority, miscalculated the extent of his gratitude and grew bolder. Steunenberg favored unionism. When elected, he was publishing a Democratic newspaper in Caldwell, Idaho, and before coming to Idaho had been a member of a typographers' union. The Boise Typographers elected him an honorary member. To the Western Federation of Miners, the new governor appeared to be a friend in Idaho's most strategic office. He seemed to represent a break in management's traditional alliance with political influence.

The events of the mid-nineties rippled past Charles Sweeny without involving him, for the time being, because he was engrossed with his Rossland mines, with using Last Chance tunnels to exploit adjoining claims, seeking new capital, and soothing Jeremiah O'Connor. Between 1896 and 1898, Sweeny seems to have left even the talking to others of the Mine Owners Association, notably Campbell and Finch, although he continued to take part in its affairs.[29]

Without intending to, Sweeny and the unions joined in an offhand alliance, for while Sweeny fought the Bunker Hill and Sullivan in court, the unions fought it in the streets and meeting halls. Because the Bunker Hill battled competitors and union alike, the *Spokane Daily Chronicle* alleged that a group of Coeur d'Alene mining men offered to buy the company, pay "handsome dividends" to Fred Bradley, who was promoted to president on June 17, 1897, and thus end the incessant labor disputes that upset the whole district.

Sweeny disliked what he called "the Bunker Hill crowd." "They . . . have encouraged everything that would injure us," he once wrote his manager. His opinion seems typical of that of the other mine owners at the time. A request to the governor from the Shoshone County commissioners in June, 1897, to disband two companies of the National Guard at Wardner "as a continual menace to the peace and good order of the country" was considered an attempt to disarm the Bunker Hill, which sustained one of the units.

Of perhaps twelve hundred men working in Coeur d'Alene mines by the end of 1898, the Bunker Hill employed approximately four hundred, mostly nonunion, at wages of $3.00 and $2.50.[30] The union continued to display its power by punishing individual miners and occasionally a company, so that Governor Steunenberg was to tell congressional investigators in 1900, "Men were driven out of camp from day to day, scarcely a week passing without some outrage being committed upon law-abiding citizens." And John Finch would say, "The fact is, in that canyon in the last five years, no man, whether he was merchant, saloon keeper, miner, or in any other employment, has tried to criticize even mildly any act of the union . . . and so complete has been the tyranny . . . that no criticism has been indulged in by anyone regarding the acts supposed to have been ordered or authorized by the miners' union. . . . We, of course, felt powerless to do anything to protect our men, and have borne whatever they have seen fit to inflict upon us or our men and have said nothing."[31]

The ultimate crime of unionism was not terror, however, but the unpredictable behavior that prevented a steady flow of profit to shareholders in the Coeur d'Alene mines. The Bunker Hill, for one, paid approximately 2 percent annually on its capital stock—not the return investors expected.[32] The companies, and perhaps the unions as well, determined on a momentous showdown. It came in the spring of 1899.

By then Charles Sweeny had organized the Empire State–Idaho. Only 8 of its 140 miners were nonunion, and the company permitted its men to trade and live where they pleased. The Bunker Hill, accused of reopening its company stores, answered that it merely held an interest in certain ones but did not require its men to patronize them.

In April, 1899, the Wardner local of the Western Federation of Miners, composed chiefly of Empire State–Idaho workmen, resolved to force union recognition on the Bunker Hill and Sullivan, partly to eliminate permits that the company required of men who applied for work.[33] These permits showed past employment and union affiliation, among other information, and the union averred the Bunker Hill used them to blacklist union applicants.

Beginning April 19, the union posted notices in Wardner calling on nonunion men at the Bunker Hill and Sullivan to join the union at once. On Sunday morning, April 23, the Wardner union met, determining that the mine owners must recognize the union and restore the $3.50 wage to all underground workers. The union sent a delegation to the company offices. Fred Burbidge, acting manager of the Bunker Hill, refused to accept the union committee as representing his employees, and his superintendent, Albert Burch, told them the company would "shut down and remain closed for twenty years" before it would recognize the union. The Bunker Hill did reinstate its 1892 wage scale of $3.50 for miners and $3.00 for carmen and shovelers.

When the union replied that the increase was not concession enough, the Bunker Hill management advised the Shoshone County commissioners that a mob was interfering with its work and wired Governor Steunenberg, who replied with a suggestion that the company refer its problems to the state board of arbitration, established in 1897 but not yet faced with a stern trial.

After the example of the Bunker Hill, the Empire State–Idaho announced the same increased pay scale, but Charles Sweeny, hurrying to Wardner from Spokane, locked his Sweeny Tunnel and mill at the end of the Tuesday day shift, fearful of violence to his property. It remained closed for two days, until the union (and the central executive committee) voted to accept Sweeny's new scale, whereupon the night shift reported for work on Thursday. Edward Boyce, the Wardner union president, explained, "The members decided it would be best to hold our old crowd together by letting them go back to work at the increased scale of fifty cents."

The union balloted to strike the Bunker Hill, however, and Burch then declared that not only would the company maintain its previous lower wage rate but that any employee who joined the union would be discharged. A dispatch to the *Spokesman-Review* now described Wardner as "an armed camp" and related that on April 26, the morning shift for the Bunker Hill, stopped on the road through the Last Chance, had been given four minutes at gunpoint "to go back down the hill." The union captured and stopped the Bunker Hill tramway for one day but did it no harm.

While the union met all night in its hall, the night shift of nonunion men sloshed timidly uphill in a rainstorm to work under armed pickets posted along the Bunker Hill boundaries. The union itself set pickets on the Last Chance to protect it, and to spy on the Bunker Hill—although if the latter shut down, the Last Chance would also close, for it relied on the Bunker Hill's plant for compressed air to run its drills.[34]

On the morning of Saturday, April 29, 1899, between eight hundred and one thousand men—about two hundred armed and some masked —commandeered the Northern Pacific train at Wallace, ordering its engineer, Levi W. Hutton, to stop and blow the engine's whistle repeatedly at the stations between Wallace and Wardner. In response to the whistle, men emerged from each town to board the captive train, swarming onto its nine flat- and orecars. Doubtless many had no notion what was to happen; they went for whatever excitement the day might offer. Hutton was to testify that he believed few men knew the ringleaders' plans.[35]

The Bunker Hill company, where the train was directed, had heard warnings "that the union was going to blow us up," and when another alarm reached it several days before April 29, the company declared it would appeal to the district court "if the strikers show any hostile intentions." Burch now received word that the trainload of men was on its way from Wallace, and at first concluded that the mob only meant to demonstrate "to make our employees quit." When he heard about the guns and dynamite on board, he ordered the mine and mill evacuated, and telephoned the county commissioners of his apparent peril. The commissioners told the sheriff, John D. Young, who boarded the train to see what was going to happen.

At Wardner, where the night shift leaving the Last Chance warned the oncoming day shift to return home, Sweeny's mill and mine were closed as the train approached town. The saloon keepers in Wardner wisely bolted their doors when they heard the train coming—the mob's shouts and the train whistle audible before the engine could be seen. The train proceeded, Hutton's captors waving him on with a pistol, despite his protest that the heavy engine might collapse the Oregon Railway and Navigation Company trestles between the Northern Pacific trackage and Wardner.

When the train stopped at 12:25 P.M. at Wardner, some riders debarked with evident purpose while the others followed. They advanced on the Bunker Hill, a mile and a half from town, and placed Giant powder beneath the company's building. Burbidge and Burch had scampered into the brushy hills and by evening reached Spokane. Some two hundred armed men on the company's property also fled. The explosive (stolen enroute from the Helena and Frisco magazine) was set off about three o'clock, and the mill burst skyward. As the blast shook Wardner, the Bunker Hill mill settled in debris. The union men whooped back to their train, forced Hutton to return as he had come, dropping off riders at each station. By nightfall, the district was placid.[36]

Although scores of telegrams were dispatched during the train's excursion and the dynamiting, eight years later a detective paid by the MOA reported his conversation with George Allen, a member of the Burke union, who had been a telegraph operator on April 29, 1899, in which Allen claimed he "received and destroyed messages by the dozen that would have proven . . . just who the guilty parties were that blew up the Bunker Hill." [37]

Charles Sweeny rushed from Spokane to Wardner in response to a telegram and wired Edwin Packard, "Strikers destroyed Bunker Hill. Have now gone home. Everything quiet. No fight against us." He sent a similar message to H. S. Strathy in Toronto, who was on the verge of investing in Sweeny's companies.[38] Despite Sweeny's assurance, Sheriff Young and two deputies guarded the Last Chance for two days because its manager thought it, too, in danger.

Governor Steunenberg, hospitalized in Boise, wired President McKinley at eleven o'clock on the night of the dynamiting, asking for federal troops. They were immediately granted. The first soldiers to reach the district were seventy-five Negro regulars of Company M, Twenty-fourth Infantry, commanded by a white officer, Captain J. B. Bachelor. They arrived in Wardner on May 2 from Spokane where they had been stationed one month, occupied in beautifying the city's new army post. As his personal representative with power to act, Steunenberg sent his state auditor, Bartlett Sinclair, who started north from Boise with the conviction that the union's leadership was criminal and his duty was to destroy it, a view shared by Burbidge of the Bunker Hill.

Steunenberg's prompt, angry action dismayed the union, for as Judge Fremont Wood observed, "The leaders of the organized miners were evidently proceeding on the assumption that no action would be taken by Frank Steunenberg inimical to their interests; provided they immediately returned to their ordinary occupations." [39] Wood's seems the most reasonable explanation for the swift peace that fell throughout the district after the Bunker Hill dynamiting. Nearly all the union miners showed up on their regular jobs the morning after the explosion.

On his way to Wardner by train, Sinclair reached Spokane April 30 to stay the night where, went a fanciful union tale, Sweeny as spokesman for the MOA relayed an offer to back Steunenberg with $50,000 to run for the United States Senate if he would declare martial law. [40] Spokane's mine owners undoubtedly entertained Sinclair and gave him their versions of the labor situation, for not only were Sweeny, Finch, Campbell, and others on hand, but the Bunker Hill and Sullivan's president, Bradley, and its chief attorney, Curtis H. Lindley, were in the city. They had come from San Francisco for the trial of their suit against the Last Chance, scheduled to begin May 1. It was postponed, however, because papers relating to the case were lost in the mill's destruction.

Martial law was proclaimed in Shoshone County on May 3, and more federal troops poured into the Coeur d'Alenes, ordered there by Brigadier General Henry C. Merriam, commander of the Department of the Colorado. Under Sinclair's direction, the soldiers arrested wholesale the men in mining towns and captured some "Wardner rioters" (a newspaper term) as far away as Spokane. John Finch growled that a number of men he knew were not involved in the dynamiting were taken—but he supposed the arrests were necessary. Prisoners were crammed into warehouses and boxcars until a high board enclosure could be erected—another bullpen—at Wardner. For alleged failure to act, the county commissioners and sheriff were removed from office by the district court. [41]

Charles Sweeny took no direct hand in Sinclair's measures because he faced demanding problems of his own. He was involved in a delicate argument over the value of ores in the principal mine in Idaho's Buffalo Hump district, and barely six weeks earlier had formed the Buffalo Hump Mining Company which needed all the attention he could spare it.

He was able to resume work in the Last Chance at Wardner with hand drills on May 1, but his machinery lay idle because the compressor had been blown up with the Bunker Hill mill. Sweeny could brook no long interruption in the flow of his ore: he was digging in the Shoshone's contested ground which a court might snatch from him, and to attract Strathy, Sweeny's company had to maintain its enticing production rate. Conceivably the Empire State–Idaho's whole success depended on Sweeny's ability to produce ore at this moment— and that grew harder each day, for not only were hand drills slow, but Sinclair's operatives were arresting the men.

Sweeny telegraphed his father-in-law, Jeremiah T. O'Neil, in Oakland, who scouted California mining camps but was able to recruit only a handful of experienced workers willing to move to the Coeur d'Alenes. One O'Neil telegram on May 31 read, "Five men left Thursday for Wardner via Tekoa. Expect more to leave Friday. Hard work getting them. Nothing in Copperopolis." There were similar wires, suggesting Sweeny's urgent need. One, dated June 2: "Five men by steamer, two by rail, left here for Wardner via Tekoa yesterday. Think after this can get men quicker. Can you wait for steamer of seventh inst. Surest way. All good men." [42]

The Empire State–Idaho had earlier ordered its own compressor but did not anticipate delivery before mid-August. Sweeny had located another plant, however, a second-hand ten-drill compressor that could be moved from North Lapwai, Idaho, where it had been used by the Tacoma contractor, Nelson Bennett. By a stroke of good fortune Sweeny confirmed his purchase of this used compressor on the day before destruction of the Bunker Hill's. He now demanded immediate delivery of Bennett's plant, and thus was able to return the Last Chance to machine drills early in May.[43] O'Neil continued to deliver men, but he could not send them north as fast as Sinclair popped experienced hands into his bullpen.

Believing his best chance to catch leaders of the raid lay in locking up everyone and releasing the innocent, Sinclair ordered arrest of the entire male populations of Gem, Burke, and Mullan. Hearing of this, more than fifty barristers descended on the Coeur d'Alenes to offer their services to impounded miners.

"There must have been between three- and four hundred men," Sinclair asserted, "who ought to be convicted of murder in one of the degrees, or for arson, and perhaps seven hundred for conspiracy." He was determined to stamp out unionism because "the State cannot endure these revolutions happening every three or four or five years; the State does not wish to and cannot stand the expense of suppressing these riots." [44] The men he wanted most fled into Montana, however, eluding his deputies and soldiers.

Sinclair's most difficult task lay not in roundups but in crushing the spirit of unionism. The *Spokane Daily Chronicle* remarked that Montana union officers feared that wage cuts in the Coeur d'Alenes would spread to their area and that recent consolidations of mining companies at Butte and Anaconda would forge the owners together with added strength. Indeed a 1900 congressional inquiry was to reveal that wages in Montana, Idaho, Colorado, and Utah mines "have decreased somewhat during the past twenty years." As a consequence of such fears, the Coeur d'Alene captives were under constant pressure from Montana to stand firm against the state and the mine owners, lest their capitulation weaken the Western Federation of Miners throughout the West. The federation had maintained their vigor at Cripple Creek in 1894, Leadville in 1896 and 1897, were beset at this moment in Utah as well as in Idaho, and did not relish a collapse at any point.

Sinclair, General Merriam, and the attorney, Lindley, collaborated on a proclamation to the mine owners issued May 8 that said, in part, "You are . . . notified that the employment of men belonging to . . . unions or other criminal organizations during the continuance of martial law must cease. In case this direction is not observed, your mines will be closed." The proclamation appointed Dr. Hugh France, the county coroner and Bunker Hill company physician, as agent of the State of Idaho to issue permits "authorizing [applicants] . . . to seek work," and required mine owners to refuse jobs to men without permits. Among the mines and companies listed under the permit system were the Last Chance, Empire State–Idaho, and the Consolidated Tiger and Poorman for which Sweeny was negotiating. The form of the permit was like that used for several years by the Bunker Hill and Sullivan.

In the permit Sinclair discovered his devastating weapon against unionism. Imposed by military force, the permit destroyed the Western Federation of Miners in the Coeur d'Alenes. It proved so effective that the Mine Owners Association, when the permit had been discontinued in January, 1901, was to establish an employment bureau at Wallace to screen applicants for mine work anywhere in the district, and through the bureau, to winnow the Coeur d'Alene labor force for twenty years after.[45] In this manner, the MOA perpetuated the usefulness of the permit if not its form.

Except for Sweeny's Last Chance, which was working with a total payroll as small as 25 men, and the Bunker Hill, with perhaps 150, virtually every mine in the Coeur d'Alenes had closed in the weeks following proclamation of martial law. The *Spokesman-Review* on May 8 estimated 1,530 men out of work as a result of the shutdown. By June 2, however, small crews of timbermen reopened some Canyon Creek mines and the Standard was operating drills with a handful of imported men. Nearly eight hundred permits had been issued for underground work to men who stopped at Wardner to obtain them before going upriver to Canyon Creek. Sinclair, in a frenzy of administration, urged haste in the interminable hearings to free innocent men from the bullpen, but the process ground slow. Of 586 men he counted in the stockade, Dr. France estimated 75 percent were of foreign origin.[46] Many of them were scabs of 1892, converted to unionism.

As the task of prosecuting the men in the bullpen wore through the summer, Charles Sweeny busied himself with his mines. All but one shift boss walked out of the Last Chance when bosses were ordered to sign permits with their men, but replacements came from Joplin, Missouri, where the Missouri and Kansas Zinc Miners' Association had shut its mills for two weeks in a price war with smelters. Others came from Montana, Utah, and Colorado.

By September the Bunker Hill had rebuilt its mill, and half its new equipment was running. In November ten of thirteen men tried—of the hundreds arrested—were convicted not of murder, arson, conspiracy, or dynamiting, as Sinclair had hoped, but of forcible seizure of a train carrying United States mails, for which they were fined one thousand dollars each. Nine were sentenced to twenty-two months in prison, the remaining one to twenty months.[47]

As a consequence of the permit system, the Western Federation of

Miners was crushed in the Coeur d'Alenes by the time martial law ended on April 11, 1901. Dr. France had compiled a table of workmen from the November, 1899, payrolls of mining companies to demonstrate that "the mines are not filling up with old dynamiters"; he reported that of 2,073 men hired, only 99 had been "members of the style of union governed by the Western Federation of Miners," and 1,357 had been born in the United States. In an introduction to his tabulation, the doctor asserted that "only one-fourth of the men employed under miners' union rule were American." [48] A congressional commission found that of perhaps 7,000 permits issued in the twelve months after April 29, 1899, only 130 went to men previously affiliated with a Coeur d'Alene labor union.

Union men continued to work and to scheme in the Coeur d'Alenes, and from time to time gun shipments were uncovered, plots thwarted, and clandestine meetings discovered, but the mine owners kept control through their detectives and their employment bureau. In 1909 Charles Sweeny was to leave the Coeur d'Alenes—and to that time there would be no union outbreak to rival those of 1892 and 1899.

It is perhaps notable that the report of the general manager to the stockholders of the Empire State–Idaho company for the year ending April 30, 1901, did not mention that organized labor affected production or profit. Stanly A. Easton, then general manager of the Bunker Hill and Sullivan, wrote of the year 1903, "From a turbulent and lawless country, with correspondingly intermittent operations, the Coeur d'Alene has now become one of the most prosperous . . . fields in the West, giving steady employment to 2,000 men . . . and not less than 1,000 additional at the smelter plants . . . and allied industries." [49]

Five years after the dynamiting of the Bunker Hill mill, wage rates were no higher in the Coeur d'Alenes than they had been in 1892, although all over the West the eight-hour day was gaining acceptance. By 1905 three of the principal mining companies of the Coeur d'Alenes were to endorse an insurance association covering mine workers.

But concern for the workers diminished in the early years of the twentieth century. The Coeur d'Alene district, after 1899, was characterized by corporate expansion, improved technology, and monopoly —not by labor's struggle for unity or recognition. Employee relations in 1910 were nearly as antiquated as they had been in 1890.

# V

## TEN-FOOT HOLES
## AT BUFFALO HUMP

$O$NE of the last pell-mell mining stampedes in the western United States was the gold rush to the Buffalo Hump in north central Idaho in the final eighteen months of the nineteenth century. Outside the inland Pacific Northwest, little of its story is known. Before the golden gleam flickered out, the Buffalo Hump became virtually Charles Sweeny's camp.

The Buffalo Hump itself is a bold, bare, granite peak rising 8,926 feet above sea level on the divide between the Salmon River and the north fork of the Clearwater—the one stark, conspicuous hump in the mountainous primitive country along the western border of the Clearwater Mountains.

Prospectors who had flooded into Florence, Elk City, and Warrens in the gold madness of 1861 named the peak because it looked to them like the humped back of an angry prairie buffalo. They displayed a penchant for picturesque names: Pig Whistle Canyon, Thunderhead Mountain, Moose Butte, North Pole, and Gospel Peak. Lured by tall tales that gold dust was so plentiful that it was being "stored in gum boots," those 1861 prospectors dashed by the thousands into the wild country, many a one on his first innocent search for ore. The rush collapsed in a short time. Most prospectors left within a year or two of the original discovery, some retreating headlong before a wild snowstorm that whipped the country on July 4, 1862, and others beckoned by newer gold finds in southern Idaho. Only the hardy and experienced stayed, and a few placer claims continued to produce. Three decades later, the Idaho Mining and Developing Company at Elk City continued to operate its hydraulic plant, and companies persevered at Florence, Warrens, and Dixie, fringing the Buffalo Hump at distances of thirty to fifty miles.

Despite the deflation of the 1861 rush, the search for gold did not entirely subside in the years after the Civil War, and seekers tramped the region in summer, spurred by the usual legends of lost mines that halo old gold camps. In 1895, a gold claim, the Banner, was located near Florence, and sold to a group of Spokane and Idaho investors who also bought the nearby Gold Bug. The president of the Banner company was Stephen S. Glidden, and its secretary, his son-in-law, Frank R. Culbertson, both veterans of the Coeur d'Alenes. Because the Banner yielded some ore in 1896, during the following year the company hauled in a twenty-five-ton mill, piece by piece on horseback, to expand its operation.[1]

Then on August 8, 1898, two prospectors from Colorado, Charles H. Robbins and Kenneth B. Young (alias Bert Rigley), located two claims they named the Big Buffalow and the Merrimac. Rigley later related that they had been hunting deer when he picked up an intriguing forty-pound chunk of rock to roast in the evening campfire. Charred, it was revealed as sulfide ore with gold visible to the naked eye. The next morning, the two men staked their claims. The Big Buffalo — others soon corrected the original spelling, "Buffalow"—lay only five hundred feet downhill from the summit of the hump. With the Merrimac, it followed a vein that, once seen, was readily traceable from its outcrop for the entire length of both claims, each the regulation six hundred by fifteen hundred feet. Two days later the two men staked the Oro Fino, a southerly extension of the Merrimac.

Reports that circulated after the pair filed their claims attracted a flurry of prospectors from northern Idaho and, what was more significant, brought agents of the major mining companies in Idaho, Montana, Utah, and British Columbia who scouted the locations on the south foot of the bare peak. The district organized a short time later was named the Robbins Mining District, but it was always popularly known as the Buffalo Hump from the eminence that glowered above it.

Soon after recording their claims, Robbins and Young dug three tons of ore from two holes about ten feet deep and shipped the ore on horseback fifty-five miles to the Banner's Huntington mill at Florence to have it treated and assayed.[2] The Big Buffalo's ore assayed six ounces of gold and seven ounces of silver, yielding four ounces of fine gold and 360 pounds of concentrates. The concentrates, consigned to the Tacoma smelter, returned a gross value of $2,800 a ton.[3]

News of the smelter report brought more prospectors scrambling to the Hump by way of Grangeville, Idaho. They hurried over the rude paths of earlier gold hunters to record 280 claims before the snow fell. How to transport ore in quantity from this sharp, broken country, no one knew. The nearest railroads were the Northern Pacific at Lewiston, Idaho, and the Oregon Short Line at Weiser, Idaho, each a hundred miles away.

On the heels of the prospectors trailed promoters, among them an indefatigable Russian Jew, Samuel I. Silverman, a one-time cook sent west for his health, who had been wealthy and bankrupt several times during his career in mining. At that moment, he owned the Badger Mine, thirteen miles from the Hump. Silverman had vied in the Okanogan, Rossland, Slocan, and Boundary mining developments, establishing his reputation as a shrewd judge of ore and avarice. With John Burke, Ross Thompson, and others, he had been an incorporator of the West Le Roi and Josie Consolidated Mining Company, whose ringing name echoed those of Rossland's best producers. After the silver-price crash of 1893, Silverman was reduced to working as a Burke millhand, but two years later he was promoting again, living expansively.

In the fall of 1898 Silverman interested two Spokane men, W. S. Norman and James F. Cameron—the latter a stockholder in Sweeny's Rossland Red Mountain—in the Jumbo claim, apparently one of the best in the Hump district. Silverman's workmen dragged supplies through the snow from the Badger to the Jumbo to begin digging. When they bored down a hundred feet, the Jumbo's ore assayed a capricious range from twelve to seven hundred dollars a ton. Naturally, Charles Sweeny heard about the Jumbo. On November 29, 1898, he joined Cameron, Norman, H. W. Casey, and C. P. Robbins of Rossland, in organizing the Buffalo Hump Development Company to buy the Jumbo.[4]

Silverman also sent his engineer, Walter Hovey Hill, to inspect the properties located by Robbins and Young. Between the Big Buffalo and the Merrimac Hill found a 140-foot fraction, which Silverman bought for four thousand dollars. Then Silverman began negotiating to buy the Big Buffalo, Merrimac, and Oro Fino from Robbins, Young, and five other men who now held shares because they had grubstaked Robbins or claimed portions as his former partners.

Accustomed to regarding its gold boom days as past, the slumbering farm village of Grangeville had needed no town government for twenty years. Now it suddenly again became an open mining town, bustling with prospectors, investors, promoters, and newspapermen. Overnight Grangeville bulged with an itinerant population of two thousand who lived in tents, under wagons, or in huts, repeating to each other the words of the *Idaho County Free Press* that the Buffalo Hump was "a monster 'hump' of ore . . . untouched while prospectors passed over it for years." The newcomers apparently forgot that experienced miners had despaired of the Hump as too isolated to be exploited.

Although the Big Buffalo, Merrimac, and Oro Fino had been located late in the Buffalo Hump's short summer, and snow soon clogged trails, the rush gathered momentum. Prospectors fought blizzards and snowdrifts to reach the Robbins district, then drove their stakes into the snow and tacked their notices on trees to claim ground they could not hope to see for months. When the snow melted, location notices fluttered high above reach in the trees, fastened fourteen to twenty feet from the ground. In the rugged Hump country, snow fell twelve months of the year and stayed eight or nine.

Two men opened a rawhide supply route—a single cowhide loaded with supplies, sewed shut, hitched to a cayuse, and skidded over the snow. Pack trains carried food and freight from Grangeville for four to six cents a pound; freight from Lewiston to Grangeville, "hauled over a range 5,000 feet high," cost two cents a pound. The Northern Pacific and the Oregon Railway and Navigation companies both surveyed routes toward the Hump during 1899. The OR&N held a right of way up the Clearwater to Grangeville.

By February, 1899, Robbins, Young, and their assorted shareholders had received two offers for their properties, one from Silverman, and the other from Hartwig A. Cohen, recently restored to his position as general manager at Salt Lake City for the De Lamar Mining Company. The company's owner was Captain Joseph R. De Lamar, a former sea captain grown rich and living in Paris; he owned a number of mining properties in the intermountain West, including the

De Lamar Mine in Owyhee County, Idaho, then a world-famous gold producer. After sending his reports in coded telegrams carried by pony to Grangeville to be wired to Salt Lake, Cohen bid $500,000 for the Big Buffalo, Merrimac, and Oro Fino. He apparently could not arrange terms for payment suitable to the owners of the claims, however, and he had never seen the locations in person. When he rode into the Hump country, Cohen became ill and fell from his horse. He canceled the inspection, returned shaken to Salt Lake City, and refused to negotiate further for Hump claims.[5]

Silverman, meanwhile, touted the district extravagantly to F. Lewis Clark and Charles Sweeny, who agreed that he should act as their agent. On their behalf Silverman bid $575,000 for the three claims—Big Buffalo, Merrimac, and Oro Fino—agreeing to pay $25,000 down on February 1 and a similar amount on April 1.[6]

The Portland *Oregonian* pointed out that the valuation of the properties depended solely on two crosscuts—two ten-foot spade trenches—and that "hardly enough work [has been] done to form an opinion of the ore shoots or dip of the vein, as the greatest depth obtained is only ten feet. The general character of the ore in the district is identical to that of the Alaska Treadwell mine or ores from the Mother Lode in California." The *Oregonian* reporter, caught by the enthusiasm of the moment, thought when he looked into the two ten-foot holes that their owners could reasonably expect to take out 75,000 tons of ore worth $1,250,000.[7] With newspaper estimates and excited prospectors' predictions, the myth of the Buffalo Hump grew. Its promoters forecast that this would be the biggest gold camp of all. Already the Jumbo, about four miles southwest of the Big Buffalo, was being worked by adit driven from a canyon, as many of the Hump's mines were to be worked.

The Northern Pacific's periodic guidebook, *Wonderland '99*, described the attractions for travelers along the railroad's route. Of the Hump, editor Olin D. Wheeler wrote:

The present outook is that the [Buffalo Hump] region will become a permanent mining camp, eclipsing all others. W. Clayton Miller, a well-known mining engineer, states that he never before found such a showing for gold. . . .

First-class six-horse stage coaches leave Lewiston daily for the Buffalo Hump region. . . .

It is stated . . . that a property . . . upon which not more than $5,000 had been expended by the original owners, was sold to expert mining men of Spokane for a sum exceeding half a million dollars. . . .

Buffalo Hump and the surrounding country will out-Klondike Klondike unless all signs fail.

Early in 1899 there remained no valid claims to be staked in all the Buffalo Hump country. Naturally a few were nevertheless "located" as stock promotions or for sale to gullible rich, and one company sold stock in a scheme to drain Crystal Lake for claims supposed on its bottom.

By this time the Hump boasted three towns, Buffalo, Callender, and Concord, the last a supply base for the Jumbo Mine. Callender was named for one of Sweeny's brokers, Thomas O. Callender of New York, who accompanied Sweeny on an outing to see the mines. Of the Buffalo Hump, a traveler wrote the *Idaho County Free Press* that there was "not a habitable house in the camp, but some tents and shacks all under two to ten feet of snow. . . . It storms incessantly and traveling in the light snow, breaking trail every time, is work of the hardest kind."

No hardship deterred those who envisioned gold. Clark and Sweeny organized two new companies to exploit the Buffalo Hump. They called one the Buffalo Hump Syndicate, organized in Spokane, and the other the Buffalo Hump Mining Company, a New York corporation that included many of the figureheads who served as directors of the Empire State–Idaho. The New York company issued a fine-printed prospectus circulated in the East and Canada, sold a good deal of stock— perhaps $750,000 worth—to speculators, paid over the first $25,000 that Sam Silverman had promised the Robbins-Young group, and sent Sweeny's engineer, Miller, with Charles M. Fassett, a Spokane assayer, to look over the country. Miller found "the oxidized ore at the surface was quite free and averaged twelve dollars per ton in gold." [8]

Lane C. Gilliam, a Spokane real estate broker and mining promoter, already had examined the Big Buffalo, Merrimac, and Oro Fino to assist Clark and Sweeny in promoting the mines. He took four samples of ore, the deepest from six feet down, had them assayed, and wrote, "It has all the indications of the greatest gold producing camp ever discovered in America." [9]

With a down payment on the three original discoveries, Clark and Sweeny spent upward of $50,000 opening two veins during the worst weather of the winter, and had completed a seventy-two-foot shaft and crosscuts totaling perhaps one hundred feet, when Charles Sweeny visited the Buffalo Hump to negotiate in person.

Suddenly at the height of Grangeville's confidence in the Hump, Sweeny deflated their hopes. He called together the owners of the Big Buffalo, Merrimac, and Oro Fino, and as one of them, Frank Mc-Grane, recalled, Sweeny declared, "There are no three ten-foot holes . . . in the world that are worth one half a million dollars. However, I am now developing the claims and I am willing and anxious to continue development work and take a chance. I will write you a check now for $250,000 and take your deeds." [10] Astounded at Sweeny's bold attempt to buy them off for half the price agreed, the owners turned him down peremptorily. They were convinced that De Lamar would pay $500,000 for their properties and believed that Sweeny had raised $780,000 in New York and Toronto—using their claims as bait to stock buyers—to acquire and develop mines in the Hump district. Now, they thought, he could only be trying to increase his potential profit.

Sweeny told Grangeville's stunned citizens, meanwhile, that when the Big Buffalo reached a depth of thirty-five feet, the ore thinned. In his opinion, the vein was pinching out. But he protested that he "did not condemn the camp because we could not see our way clear to take the Big Buffalo group, for as a matter of fact we are today spending $5,000 to $6,000 a month" on other properties. [11] The *New York Sun*, reaching Grangeville, carried a paragraph that quoted Clark and Sweeny as saying the Big Buffalo ore grew inferior as its shaft deepened. The *Engineering and Mining Journal* mentioned that prominent veins seemed to thin with depth, voicing its apprehension for the future of the Buffalo Hump.

The amazement at Sweeny's assertions in Grangeville was greater because other investors seemed confident that the Hump would prove itself rich. An English company spent $100,000 for the San Francisco group, consisting of the Baby Louise, Monte Carlo, and San Francisco, the first claims to be located after those of Robbins and Young. Boston capitalists took eighteen patented claims called the Concord group, and ten in the St. Louis group.

"Mr. Sweeny's statements about the shaft being in low-grade ore cuts no ice with us," declared one owner, quoted by the *Idaho County Free Press*. "Mr. Sweeny has an axe to grind. . . . It is to his interest to depreciate the value of the property. I have known Charlie

Sweeny a long time and I do him no injustice in saying that he is 'onto his job' when it comes to a mining deal." [12]

Despite Sweeny's disparaging report, three shifts of his men worked with a steam hoist to lift ore from the Big Buffalo shaft. Grangeville preferred to think that Clark and Sweeny discredited the claims shamelessly so they could drive down the owners' price, pay off grubstake claims cheaply, and dissuade other capital from coming into the Hump area.

On May 10, 1899, the *Grangeville Standard's* editor, A. J. MacDonald, had written acidly that Charles Sweeny's statement printed in New York newspapers

has already told with baleful results to the mining, commercial and farming interests of the Clearwater region. . . . It has scared capital from closing purchases at the Hump. . . .

The ruse of Clark and Sweeny has several purposes. It is a well known trick among the speculators on the stock exchange, who wreck railroads and other great enterprises to profit by it. . . .

The poor-showing report is designed to depress the value of the Hump properties for several reasons—to prepare for a low valuation in the event that the grubstake suit should result in a verdict for Rice and Mallory; to obtain a reduction in price from the original owners of the Big Buffalo, Merrimac, and Oro Fino . . . and to enable them and their colleagues to purchase cheaply other choice properties in the vicinity.

Sweeny remained adamant. He spread his opinion that the Buffalo Hump veins pinched out at depth, and on January 1, 1900, he and Clark failed to pay the third $25,000 due under their agreement with the Big Buffalo owners. Missing a payment automatically threw up the bond. Indignation followed astonishment at Sweeny's actions.

Notwithstanding their dramatic withdrawal from the Big Buffalo group contract, Clark and Sweeny continued—as Sweeny had pointed out—to invest in the Hump district itself. To Grangeville citizens, the partners' continued activity in the mines simply proved that Sweeny's covert purpose was to buy the best claims at depressed prices. In July, 1899, Clark and Sweeny had bonded the Jumbo and Crackerjack and held them until October, installing Charles' brother, Mike Sweeny, as manager with instructions to reveal nothing about the properties. In August, Clark and Sweeny had put ten men to work on the Buffalo Bull, a northerly extension of the Big Buffalo, and Edward J. Roberts, who had been offered the general managership of Sweeny's mining empire, visited the camp on an inspection tour.[13]

In retrospect, the impetus for Clark's and Sweeny's continued participation in the Hump's development seems to have emanated from the Coeur d'Alene district. There Sweeny bought the historic Tiger-Poorman, one of the first producing mines of the south fork. He obtained the mine, located as two silver-lead claims on Canyon Creek but now joined by a network of adits, by buying the option of Joseph Mac-Donald on six hundred thousand of the Tiger-Poorman's million shares at thirty-five cents a share. MacDonald, who had been general manager of the Helena and Frisco, joined Sweeny as a consultant. Sweeny had undertaken discreet diamond drilling in the Tiger-Poorman before dealing with MacDonald, and now bet his observations against the belief of the Tiger-Poorman's owners that the property was worked out.

The Tiger-Poorman had not paid a dividend in years as the result of a mill fire in 1896 and a flooded shaft. But Sweeny told a Grangeville resident that "he would not give it up for the entire Buffalo Hump," estimating the Tiger-Poorman "would pay him $50,000 a month" after restoration. Sweeny was right. Shortly after acquiring and refurbishing the Tiger-Poorman, he hit a rich vein east of the exhausted one, and the mine began paying handsome dividends again, as much as $210,000 in the first eight months of 1900.

Patrick Clark, who had been instrumental in the sale, cried fraud. A group of former stockholders from Butte sued to set aside the sale of the Tiger-Poorman to Sweeny, whereupon Sweeny engaged Van B. De Lashmutt, a former Portland mayor and now a Spokane mining broker, to settle with the Butte contingent. De Lashmutt, after negotiations, bought them out for another $250,000.[14]

At the time of its purchase, Sweeny placed the Tiger-Poorman in the Buffalo Hump Mining Company as a subsidiary, and his enthusiastic eastern shareholders in the Buffalo Hump company demanded that Sweeny broaden their profit by extending their control in the Buffalo Hump district. Clark had resigned his partnership with Sweeny, and, now on his own, Sweeny reluctantly asked De Lashmutt to see if the owners of the Big Buffalo, Merrimac, and Oro Fino would consider a new, lower price for their holdings. Caught by his own expansive promotion of the Hump, Sweeny could not well reveal to his eastern supporters his hesitance to invest there. The easterners would merely point to his revival of the Tiger-Poorman and direct him to work the same magic with the barren, snow-swept claims of the Hump.

For Sweeny, it was a good time to ask about buying the Buffalo

Hump group. The summer at Grangeville had been long and melancholy. The De Lamar company, busy in Utah copper, reviewed its interest in the Buffalo Hump and again declined to buy claims. Various English companies reacted timidly due to uncertainties connected with the Boer War. No matter how bravely they talked about the future of the Hump, investors shied from contracts. De Lashmutt found many of the mines idle, but the courts busy with niggling suits over ownership, shares, and claim boundaries. He also discovered that the owners of the Big Buffalo group had spent their stock as negotiable and had taken into their company various creditors, friends, and relatives, who now numbered thirty or forty persons. When De Lashmutt attempted to bargain on Sweeny's behalf, he dealt with approximately three dozen scattered, suspicious men who held, or thought they held, a direct or indirect interest in the properties. Some of the presumed stockholders were not sure of their rights and filed grubstake suits in the district court to clarify their positions. Among these, Jacob Rice and Perry S. Mallory were awarded half of the three Robbins-Young claims by the court. This decision was being appealed when De Lashmutt entered the scene.

De Lashmutt talked to his first Big Buffalo stockholders on February 10, 1900, and spent the next two full months rounding up the others who seemed to hold some kind of interest in the Big Buffalo, Merrimac, and Oro Fino. He finally came to terms with those whose equities seemed valid, settling on a total price of $125,000 cash.

Inevitably the news that Sweeny was finally going to buy the Big Buffalo group leaked out. Grangeville was elated, De Lashmutt would recall, because much of the expected payment had already been pledged to bars, hotels, and stores, and "a sort of conviction had settled down upon the whole community that the consummation or failure of this particular deal would demonstrate whether quartz mining was to be a success or failure in this section."

Three days passed while the participants in the sale discussed details, pens almost poised to sign. Friends and newspapermen clustered about the rooms of the owners and their attorneys, tugging the sleeves of men who came and went from the conference chambers, trading rumors and bits of conversation overheard, and trying to guess how the business went from the expressions on the faces of those involved. Finally all the papers were signed. De Lashmutt paid over the $125,-000—and a good deal more.

Two principal owners of the Big Buffalo group had died since the claim's discovery: Robbins, whose estate collected $16,601 in the sale to Sweeny, and Del Butterworth, whose estate received $15,290 for shares given him by Robbins. In addition, among the living shareholders, A. F. McKenna received $14,893; Mike Green, $6,000; Frank McGrane, $9,258; Henry Wax, $3,898; and Young, $44,882.[15] The owners' attorney, W. N. Scales, received $10,000; Perry Mallory, $7,500; James Justice, $7,500; Jacob Rice, $25,000; and even Lane Gilliam, $2,250. A man named Charles Moore dropped a suit against Rice on payment of $750 by De Lashmutt. Albert Allen, the Spokane attorney who represented Mallory in his grubstake suit, was paid $10,-000, and his assistant, Vic Bierbower, $750.

The $125,000 cash and other payments added up to more than $150,826, all from Charles Sweeny's pocket. One investigator estimated that Sweeny spent $350,000 to gain his uncontested title to the Big Buffalo, Merrimac, and Oro Fino. There could have been others to pay. Harry Glidden demanded a high price for his supposed interest until the court ruled that he held no share of the properties. Silverman sued for his share, contending that Sweeny had used Silverman's maps to sell stock in the East; he compromised for a block of stock in the company before going to Alaska to seek new fields.

Whatever the true cost, whether he wanted it or not, after nearly two years of cat and mouse, Charles Sweeny owned the heart of the Buffalo Hump.

As the months passed, Sweeny continued to buy claims until he, or someone associated with him, owned no fewer than seventy locations of varying size and value—the select claims of more than four hundred in the Robbins Mining District—among them the Vesuvius, Buffalo Bull, Andover, Bluebird, Clipper Bullion, Orphan Wedge, Timber King, Red Star, Blue Ribbon, and scores of others. Sweeny ruled a wintry domain three by seven miles, an empire of granite, snow, timber, and gold.

Sweeny declared he would spend a million dollars developing his fief. By October, 1900, the Big Buffalo shaft was down two hundred feet with three crosscuts, and the Vesuvius ran ore to its own mill over a new 2,200-foot tramway. There were 180 men working in the Sweeny mines at the Hump when Clendening reported that the Buffalo Hump Mining Company produced 2,000 tons of mineral in November, valued at $71,000, for net earnings of $21,000 (although this figure

also included receipts from the Tiger-Poorman in the Coeur d'A-
lenes).[16] The company proposed tapping Crystal Lake, fed by snow, for
500 horsepower to run a compressor, and was to purchase water rights
from various owners during 1904 to Sheep Creek, Buffalo Lake, and
the Basin Fork. It also planned a 4,700-foot adit costing $20 a foot to
penetrate the Big Buffalo at the 1,200-foot level. Ore would then fly
to a mill over a gravity tram.[17]

Future plans notwithstanding, the Big Buffalo closed during the
winter of 1900–1, its pumps were turned off, and water and ice filled
its shaft. "The reason assigned for the shutdown," said the *Spokesman-Review*, "is that under the present conditions of climate and the
stage of development . . . expenses were too heavy to justify continued operations." The shaft was now down 267 feet; the hoist, boiler,
and steam engine were no longer adequate, and so much wood had
been cut from nearby stands that fuel, brought from a distance, cost
up to forty dollars a day.[18]

Sweeny's foremen maintained a snow trail to the Buffalo Hump
through the winter by putting snowshoes on their pack horses, which
the *Idaho County Free Press* described as "heretofore unknown in
this country." The shoes were merely boards with a skin covering,
lashed to the horses' hooves.

Six trails had been beaten to the Hump, but the need for adequate
roads was acute. Sweeny promised Grangeville's merchants a profitable market for Camas Prairie farm produce among the mining towns
if they would build him a road. By October, 1900, the town had raised
$20,000 in public subscriptions and had hewn a passable wagon road
up Twenty-Mile Creek, part way to the Hump. The United States
Forest Service had applied for permission to construct a nine-mile
road of local materials from Lake Creek to Badger to open the mining
area, and was granted its request near the end of August, 1900. But
both proposed roads left to Sweeny the completion of twelve miles
over the rocky hills to connect with his shipping point, Ore Grande.

As the transportation to the Hump improved—it was never to be
satisfactory—a farming boom materialized. Until that time, perhaps
one-tenth of the arable land around Grangeville had been cultivated;
the rest lay virgin because the high cost of shipping precluded raising
hay, vegetables, or grain for sale outside the immediate area. The
farms grew apace with the influx of miners to work at the Hump.

By the summer of 1901, five stamp mills were erected in the Buffalo Hump camps, the largest a twenty-four-stamp mill at the Jumbo. (Stamp mills crushed the ore so that gold could be recovered by either a flotation or an amalgamation process.) A ten-stamp mill, purchased from the Badger and dismantled by Walter Hovey Hill for the Big Buffalo, had been hauled piece by piece through the snow in December, 1899, and had lain unassembled from the time Sweeny threw up his bond in January, 1900, until the day he bought the mines on the terms arranged by De Lashmutt.[19] Now this mill was set up.

In that summer of 1901 produce, hogs, cattle, and sheep from Camas Prairie brought high prices as the Buffalo Hump renewed operations. Grangeville throbbed again in an atmosphere of confident prosperity. It all gradually slowed down, however, as one after another of the mining companies found that they could not recover the high costs of carrying their ore or its concentrates out of the rugged country. Clendening wrote Sweeny that, after paying all its debts, the Buffalo Hump company was down to $20,000 in its bank account.[20]

There were, it is true, difficulties other than transportation. Little of the Buffalo Hump ore was free-milling, that is, ore in which sulfide had been oxidized by exposure so that the gold could be extracted by simple washing or chemical treatment of the crushed rock. The Buffalo Hump's was refractory ore, hard to treat by ordinary methods. The rich surface ores had been treated easily but the deeper the mines were drilled, the harder it was to recover gold. No sure method of extraction appeared, necessitating costly experiments. Nearly all the gold recovered from the Buffalo Hump was extracted by amalgamation, which collected not more than 50 to 60 percent of the value in the ore. Few Buffalo Hump mines recovered more than eight to fifteen dollars worth of gold from each ton of ore. The Jumbo tried a chlorinating process for a short time. Cyaniding was attempted. Both failed.[21]

Jumbo mill reports for the period June, 1902, to February, 1903, show that only 57 percent of the gold was taken from its ore. The average ton of ore was worth approximately $14.90, but no more than $8.52 of this stuck to the amalgam plates. In many camps of the West, ore worth less than fifty dollars a ton had been deliberately abandoned as not worth processing. Mining costs at the Hump averaged $3.29 a ton, and milling, $1.44. The Vesuvius, for a while one of the most active mines, reported its ore in 1903 worth $18.15 a ton. Its mill saved only 57 percent of this.[22] During 1903, concentrates from the

Crackerjack, Jumbo, and Del Rio mines were worth an average of $115 a ton. Even at $115, the concentrates were too low-grade to pay the cost of shipment to smelters.[23] For a time, the three mines worked their mill tailings, valued at $2.50 to $3.75 a ton, in a fruitless endeavor to profit.

So the Buffalo Hump, hailed at its discovery as possibly the richest camp of all time, faded in less than a decade. It receded from public concern like a languishing hero, to be mentioned in guarded tones with forebearance.

The Buffalo Hump declined for three principal reasons: lack of transportation, rudimentary processes that extracted too little gold from its ore, and Charles Sweeny's increasing attention to his other interests, which deprived the Hump of its chief promoter. Sweeny began scheming to merge the major mines of the Coeur d'Alene district into one giant corporation with money supplied by John D. Rockefeller, Jr. As his friends would have put it, when Sweeny realized the Hump was not a sure thing, he turned his back on his granite empire. In any event, perhaps his zeal alone could not have sustained the Hump.[24]

Even as the Hump withered, new schemes budded. Walter Hill surveyed the route for an electric railway, the Lewiston and Southern, during 1901, to cost $900,000—but it was never built. C. S. Mellen, president of the Northern Pacific, talked with a Grangeville delegation in May, 1901, after he had acquired the rights of the Oregon Railway and Navigation Company to the Camas Prairie route and had filed a plat of a proposed branch line to Grangeville. The railway did extend to Stites, Idaho, forty miles from the Hump, but further construction of the Grangeville, Culdesac, and Lewiston branch into Grangeville was delayed for some years.

Transportation did not reach close enough or come soon enough— and perhaps even with adequate transportation the Hump would have waned. The Buffalo Hump probably produced no more than a million dollars worth of gold in all its brief life—some men think half that amount—with the Jumbo and Big Buffalo yielding the major shares. Whatever the Hump gave up in gold, it was less than the thousands of dollars spent to develop its claims.

Except for a short-lived gold delerium in 1902 at Thunder Mountain, Grangeville settled back into its quiet routine as a farming town, wagons rattling along its dirt streets, its brick buildings recalling the flurry of construction in its gold-rush days. On the strength of its brief prominence, Grangeville won the Idaho County seat from Mount Idaho, and the railroads intended to serve its mines opened the outer world to Camas Prairie farm products.

The Big Buffalo closed on March 19, 1903. The Crackerjack ran with irresolution for six more years, working occasionally through a winter, and it operated a ten-stamp mill for five years until its owners, as had others, acknowledged at last that the mine would not pay. Even as the decline hushed the camp, six new companies were formed in the last months of 1903; the Colonel, Granite, Lucky Lad, Buffalo Lake, Buffalo Chief, and Prudential. The Jumbo and Crackerjack companies continued to build water-power systems. But in the high Hump country, the streams froze in winter months, cutting off water flow.

In 1902 Sweeny's Buffalo Hump Development Company agreed to sell its stock for five cents a share to Richard H. Hughes, although the important claims of the Hump were consigned not to it, but to another Sweeny company, the Buffalo Hump Syndicate, which in turn belonged to the Empire State–Idaho Mining and Developing Company. In 1908 the syndicate was to contract with Andrew Prader to refurbish and reopen its Callender stamp mill in response to his offer of $4,501 for permission to work the abandoned claims.[25]

The Jumbo closed, and was to reopen for a few months in 1912. It contained four tunnels, owned a twenty-four-stamp mill, and its ore was assayed as worth from sixty to eighty dollars a ton. This was not enough to pay transportation, so the Jumbo closed again, perhaps forever.

Strangely, the Buffalo Hump seemed merely slumbering in its twilight. A dozen years after the mining companies had laid off their last crews, cut off power, and padlocked their buildings, their directors continued to pay taxes on the properties and to maintain the buildings and equipment on the larger claims as if the Hump might rouse itself again. As late as 1932 W. Clayton Miller reported to the Sweeny Investment Company that the Bunker Hill company had re-assayed ores from the Hump and expressed interest in reopening certain mines, but nothing came of it. By the thirties, visitors who followed one of the two old rutted wagon roads found the mines caved in, shafts filled with water, timbering charred by brush fires, and only surface ores accessible for ready processing.

"In the last analysis, the present stagnant condition of the camp can be traced to but one cause," wrote Arthur L. Flagg in the *Mining and Engineering World* for April 26, 1913, "the extremely unfavorable physical and economic conditions. The greatest obstacles to be overcome are expensive and difficult transportation, high power costs, and the cost of mining."

Investigators from the United States Bureau of Mines visited the Hump in 1917, reporting values from $8 to $15 dollars a ton in ore, and tailings carrying $2.50 a ton. The veins averaged eight feet wide and were long enough to indicate value, from a geological view. How deep did the gold deposits go? The Jumbo had bored eight hundred feet into the earth with little change in the quality of its ore.[26] Such reports were infected with the germ of gold fever that had swept the Hump two decades earlier. But by now there was no Charles Sweeny to exploit the punishing country. The Hump merely slumbered.

Sweeny was not forgotten, however, for a geologist wrote in 1909: "Much misinformation about the Buffalo Hump district has been vigorously circulated . . . a great deal of which has no doubt been intentional. Mr. Sweeny has often expressed a deep grief . . . over his Buffalo Hump venture, but the fact this gentleman and his satellites have obtained title to over seventy claims in the district through predatory tactics . . . would warrant the belief that Mr. Sweeny's disappointment is only a part of his big bluff at high finance." [27]

With this refrain, many an old-timer nursed his flickering fancies for the Hump, and many imagined bitterly that Charles Sweeny had snuffed out the spark that would have ignited the Buffalo Hump, made it famous, and its miners rich.

# VI

## LONG COPPER WIRES

*F*OR fifteen years after their discovery, the Coeur d'Alene district mines operated on a seasonal basis, their production interrupted by labor war, merger, and by frozen streams that cut off water power or dwindling wood supplies that limited steam-power generation. Sometimes the mine managers shut down their workings as a weapon against labor or the railroads. By 1900, however, so much money had been invested in the mines, and their development required such a continued flow of capital, that the companies could not operate without a reliable source of power twelve months a year. Seasonal operation was intolerable to stockholders, particularly after the threat of disruption by labor organizations had been dispelled.

The wood, once plentiful and cheap, had been cut for timbering or for fuel, or had been burned off. In a widening area around the mines, the mountains were balding. Some of the mines, and several towns, raised awkward water-power plants on the mountain streams, but in winter the creeks froze, stopping water wheels, and in spring the streams gushed silt and waste. When the forests receded, the streams, too, dwindled. As a consequence, the mining companies could no longer combine water with cheap wood-fired steam power to run their compressors, hoists, and mills, even on a seasonal basis.

The towns and mines had begun to experiment with electrical plants early in the district's blooming, despite the uncertain water and wood supplies. The first electric plant in the Coeur d'Alenes consisted of two Edison bipolar generators of twenty kilowatts each, installed in

112

1890 by Charles Sweeny to light the Last Chance Mine. This plant was replaced by a larger one when Sweeny organized the Edison Illuminating Company of Wardner on May 21, 1891, and contracted with the Edison General Electric Company of Portland, Oregon, to install a 100-kilowatt dynamo to furnish 160 horsepower for Marvin drills in the Last Chance, new lights underground, and the company's mill.[1]

Sweeny's original Last Chance generator was bought by Robert Cheyne, who ran it with a water wheel during the spring and a steam engine the rest of the year, to supply the Bunker Hill and Sullivan with electricity. This diminutive plant was dismantled in 1897 as too limited in capacity.

When Sweeny erected his own compressor plant at the mouth of his Sweeny Tunnel, two small boilers furnishing steam for the compressors also drove a high-speed engine that operated a dynamo to light the town of Wardner with 350 incandescent globes. Arc lights first twinkled on Wardner's streets the night of July 27, 1891. The town council, shortly after, granted a franchise to F. Rockwood Moore for an electric street railway two miles long between Wardner Junction, on the Northern Pacific, and the Bunker Hill. (It was never built.)

Although Sweeny operated the pioneer dynamo in the Coeur d'Alene district, the first franchise for an electric system was awarded by the town of Wallace to the Wallace Manufacturing, Electric and Water Power Company on October 15, 1889. Home-owned, this company sold its stock at twenty-five cents a share to finance its eight-thousand-dollar plant, including a one-mile wooden flume from Placer Creek. Wallace turned on 650 sixteen-candlepower bulbs for the first time on July 4, 1891, and the display, outdazzling the traditional parade, climaxed a boisterous Independence Day.

In April, 1891, a man named O. B. Hardy had completed a station with two Edison bipolar dynamos generating 150 kilowatts; he used his power to test electric drills in his Black Bear Mine while their inventor, M. H. Marvin, watched. The men agreed that the electric drill struck faster than one run by compressed air, but did not strike as hard. Hardy declared that electric drills were lighter, more durable, and in the long run, would prove cheaper. Moreover, they remained cool in operation. Compressed-air drills became so hot that miners could hardly hold them. As a further demonstration, Hardy contracted with William T. McCaskey, traveling agent of the Portland Edison General Electric Company, to manufacture ten drills for approximately eight thousand dollars. These were the first electric drills in the district.[2]

Patrick Clark, manager of the Poorman Mine, meanwhile bought an Edison plant from McCaskey to operate drills, the pump, hoist, and mill, and to light his mine and mill at Burke. Shipped from New Jersey, the plant equipment filled eight railroad cars. McCaskey declared it "the largest single shipment of electric machinery that has ever come west of the Mississippi and the most extensive electrical mining plant in the world."[3] The Poorman set its powerhouse on Canyon Creek, a mile and one-half above the mine and mill, with a flume to carry water in a fall of eight hundred feet in two miles. The flow turned two 225-horsepower dynamos. Six bare copper wires on cedar poles connected the station to four more dynamos in the engine-room of the concentrator—among these, McCaskey bragged, "one of the four largest [dynamos] in America."

Even though this electrical system cost fifty thousand dollars, Clark told the *Wallace Press* that the Poorman would save thirty thousand dollars a year in fuel costs. Wood sold so dearly that the Poorman had been spending one hundred dollars a day to fuel its steam boilers, and had had to shut its mill at times because wood could not be bought at any price. The cost of coal, shipped to the mines by railroad, was also considered prohibitive.

While these and other electrical plants—one at the Morning Mine attracted a large measure of publicity—were being planned and built, the Coeur d'Alenes changed. In 1890, many of the mines had simply been holes worked by a man with his partners. By 1900, the mines were controlled by companies with stockholders, managers, consulting engineers, and the related satrapy of corporate enterprise. During the war with the miners' unions, the financial panic of 1893, and depressed lead prices, claims were gradually consolidated. Sweeny's Empire State–Idaho, for one, embraced more than thirty separate locations.

By the turn of the century, consequently, the mine owners often discussed an uninterrupted source of electric power, considering whence it might come, and envisioning a mammoth plant at a central location. So caught in this myth was one that he attempted to promote such a station, proposing to pay his workmen with shares of stock.

As the Coeur d'Alenes turned to electricity for constant power, so did mines in every section of the West.[4] In the last ten years of the nineteenth century, electricity became an established tool of mining. Alternating current, which allowed transmission of high voltages over many miles, indicated that the Coeur d'Alenes might find its source of power beyond the local streams. Charles Sweeny, in his 1899 report to stockholders of the Empire State–Idaho, prophesied that "with cheap electric power later on for pumping and general purposes, there is no reason why this property [Tiger-Poorman] should not be worked profitably to a depth of 5,000 feet." [5]

In this climate of interest, R. K. Neill, the general superintendent for Finch and Campbell, in 1900 organized the Coeur d'Alene Transmission Company to promote a power plant big enough to serve the Coeur d'Alene mines. Neill at first visualized a central compressor plant to deliver air by a web of pipelines across the mountains, and sought to write his contracts with mining companies on that premise, stipulating, "Whereas the party of the first part [Neill] is about to construct an electric power plant, at Post Falls, for the purpose of delivering electric current and compressed air, to the mines of the Coeur d'Alenes," the companies must agree to buy power for one year. Neill bound himself to begin construction by November 1, 1900.[6] Among the men associated with Neill in this enterprise were William S. Norman, former manager of the Washington Water Power Company at Spokane, Amasa Campbell, John Finch, Frank Culbertson, and Charles Sweeny. Campbell, a Washington Water Power stockholder, extracted a promise from the power company not to obstruct Neill's scheme, as Henry M. Richards, president of Washington Water Power, acknowledged: "Our arrangement with Mr. Campbell and his friends . . . was that we were not to interfere with him in the purchase of property to be owned and used for transmitting power to the Coeur d'Alenes only." [7]

As his power-station site, Neill chose the cataract of the Spokane River twenty-four miles east of Spokane at Post Falls, Idaho, about sixty-five miles west of the mining district. On August 1, 1900, he bought the land and water rights. For $25,000 Neill acquired an area totaling 270.3 acres (more than half in water surface) and 3,500 horsepower not previously sold by the falls' owner, Frederick Post.[8] To Norman this was familiar ground; eight years earlier, he, Frank Moore, James Monaghan, A. A. Newbery, and Dan Drumheller had projected an electric railway using power from Post Falls, but their scheme had fallen through. An engineering report on Post Falls by

Byron C. Riblet, delivered to Neill, described a flow of not less than 1,950 cubic feet per second, and recommended using Coeur d'Alene Lake as a natural reservoir to increase the flow by 69 percent, to provide 15,120 horsepower at a minimum. Dams, powerhouse, and a transmission line to the mines brought the project's estimated cost to an estimated $1,191,270.[9]

Once Neill's associates in promoting a power station had approved his purchase of Post Falls, they sought a competent engineering firm to design their system. Charles Sweeny, during his travels in the East, called on General Electric and Westinghouse. So did Amasa Campbell, who also discussed the project with William A. White of Brooklyn, a vice president and financial chairman of the Washington Water Power Company. Both General Electric, which held some WWP stock, and Westinghouse were hesitant to build a station at Post Falls and a transmission line into the mining country.

Deliberations with possible builders took so much time that Neill's deadline for beginning construction, November 1, passed. Most of the mining companies agreed to extend their contracts, and the transmission company was reorganized to eliminate Norman, who apparently had been trying to sell his private property near Post Falls directly to Westinghouse.

At the mines, meanwhile, the acute need for electrical energy grew. The Empire State–Idaho company halted work on its ten-mile Pine Creek flume which was to cost $96,676 and require two years to complete. The company's general manager, Edward Roberts, felt the flume could not compare in economy with steam power. "I think that the time is now ripe," he wrote Sweeny, "for the organization of an electric power company for the purpose of supplying the entire Coeur d'Alene district with power at fifty percent of the present cost." [10]

During reorganization of the Coeur d'Alene Transmission Company, the reason for the reluctance of General Electric or Westinghouse to write a construction contract became evident. Despite the Washington Water Power Company's agreement not to interfere in the Post Falls project, both General Electric and Westinghouse regarded northern Idaho as WWP territory. So did W. A. White, who actively opposed erection of a power station by mine owners, and wrote WWP President Richards, "I think I have considerable influence with the General Electric people and might perhaps through them be able to steer matters somewhat with the Westinghouse," adding that General Electric was "anxious to protect our interests." [11]

During reorganization, the principal supporters of Neill's plan had fallen to squabbling among themselves. An informant now assured White, he wrote Richards, that Westinghouse would not build the power plant, and that "he got the impression out West that the Post Falls water power could be bought at a pretty low price. He suggested $20,000; but I suppose . . . that it is unlikely that it could be acquired at that price. If it could be, I should think it might be worth considering." [12]

Post Falls was indeed for sale, as White had been advised, but for sale only to someone who would convert it to a power station for the mines. The mine owners had concluded, as the Washington Water Power's general manager, D. L. Huntington remarked, "that their business was mining, not electricity." The principal members of Neill's combine had other interests: Finch was busy with British Columbia mines; Sweeny flirted with political office and bustled about trying to buy the Bunker Hill and Sullivan.

When Neill's associates had evidently given up hope of building a power station, Sweeny directed Roberts to approach Huntington with a suggestion that the Washington Water Power Company buy the falls and build a transmission line to the Coeur d'Alenes. Fred Burbidge advanced the same counsel, as doubtless did other mining men. Turning over Post Falls to the Washington Water Power might sound like the next inevitable step in a well-laid plot, but in Roberts' opinion, Huntington seemed awed by the scope of the proposed project and not at all sure of his company's capacity to finance it. If the WWP was merely waiting for Post Falls to fall under its control, Huntington hid his anticipation well from Roberts. Roberts had to insist that Huntington at least look over the ground, arguing, "Power has to come into the Coeur d'Alene region. We're using coal all the time now." Perhaps less surprised and reluctant than he seemed, Huntington agreed to consider the proposal.[13]

It may be well to review the Washington Water Power briefly, for in 1901 it was only twelve years old and had been recently reorganized by eastern stockholders. It was successor to other water power and electric companies, and in 1888 had acquired various individual power rights on the Spokane River within the city's limits, and most

of the city's electrical services, as the result of Billy Norman's efforts
to consolidate electrical generation and sales into a single company.
The new, consolidated company had barely completed its unification
at a cost of approximately $485,000 when the Panic of 1893 struck.
After Frank Moore's First National Bank failed—Moore also was
president of the power company—the Washington Water Power's
officers borrowed money wherever they could, offering stock as collateral at half its $100 par value. In this manner, WWP stock fell into
the hands of such diverse lenders (at 9 to 12 percent interest) as
Abiel A. Low and William White of Brooklyn, and a great many
others.

Moore's personal pledges of power company stock and his own
financial collapse brought the firm close to bankruptcy. White saved
it by persuading the creditors to contribute toward its survival.[14] As
chairman of its financial committee, White installed Henry M. Richards as president of the Washington Water Power, and put in his
hand-picked choice, David Lynde Huntington, as general manager.
Huntington, the twenty-six-year-old son of White's close friends in New
London, Connecticut, had come to Spokane in 1894 (with the title of
treasurer of the company) as White's personal representative. He had
been briefly employed previously as an assistant engineer with the
General Electric Company.

Huntington was to say that in his first year with WWP, "We had
gross earnings under $200,000 with no profits." But by the time
Sweeny, Campbell, Neill, and their emissaries approached the Washington Water Power to buy Post Falls, the company was expanding
on the crest of revived good times, showing steady growth and profits.[15]
The company was studying a 22,000-volt line it proposed to build
from Spokane to Ritzville, Washington, to serve mills and local utili-
ties.

Post Falls held a peculiar attraction for the Washington Water
Power Company in addition to its power potential, because an adequate dam at Post Falls could control the flow of the Spokane River
at the company's two other power sites, the upper falls and the Monroe Street plant. With Coeur d'Alene Lake as a storage reservoir, the
dam could release water during slack periods, and contain floods
like those which twice had inundated the Monroe Street station.

The mines demanded power in a hurry. To serve them, the water
power company proposed to transmit electricity from Spokane while

the Post Falls station was being built. But the first step in construction of a high-voltage transmission line more than 100 miles long was to determine whether it could be built at all. There existed in the world only one system of this magnitude, that of the Bay Counties Power Company, a 142-mile line completed in 1901 in California. Before that time the Tellerude Power Transmission Company's system, carrying 40,000 volts 105 miles to Utah mines, had been the longest.[16]

David Huntington asked the advice of each of these companies and sought the opinion of Charles P. Steinmetz, the dwarfed genius of General Electric. Steinmetz, then the leading authority on alternating current, had published a book on transmission in 1900 and had written articles for professional journals; he had hinted, in an essay in *Electrical World,* that climate might be a consideration with current higher than 10,000 volts. As the climate of Idaho patently differed from that of California, or even Utah, Huntington went to talk to Steinmetz at his laboratory in Schenectady.

Sitting cross-legged on his table, Steinmetz checked Huntington's data on wire size and insulator spacing, and then declared the line could be built. He estimated that resistance would diminish current 9.4 percent in transmission, and voltage 11.1 percent. Huntington tucked Steinmetz's penciled notes away with his own, brought them to Spokane, and deposited them proudly in the Washington Water Power files as a trophy.

With assurance from Steinmetz, the Washington Water Power Company took an option on the Post Falls property and signed tentative contracts to deliver power to six mining companies: Sweeny's Empire State–Idaho, the Bunker Hill and Sullivan, Finch's and Campbell's Coeur d'Alene Development Company, the Hecla, the Standard, and the Mammoth. According to the minutes of the Empire State–Idaho company for December 11, 1901, "The proposed contract with Washington Water Power Company was presented for furnishing electrical power at a cost of $20,000 a year for a period of six years. Mr. Sweeny explained the terms of the contract, stating that the cost would be $50.00 per horsepower, the present cost for creating our own power being considerably over $100 per H.P. Moved, seconded and resolved that the proposed contract with WWPCo . . . be referred to a committee consisting of Mr. Packard, Mr. Sweeny and Mr. Cox with power to act." [17]

Washington Water Power's directors authorized buying Post Falls at their meeting in September, 1901. Early in 1902 the company bought the property for $31,465, obtaining all the rights Neill had previously purchased from Frederick Post. Neill himself had held the major share in his transmission company, three-tenths, for which he took WWP stock. The remaining shares had been owned by Finch, Frank Culbertson, and two Wallace merchants, Henry White and Charles Bender.[18]

On June 20, 1902, Washington Water Power notified the six mining companies that it would definitely undertake a transmission system to the Coeur d'Alenes. Now Huntington proposed to inspect the line's route and with John B. Fisken, the company's engineer, traveled through Fourth of July Canyon, a narrow, winding furrow in the mountains, the route of the old Mullan trail.[19] They found, said Fisken, "heavy timber, hills of thirty percent grade, no roads," and resorted to driving their buggy along creek beds. The trip was unsatisfactory. Huntington declared that this route, although the most direct, was impractical; he decided instead on one running over meadowland and through marshes south of Lake Coeur d'Alene and up the valley of the Coeur d'Alene River. This was the old Jackass Trail from the lake. Along the riverbank lay the trackage of the district's first railroad, D. C. Corbin's narrow-gauge "chippy" line.

As finally mapped, the power line ran from Post Falls westerly back toward Spokane to Chester, Washington, then southeasterly through Rockford to a point near the mouth of the St. Joe River, which flowed into Lake Coeur d'Alene from the south, and then along the lakeshore to the Coeur d'Alene River and up its winding valley to follow the south fork to Wallace, Idaho.

To provide capital for the Coeur d'Alene project, the Washington Water Power Company on August 6, 1902, increased its stock from twenty thousand to twenty-six thousand shares, thus raising its capitalization to $2,600,000. The mining companies had agreed, in their contracts, to take 60 percent of the capacity of the proposed system; others would sign agreements when the line was completed. (The Big Bend project was shelved until 1908, despite daily inquiries from mills down country.)

While the route was being surveyed in 1902 and 1903, the Washington Water Power increased its Monroe Street station in Spokane from 1,739 to 7,920 kilowatts, installing oil insulators around the huge coils of the transformers that would step up the power for the Coeur d'Alenes. A corrugated-iron temporary substation went up at Post Falls, connected to Spokane by wire to provide power for rock crushers, cableways, concrete mixers, and other equipment to build dam and powerhouse.

During April, 1903, Fred Phair of Spokane, under contract to WWP, erected six brick power stations, each eighteen feet square and thirty feet high, to serve the mining companies with step-down transformers: one station at Burke for the Tiger-Poorman and Hecla, another near Mace for the Standard and Mammoth, others at Wardner to serve the Last Chance, at Kellogg for the Bunker Hill and Sullivan, at Sweeny, approximately one mile below Kellogg, for the Empire State-Idaho mill, and one on the railway a mile from Sweeny for the Coeur d'Alene Development Company.[20] At these brick substations current would be stepped down for individual mines. The biggest user, the Tiger-Poorman, took approximately twelve hundred horsepower, and the others lesser amounts, down to the Last Chance Mine and the Sweeny Mill, two hundred each. When these were connected, the Frisco and Hercules would be the only major producers without power from Spokane.

A crew of perhaps forty men struggled eastward from Spokane through the dry heat of late summer in 1902, setting poles and stringing wire for what came to be called Coeur d'Alene Number One.[21] Poles had been dropped from wagons of the contractor, M. D. Wright, along the cleared route. Once a post hole had been bored by hand, the workmen snaked a thirty-five-foot cedar pole by team to the lip of the hole, used pikes to lift it upright, and dropped it in. To insure that the pole would not topple during erection, a wooden tripod of two-by-six-inch beams was shouldered under it as the pole rose. Such a tripod weighed 150 to 200 pounds. The biggest man on the crew put his weight behind it, keeping the tripod tight against the post until it thumped into its socket in the ground. Then five or six men dragged the tripod to the next hole.

The construction crews lived in tent camps that followed them across the relatively flat land, south of the lake, and up the river valley. Laborers were paid twenty cents an hour; linemen, the darlings of the outfit, forty-five cents. They worked nine hours, six days a week, paying the company $4.50 a week for their board.

Before starting to work on the wires, the men telephoned the power station at Spokane to have the switch pulled, and then hung heavy iron chain across the copper strands to short-circuit any current that might be thrown on accidentally. Generally the wire crews worked at night so that power could be transmitted during the day.

In preparation for the electrical service, the mining companies installed new equipment. Roberts wrote Packard, of the Empire State–Idaho, "We are about closing contracts for the electrical machinery for the carrying out of the contract of the Washington Water Power Company. Total cost of installment will be somewhere in the neighborhood of $20,000. This amount, however, we expect to save during the first year's operation." [22]

Before the end of August, 1903, three naked strands of copper wire gleamed thirty feet in the air on yellow-bare poles with crossarms and petticoated insulators. On August 25, the Sweeny Mill and the Bunker Hill and Sullivan took the first experimental power deliveries. The town of Wardner blazed on the twenty-seventh with electric lights hooked to the Bunker Hill, which had acquired Sweeny's illuminating company. The town's lighting, and the spontaneous celebration that greeted it, were premature. The connections had been completed and motors turned on for a test. Regular electric service began shortly after September 1, 1903.

At first the voltage on the Washington Water Power line was forty-five thousand; it was increased to sixty thousand volts as soon as demand warranted.

Although Charles Sweeny's new mill at Sweeny, completed early in 1901, was one of the first connections, the Last Chance Mine was the last of the original six customers to be served. Its pumps began turning with Spokane-generated electricity on November 14; its compressor was connected a few days later. The Last Chance substation was the last in which the transformer was installed; the Burke, the next to last. Burke lay 114.5 miles from the Monroe Street power station in Spokane. Some of the mining companies, like the Bunker Hill and Sullivan, continued to operate their own steam or water-power plants, drawing on the Washington Water Power as supplemental service, but this proved expensive. By February 2, 1905, within fifteen months of completion, Coeur d'Alene Number One was carrying its full capacity of sixty thousand volts—after an experimental surge of seventy thousand to see how the line would stand it.

The mining companies used their current in various ways. In addition to running drills, pumps, railways, and mills, the Standard designed a signal system for its hoist not unlike elevator indicator boards in office buildings. The Morning illuminated not only its shafts and stopes but a three-hundred-man company hotel.

In the meantime, the Washington Water Power Company had begun construction of its dams and powerhouse at Post Falls. The plant was to cost more than $1,208,000 and to go on the line January 29, 1907. A second power line to the mines would be built along the canyon route Huntington earlier had deemed impractical.[23]

The company's great burnished wire, shining across a hundred miles of meadow and mountain to the mines, captured the popular fancy. In its review of 1903 the *Spokesman-Review* declared, "One of the principal achievements of the year for Spokane and one of the great engineering achievements of an engineering age was the successful transmission of electric power from Spokane falls to the Coeur d'Alene mines." The newspaper described the system and reflected on it as a marvel. It might have reported that Washington Water Power Company stock, offered ten years earlier as collateral at $50 a share, now sold no lower than $124 and paid 6 percent dividends.

When electricity came to the Coeur d'Alenes, mining operations became possible twelve months of the year. The first deterrent to continuous operation, unionism, had been stifled, and the second, a lack of steady power, removed. In each of these steps, Charles Sweeny played his role. As electricity came to the mines, Sweeny was devising other changes in the structure of corporate mining in northern Idaho.

# VII

## DIGRESSIONS:
## POLITICS AND REAL ESTATE

*R*EAL estate and politics constituted Charles Sweeny's major digressions from mining promotion during the years of his broadest influence and fame. His name was to survive him in his Sweeny Investment Company, organized to hold his real estate, but his quest for appointment to the United States Senate has been forgotten for many years. In politics Sweeny confounded his detractors by putting honor above gain.

Sweeny's interest in land began in 1882 in Portland. He was not systematic as a buyer and seller, however, until his apprenticeship with the artful F. Lewis Clark. After that Sweeny invested substantial sums in Spokane and Portland ground. Nearly all the well-to-do men of Sweeny's acquaintance plowed money into the land, believing it alone of enduring value. For Sweeny, real estate held its own surprise: his Emeline proved to be a shrewd dealer, too, and she was to appraise and buy much of the property that subsequently was vested in the Sweeny company.

Sweeny's close attention to real estate endured for ten years; he folded his political aspirations into three.

Because no one cared about his politics until he became wealthy, the evolution of Sweeny's ambition to sit in the United States Senate is shadowy. He probably fired his fancies with his increasingly generous contributions to the Spokane County Republican organization. In 1902 the Republicans were divided on endorsing a proposed state railroad commission. The party's leaders and Republican

124

governor wanted a commission to regulate the rates and practices of the railroads, but former Senator John L. Wilson, defeated in 1899 and running again for the Senate, opposed a commission and fought it through his newspaper, the *Seattle Post–Intelligencer*, which he had purchased with financial aid from James J. Hill of the Great Northern Railway.

Hill, with Mellen of the Northern Pacific, had visited Spokane to confer with mine owners; both had agreed to build a second track into the Coeur d'Alene district and to haul ore at lowered rates. During his visit in 1899, Hill had promised Spokane a smelter, and in 1902 that pledge remained fresh. Most mine owners, therefore, supported the railroads and opposed the commission. (Amasa Campbell, for example, advanced the argument that the railroads would only react to regulation by treating everyone worse than they already did.)

Sweeny, on the other hand, despite his interest in lower ore-hauling rates, gingerly admitted that he favored a commission. This probably signaled his conscious enlistment in the ranks of the politically ambitious.

Other mine owners were openly pursuing public office. Campbell nursed a desire for the Senate or high state office. William M. Ridpath strove in vain for Congress in 1902 and was to fail in 1904 to capture the nomination for governor. Because Campbell opposed the railway commission and Ridpath was harrassed by the *Spokesman-Review*'s stern voice of the party, the anti-Wilson Republicans chose the most prominent man available at the moment, Charles Sweeny, as their candidate to unify Spokane County party members. The anti-Wilsonians had organized a rump unit, the Spokane County Republican Club, for the purpose of "rehabilitating the party in Spokane and electing a Republican administration stripped of factional strifes, deals, and controversy." [1] Their selection of Sweeny was something of a surprise to the public because he offered no record of political activity other than campaign contributions.

Led by Cyrus Happy, the executive committee of the Roosevelt Club offered to nominate Sweeny for senator in the county convention, saying they wished their candidate to "harmonize" the party and believed that Sweeny's name might inspire a general anti-Wilson reaction. Although Sweeny had not previously offered himself for office, the committee must have known that he would not turn them down summarily. Sweeny asked for a few hours to consider their proposal, then declined with the statement: "I have never had any notion of becoming a candidate for senator and could not entertain the proposition made to me today. My business interests are so great that they are almost too much for me to attend to as it is. My refusal is final and absolute."

Some citizens may have regarded this as the classic equivocation of the eager candidate, but Sweeny probably meant what he said. He truly was busy trying to merge the Coeur d'Alene district mines. More to the point, however, the convention was to open the next morning, and in his few hours of deliberation Sweeny doubtless learned by diligent inquiry that he could not win the nomination with an overnight campaign. He therefore declined the Roosevelt Club's entreaty. In fact, Sweeny donated the entire twenty-five hundred dollars that Wilson spent on his campaign in Spokane County.

Wilson won the county's vote without notable opposition other than the aversion of the *Spokesman-Review*, which observed editorially that "the railroad creature," Wilson, had done nothing for Spokane during his ten years in Congress ending in 1899. Singly or in conclave, the Republican delegates seemed perverse in 1902—one shot another over a woman, and the convention, after endorsing Wilson, voted to support the state railroad commission that he opposed.

The events of 1902 bent Sweeny's thoughts toward political office. Now he contrived toward 1905 while his friends began seeking ways of keeping his name before the public. He was elected a delegate from Spokane County to the state convention, and then chairman of the delegation.

Charles B. Hopkins, United States Marshal in Spokane, assumed direction of the Sweeny design. It was arranged that despite his financial aid to Wilson, Sweeny would support Levi N. Ankeny, the Walla Walla banker, for the senatorial nomination in the 1902 state convention in return for a promise that southeastern Washington would rally to Sweeny's banner at the proper time, either in 1905 or when Ankeny's term would end in 1909. Such an alliance of eastern Washington political forces was imperative, because the state was split politically in almost the same way as it was geographically. The Cascade Mountains formed a natural barrier between the western seaboard with its shipping, fishing, timber, and humid farming districts and the eastern plains with irrigated orchards and wheat fields. The mountains barred political and commercial unity so effectively that for years serious attempts were made to form a separate state by joining northern Idaho to eastern Washington, whose concerns were mutual.

In the months between Ankeny's election to the Senate in 1902 and the campaign that preceded the election of 1905, Sweeny kept himself in the headlines of Spokane newspapers. He organized the Federal Mining and Smelting Company, became its president, bought a granite mansion in the city's largest residential purchase to that time, and set editors guessing how many boxcars his fortune would fill if it were converted to silver dollars. None of these activities were political in intent, but they nevertheless enabled Sweeny to adopt his hearty role as tycoon, benefactor, and financial seer. All of these poses enhanced his campaign for the United States Senate.

In the meantime Washington's incumbent senator in 1905, Addison G. Foster of Tacoma, boasted that he could be re-elected without eastern Washington votes, while John Wilson incurred President Roosevelt's disfavor in distributing patronage. With eastern Washington indignant against Foster, and Wilson derogated, Sweeny's opportune moment seemed to have come. He visited Spokane from New York in mid-January, 1904, to issue a statement favoring Roosevelt's renomination and allowed himself to be drawn into a "guarded admission" that he would seek a place on the Washington State delegation to the Republican national convention in Chicago in June. He would attend, naturally, at Roosevelt's invitation, saying, "I am too busy with my private affairs to pay much attention to politics. In New York, several friends of President Roosevelt suggested that I go to the national convention in his interest. Of course I am for Roosevelt. Most western men are." [2] With this, Sweeny was in the race. His opponents charged that he proposed to control state expenditures by putting the assistant cashier of his Exchange National Bank on the ballot as a candidate for state treasurer; they intimated that Sweeny supported F. K. Pugh for Spokane police chief because Pugh could deliver Sweeny the slum vote, as he had turned it previously to Wilson.

Railroad representatives worked to keep Sweeny off the state's ten-member delegation to Chicago, while the *Tacoma Forum* fulminated, "Charles Sweeny . . . absolutely has no claim on the Republican Party that entitles him to any consideration." Sweeny was appointed a delegate, however, upon pledging five thousand dollars toward the campaigns of state candidates controlled by railroad interests.

Some weeks before the Chicago meeting, Sweeny hinted openly at his availability for the Senate. He left New York in time to join the Washington caucus at the Palmer House, handing each member a souvenir badge struck for the occasion. In return his Washington cohorts wrote him a resolution of thanks, framed it, and presented it to Sweeny on the last day of the convention when he treated them to lunch. Early in the delegation's business, Sweeny's hidden commitment to Ankeny emerged. He cast the deciding sixth vote to elect Ankeny to the Republican National Committee, defeating Wilson's candidate who mustered four. The *Spokesman-Review* observed, "This will come as news to those who have been accustomed to seeing Mr. Sweeny and Mr. Wilson drill together."

Sweeny served on the convention's committee on permanent organization. During the convention the Republicans acclaimed Teddy Roosevelt, named Charles W. Fairbanks of Indiana as his running mate, and wrote a platform expressing views on polygamy, the admission of Arizona and New Mexico as states, establishing Oklahoma Territory, and trade with the Philippines. Two weeks later, the Democrats were to consider George Turner of Spokane as a vice presidential possibility, then to abandon him when his own delegation split between Turner and William Randolph Hearst.

His experience in Chicago solidified Sweeny's determination to run against Foster. On his return to Spokane, he acknowledged he would not wait until 1909 but would run in 1905 because the convention had "scorched" the other prominent candidates. Perhaps as a new face he could consolidate the state party's disputing factions.

Sweeny's decision was bold; he counted on the endorsement of outgoing Governor Henry McBride, who had been repudiated by the party's state convention in May. Not only had the conclave, rigged in Seattle hotel rooms before it opened in Tacoma, ignored McBride, it had disdained eastern Washington, rejected a platform plank favoring a railroad commission, chosen the Bellingham attorney Albert E. Mead to succeed McBride in a high-handed maneuver against David T. Ham of Spokane, and tossed eastern Washington a nomination for a judgeship as the eastern side's sole representation on the slate.[3] From well-organized western Washington, clearly, Sweeny could anticipate little generosity.

In 1905, as it would until 1913, the Legislature elected the state's senators. In addition to Sweeny and the incumbent Foster, John Wilson contended, as did the Seattle banker Jacob Furth, and the protege of Seattle's business community, a young Kentuckian named Samuel H. Piles. Piles had once put ten thousand dollars into a Yukon exploring party and then had come West to check on its progress. His investment had vanished. He was forced by indigence to stay in the Pacific Northwest, and began by working two days as a cook, then briefly as a Northern Pacific laborer carrying brush cleared from trackside. Next he opened a law office where he slept on the floor and existed on one meal a day. Piles had entered the King County prosecuting attorney's employ without pay, stumped for Republican candidates throughout western Washington, and had finally risen to a partnership in law with the prosecutor, J. T. Ronald, who promptly dissolved their association to become Seattle's mayor. Enduring his hard knocks, Piles won a reputation for party loyalty. He was believed one of the stronger candidates for the United States Senate in 1905.

Both Piles and Foster asserted they could win without eastern Washington. This kind of talk, abetted by Ankeny's machine, put all of eastern Washington except Whitman County behind Sweeny, so he went with strength to Olympia, the state capital. In the minds of a number of denizens of the capital city, Sweeny arrived with a recommendation more alluring than votes—money. Many guessed that Sweeny would have to buy his majority and anticipated his munificence.

The Legislature was to commence voting at noon on January 17, 1905. Sweeny arrived in Olympia a week in advance with the largest candidate's contingent of the session, including his campaign manager, Hopkins, and an advisor, D. B. Crocker, who operated the Ankeny ring from his post as collector of internal revenue for Washington. Sweeny set up headquarters in the mansion of J. C. Horr, a spacious house which stood near the capitol and suited Sweeny's program of entertainment and entreaty.[4] With him, too, were Emeline, three of his sons, and his friend John Hinchcliffe, who had been mayor of Paterson, New Jersey, for seven years.

Here in the Horr home, Sweeny laid his plans. With King County committed to Piles and commanding nearly one-third of the total vote, Sweeny aimed toward the possibility that Pierce County, with the second largest vote, would defect from the west-side ranks. If

Foster failed to rally a majority, Crocker urged that Sweeny's strategy be to persuade Pierce County to switch to him before Piles could amass enough votes to encourage a stampede to his name.

The Horr mansion was bustling with legislators answering Crocker's calls or eager to learn how much Sweeny was willing to spend to buy himself into the Senate. The struggle would be, predicted the *Spokesman-Review,* "the biggest senatorial battle in the history of the state," with little chance that any candidate might win on an early ballot.

When the session convened, Sweeny was nominated by State Senator Walker A. Henry, Spokane, who dwelt on Sweeny's business successes, his "faithful service" to the Republican Party, and his Civil War record. On the first ballot, Foster tallied forty-three, Piles thirty-two, Sweeny twenty-seven, Wilson fifteen, with the remaining votes scattered among flattered men who would soon withdraw. Nomination required sixty-nine votes. None of the leaders exhibited dominant strength, and Wilson's fifteen votes were not enough even to give him a lever. Because Wilson had broken an earlier pledge not to oppose Piles, the west side had turned against him.

Through eight ballots, Sweeny held his twenty-seven, while Foster and Piles gained or lost a vote or two with each tabulation. As the Legislature plodded toward its sixth consecutive day of voting, conferees importuned in hotels and hallways to break the impasse, with the result that on the ninth ballot Foster picked up five votes and on the twelfth, two more, to rise within fourteen of re-election. Piles stalled at thirty, Sweeny at twenty-seven. On Thursday, January 26, Foster's opponents moved adjournment early to forestall a thirteenth ballot which might have elected him. A few minutes after the gavel fell, King County's men approached Sweeny to determine whether he would be willing to throw his votes to Piles to thwart Foster.

"The Sweeny campaign has run its limit," asserted the *Seattle Times.* "No probable combination in his interest would be strong enough to force his election." It was true. Crocker had exhausted the hours of the previous Sunday trying to entice votes for Sweeny; he garnered not a single ballot. The *Spokesman-Review* sought to explain his failure:

In advance of the Legislature, Mr. Sweeny was toasted as a man who would spend money freely to be elected. Now the common expression about the hotel lobbies is that "Sweeny hasn't opened his barrel." He is liberal in expenditures, of course, but the money hasn't been spent in a way which political grafters like it spent. A good many people think that Mr. Sweeny, like Mr. Furth, doesn't want to spend his money until he is sure he will get his money's worth.[5]

Crocker had counseled Sweeny to make as strong a showing as possible, and then to accept compromise. With Foster gaining and Sweeny unable to increase, the time had come to barter. Consequently, Sweeny and John Hinchcliffe walked to see Sam Piles in his rooms, finding him "pretty blue," as Sweeny was to tell the story. Piles lamented that he "could see no chance for a poor man to be elected Senator." Understanding his visitors' purpose in coming to him, Piles appealed to Sweeny: "Unless you help me, I'm out of it." [6]

Piles's characterization of himself as a poor man may have been astute or merely lucky, but it was the most effective plea he could have made. Sweeny had become obsessed momentarily with the homily of Edward Bellamy's novel, *Looking Backward*, which caricatured society as riding an imaginary coach drawn by the poor while the fortunate perched on insecure seats. A priest who knew Sweeny recalled that he "was strong on the theory that when a man is forced to the front, the man next to him would tap him on the shoulder and tell him to go 'way back to the end." [7] Sweeny, who could be charitable as well as callous, seems to have been swayed by Piles's dejection. As the price of his support, Sweeny extracted a written promise from Piles that he would champion a state railroad commission and defend Roosevelt's proposal to enlarge the Interstate Commerce Commission. Piles also agreed to advocate a separate federal judicial district for eastern Washington and a port of entry for Spokane, and to maintain Sweeny and Ankeny men in office. These men included the United States Marshal at Spokane, the postmaster, and certain employees in the land office.[8]

Shortly after Sweeny returned to the Horr mansion with Piles's pledges in his pocket, Foster representatives called to ask his endorsement of their candidate and to offer to defray Sweeny's campaign expenses in consideration. Sweeny believed he had struck a better bargain with his poor man, Piles, than he could hope from Foster, so he sent word that he was "able to pay his own bills, and at this session, a poor man will be elected Senator."

Sweeny called together his backers, revealed his decision, and after a good deal of speech-making formally capitulated at 11:30 P.M. Senator J. B. Lindsley of Spokane rose when the Senate reconvened to announce Sweeny's withdrawal. When Sweeny entered the chambers, the senators cheered him. Not only was he out of the running for 1905; he declared he would not be a candidate in 1909. By this promise, he delivered Ankeny's organization to Piles, repaid King County for its support of Ankeny in 1903, and obligated King to accept a candidate suitable to eastern Washington in 1909. The pact sealed, Piles was elected on the thirteenth ballot with 125 votes. "The history of Samuel H. Piles' election to the United States Senate may be summarized in a single sentence—Charles Sweeny refused to be held up," reported the *Spokesman-Review*. The newspaper averred that five or six men who had been at Sweeny's side during the early balloting demanded money to keep their votes from Foster. When Sweeny turned them down, his managers recognized that he had forfeited election.

Sweeny left Olympia a hero. When Piles's carriage reached Seattle, about two thousand adherents greeted the Senator-elect, who responded to cries for a speech by summoning Sweeny, riding with him. He introduced Sweeny as "the man who has made me United States Senator." The *Seattle Times* described Sweeny as tall, erect, with "gray hair and a gray mustache, along with a look of tenacity and determination that . . . reminds one of the late Prince Otto von Bismarck." Sweeny talked for some time but the throng drowned out his words. Amid back-slapping, Piles and Sweeny were conducted first to dinner, while the band played "Dixie" for Piles, and then to a reception at the fashionable Rainier Club.

On his return to Spokane, Sweeny told his story of what happened at Olympia: "I know there were a good many Spokane people who had a wrong opinion of me. They thought I went down there to get the election, regardless of means. Well, now my campaign is over, and I've left the politics of the state purer than they've been for a long day. . . . Some of the grafters went down to Olympia expecting that they could go home with enough money to start national banks." [9]

For a short time, Spokane's habitual wariness toward Sweeny virtually disappeared. The *Spokesman-Review*, whose editors had suspected that Sweeny might buy his way into the Senate, editorialized on January 31, 1905: "Mr. Sweeny's prompt refusal to recoup his campaign expenses by throwing his influence to another candidate is very much to his credit. And still more so was his emphatic refusal to deal with a gang of boodlers who wanted to sell the United States senatorship to the highest bidder. It must be conceded that Mr. Sweeny was superb in his hour of personal defeat."

On this note, Sweeny accepted the transitory esteem that his quest for public office brought him and, sensibly, never again entered politics.

Sweeny savored politics for honor, but his activities in real estate in Portland and Spokane indulged his relish for acquisition. Nonetheless, for a time he was welcomed in Portland as the man who stemmed a disaster in land prices. During his partnership with F. Lewis Clark, Sweeny observed the stratagem of buying depressed property to hold for a rising market. Except for his five-thousand-dollar home, Sweeny obtained only one piece of land in Spokane before entering his partnership with Clark. As we have seen, this was a business lot carrying an eight-thousand-dollar mortgage on Havermale Island (in the Spokane River) bought from one James W. Bell in December, 1892, for thirteen thousand dollars.[10] At the time, Sweeny had been a modest land proprietor in Wardner, Idaho, and manager of the Last Chance Mine, which was closed in litigation with the Tyler. His expenditure of thirteen thousand dollars thus stands as a curious footnote to his circumstances. The money apparently was borrowed with a note to the First National Bank of Spokane; it had not been repaid when the bank failed.

Sweeny acquired his wealth at Rossland at a time which enabled him to take advantage of the real estate market. When a number of Spokane's early fortunes were swept away in the Panic of 1893, Dutch and German investors, organized as the Northwestern and Pacific Mortgage Company and the German Savings and Loan Association of San Francisco, had first lent and then foreclosed on desirable business property.[11] It was customary to say in 1896 that the Dutch owned downtown Spokane. Indeed, it was estimated that the Northwestern and Pacific held delinquent mortgages on thirteen blocks fronting the city's main commercial thoroughfares. The Dutch had invested as much as eight million dollars in Spokane, regarding it and the region about it as ripe for exploitation at 12 to 15 percent interest. Hollanders were to finance agricultural and commercial development in eastern Washington for many years.

By the late nineties, the mortgagees were beginning to liquidate their Spokane acquisitions at moderate prices, so that Sweeny fortunately came into his money in a buyers' market. Because Spokane was expanding with the momentum of economic recovery and farm-land promotion, astute buying of vacant land could be enormously profitable. In this clime Sweeny joined Clark in purchasing land and buildings. Their association, veiled at the outset, was abrasive to those who sought to untangle the affairs of the defunct First National Bank and the Last Chance Mine.

As overt partners, Sweeny and Clark on July 3, 1896, bought the old Commercial Hotel at Riverside Avenue and Lincoln Street, and the adjacent two-story structure that had served once as city hall, police station, jail, and water office. It had been the seat of an administration scorned as the "ham council" when its members stole hams and other supplies from relief shipments sent Spokane after its fire of August, 1889, and one councilman traded his vote for a cemetery plot. The flimsy buildings were dilapidated, but Clark and Sweeny proposed constructing a modern edifice on the ninety-by-one-hundred-foot corner. (After their rupture, Clark was to complete the six-story Empire State Building there in 1900, one of two then in Spokane containing two elevators—and the first major construction on Riverside Avenue since the Panic of 1893.) Two days after the purchase Sweeny wrote Jeremiah O'Connor that the corner had sold for twenty-six thousand, twitting him for refusing to join in acquiring another corner at Sprague and Post. It was to become part of the site of Louis M. Davenport's famed hotel.[12]

During the next four years, 1896 to 1900, Clark and Sweeny together invested upward of three hundred thousand dollars in Spokane real estate while open land was devalued and commercial property heavily obligated. It was during these same four years that Clark and Sweeny also gained control of the Last Chance Mine, monopolized the best claims of the Buffalo Hump country, and organized the Empire State–Idaho Mining and Developing Company, using for these enterprises the funds supplied primarily by the stock purchases of O'Connor, Benjamin, Strathy, and their associates in eastern Canada and the United States. Clark came from a wealthy home, but Sweeny had only the spoils of one venture to apply toward his next. In addition, these four expansive years passed in litigation or threats of suit with the owners of the Tyler, the Stemwinder, the Bunker Hill, and the creditors of the First National Bank.

The pattern of Clark's and Sweeny's real estate speculation becomes clearer when one realizes that after its major fire in 1889 Spokane rebuilt its business district along Riverside Avenue, running east and west parallel to the river and three blocks south of the river. For the next forty years Riverside at Washington, known as "the million dollar corner," was the professional and financial center of the city, boasting three of the city's major professional buildings, the Granite, the Temple Court, and the Lindelle blocks.

At the opposite end of the business district to the west loomed the Crescent Block and Review building. There was a continuous tugging toward the intersections west of Washington, and capitalists moved their investments like chessmen to bestow a temporary prominence on Howard and Riverside, Lincoln and Riverside, and the buildings near them. Along Riverside, Spokane's contest for land occupancy and position fluctuated. An announcement of purchase or expansion could inflate the price of one parcel of land and simultaneously depress that of another not a block distant. Of course there were other downtown streets and buildings, but their desirability was measured by their proximity to the action in the game played along Riverside, the broad central thoroughfare where, in Charles Sweeny's time, the city's important stores, banks, and offices fronted on converging street railway lines.

As the contest moved east or west along Riverside, peripheral properties acquired transitory values. Clark and Sweeny together chiefly bought ground on Riverside, but Charles and Emeline Sweeny invested in land east of Washington, a block or two from the most expensive locations. Today the aging small hotels, restaurants, stores, and old theaters on Riverside east of Washington present the doleful aspect of land that has always been secondary—but in 1900 these structures stood within a few steps of the million-dollar corner.

During their brief partnership, Clark and Sweeny were the most influential promoters of downtown real estate in Spokane. Seven decades later a stroll along Riverside suggests the signal role they played in the unceasing struggle to obtain the best commercial property in the city. It is an axiom among real estate men that only one location is best, and that all others crowd about it for convenience and for prestige.

Commercial "land and appurtenances," as the deeds say, sold between 1893 and 1900 for prices that compared to fine residential sites before the panic, and much downtown property bore heavy indebtedness. These were the circumstances in which Clark and Sweeny began to buy.

In 1898 they bought the ten-year-old Temple Court, an office and apartment building on the northwest corner of Riverside and Washington, from Grant and John S. Wolverton. In addition to the price of $85,000, they also assumed a $60,000 mortgage to the United States Mortgage and Trust Company of New York and agreed to pay the Wolvertons' paving assessment on Riverside to consummate the contract.[13] Clark and Sweeny moved to the other end of the commercial district in April, 1899. They invested $35,000 cash in one of the last unimproved corners on Riverside, called the Costello block, directly north of their proposed Empire State Building at Lincoln, obtaining the Costello land from the Northwestern and Pacific Hypotheekbank, successor to the Northwestern and Pacific Mortgage Company.[14] On this corner would rise Spokane's Federal Building in 1908 and 1909. To this ground the partners added the property immediately west in July, 1899, paying the Hypotheekbank $16,500 for three irregular lots.[15] In October of the same year Clark and Sweeny plucked the northeast corner of Riverside and Washington from D. C. Corbin for $30,000.[16] Here Clark was to erect the Spokane Club in 1901, a six-story $175,000 granite structure where the club leased the three top floors. At one period the Chamber of Commerce was located in the building.

The wonder of their foray into real estate was not that Clark and Sweeny acquired centrally located ground, but that Emeline Sweeny blossomed as an astute property appraiser in her own right. A family friend described her as "a sharp, shrewd woman who watched Sweeny's financial—and feminine—deals closely." As early as 1893 Charles had given Emeline title to his property on Havermale Island, and while he and Clark were collecting business property, Emeline, too, bagged downtown land as well as a good portion of the open country that Clark intended to develop for homes through his Hillyard Town-site Company, organized June, 1898, with the real estate broker, Arthur D. Jones, to exploit an area west of the original Hillyard townsite platted by Leland D. Westfall.

Hillyard had been named for James J. Hill and planned around his Great Northern shops, located in 1892 on acreage northeast of and outside the Spokane city limits to avoid municipal taxes. Hill threatened to close his roundhouse if Hillyard incorporated, and the Great Northern stubbornly listed the place on its maps as East Spokane. But despite the formidable handicaps of coercion and anonymity, Hillyard began to expand after 1893 on previously vacant land. Clark acquired two large tracts that he named Rochester Heights and Arlington Heights, west of the Hillyard townsite, and Emeline Sweeny bought every lot but three in four blocks of Rochester Heights.

Emeline recorded the deeds to this ground in her own name. It is notable that both Charles Sweeny and Clark individually bought property between 1896 and 1900 that neither contributed to their joint holdings. Emeline also received deeds to ground downtown between Washington and Division streets on Riverside (within two blocks of the million-dollar corner) from her husband, and then added to it by purchases from the Hypotheekbank in amounts ranging from eleven thousand to twenty-six thousand dollars. In this manner she held title to the land on which the Realty Building and the Washington (later Empress) Theater were to stand.[17] The various Sweeny homes and scattered residential lots in good districts bore Emeline's name on their deeds, either purchased by her or transferred to her by Charles. Emeline had no private income. She operated with her husband's money and unquestionably with his approval.

As a consequence of their own buying, Charles and Emeline Sweeny owned parts or all of a dozen fine commercial sites in Spokane before Clark and Sweeny dissolved their partnership in March, 1900. At that time Sweeny took their joint mining enterprises, Clark gradually sold Sweeny his stock in mining companies, and Clark bought their joint real estate, continuing to develop downtown and residential areas. Clark prospered at the crest of a building boom: the *Spokesman-Review* observed in 1898 that "there is more inquiry for real estate and dwellings in Hillyard than for two years past," and in September, 1900, the newspaper reported thirty new residences completed during the season with no rental property available to answer an increasing demand.

Although Clark and Sweeny separated in 1900, their affairs necessarily overlapped for some years longer. They sundered amicably, it appears, and remained cordial. Among the city's best families, the Clarks were welcome. The Sweenys were regarded as upstarts.

Clark paid the Sweenys three hundred thousand for the property that had belonged to the partnership and for Emeline's Rochester Heights ground.[18] Thus, to summarize, Clark acquired all or parts of the sites of the future Federal Building, Davenport Hotel, Spokane Club, Empire State Building, and such existing structures as the Wolverton and Temple Court buildings. He controlled two corners of the million-dollar intersection. To Sweeny fell the holdings of the Empire State–Idaho Mining and Developing Company and the Buffalo Hump Syndicate.

Sweeny continued to speculate in real estate after his separation from Clark. He had purchased a valuable tract on the river front at Howard only two weeks before their split, when a division of their holdings must have been taking place. This was the foreclosed land of Bentham B. Bravinder, one of the proprietors of the pioneer Echo Roller Mills. Sweeny acquired it for $99,049.62 at a sheriff's redemption sale on March 13.[19]

Among the assets Sweeny received from Clark was the latter's share in the Exchange National Bank, which leased the street floor of the Exchange Bank Building. In 1902, Sweeny bought the six-story building, too, for $130,000 from the Northwestern and Hypotheekbank. Standing on the northwest corner of Howard and Riverside, where three banks guarded four corners, the Exchange typified its time. Its street level was of hewn brownstone with Roman-arched doorways, while above rose five stories of red brick with the arch repeated at the third and fourth floors. Decorative brick pillars posed as if supporting a peaked facade that broke the line of the pitched tile roof. Sweeny's Spokane office occupied a second-floor corner. A stationer rented the basement, and offices of brokers and attorneys filled the upper floors.

During 1903 Charles Sweeny was busy with organization of the Federal Mining and Smelting Company. As he spent much of his time in New York City, the acquisition of Spokane property fell to Emeline. She obtained ground opposite the Northern Pacific depot, running through the block between Riverside and Sprague avenues; she bought the pretentious Glover mansion on the hill above Spokane, and negotiated toward various purchases that were to be consummated in the next three years.

These three years, 1904 through 1906, marked Charles Sweeny's zenith as a property holder. He bought in Spokane and Portland, formed a real estate management company, and in two years bestowed on it commercial properties purchased for more than two million dollars. Sweeny, now rich from mining promotion, bought when others could not. He was credited with reviving land values in Portland. And throughout these years, Emeline, who had played no comparable role in Sweeny's mining promotions, worked by his side in appraising real estate and haggling with its owners.

Sweeny's Exchange building, on the corner of Howard and Riverside, was one of the westward tugs against the million-dollar corner. Howard and Riverside was second only to Washington and Riverside in desirability, and forty years later would be regarded as the city's center. In December, 1904, Sweeny bought from Dutch mortgage holders the southeast corner of the intersection for $165,000, expanding this thirty-by-seventy-five-foot area by ancillary purchases from the Ham family and from George Turner. Thus, of four corners at Howard and Riverside, Sweeny owned two.[20]

The *Spokesman-Review* perceived these purchases as ending a Dutch era in Spokane:

Through the sale of property at Riverside and Howard to Charles Sweeny . . . the Hypotheekbank, which formerly owned nearly all of the big business blocks here under mortgage foreclosure, sold out the last of its buildings on Riverside Avenue. Sweeny, millionaire mine owner, real estate holder, and a candidate for the United States Senate, signed the contract yesterday morning to buy the Rookery Building, the Spokane National Bank Building, the Rookery Annex, and the Riverside Building.[21]

Sweeny's new ground fronted 120 feet on Riverside and 120 feet on Howard with a 30-foot strip running through the block from Riverside to Sprague Avenue. He consolidated the four into one building. The *Spokane Daily Chronicle*, noting that the insurance broker, banker, and automobile dealer, Mose Oppenheimer, had acted as Sweeny's agent, called this the "best paying" ground in town. The transaction was, observed the *Spokesman-Review*, "the largest individual real estate deal ever consummated in Spokane; the only other one approaching it was when Sweeny dissolved his partnership with F. Lewis Clark and sold Clark his interests."

The Rookery carried an $87,000 mortgage. The share in it belonging to the Ham family was one of the few large mortgages in Spokane that had not been foreclosed after 1893. With its purchase, and Emeline's property, the Sweenys owned pivotal ground both east and west of the million-dollar corner; they stood to profit whichever direction the city moved.

If Sweeny ended a cycle in Spokane with his purchase of the last major downtown holding of the Dutch, he inaugurated an era in Portland. Portland was to stage the Lewis and Clark Exposition in 1905, a trade fair of size and splendor that would not be matched until Seattle's Alaska–Yukon Exposition four years later. Portland's most spectacular structure for the fair was the Federal pavilion, for which Congress appropriated $1,700,000. Congress also authorized coinage of Lewis and Clark memorial gold dollars. Nearly two million visitors would flock to the fair, publicize Portland throughout the world, and return 21 percent profit to the exposition's shareholders. But real estate dealers forecast that after the giant show, property values would decline in Portland. Ignoring these expectations, in August, 1904, Sweeny bought the Dekum Building, a landmark in the middle of Portland's commercial district. The effect of this sale was later described by a pioneer Portland real estate broker, Henry E. Reed:

> Curious as it may seem, the prevailing opinion in Portland was that after the Exposition there would be a local business depression, accompanied by a slump in real estate values. Wiseacres told intending investors in real estate to hold off until after the Exposition and they would be able to buy cheaper. It was the purchase of the Dekum Building by . . . Charles Sweeny in August, 1904, that set off the spark and set a high pattern for Portland real estate values that was not seriously interrupted until the stock market crash of 1929.[22]

The Dekum Building stood in a three-block area that in 1905 was the theatrical, hotel, financial, and retail heart of Portland. Erected in 1892 for $235,000 by the late Frank Dekum, it was a massive eight-story structure, planned before steel skeleton framing, which rose on heavy foundations at the southwest corner of Southwest Third and Washington with one hundred feet of frontage on each. Its street floor housed a leading department store, Lipman, Wolfe and Company, and among its neighbors were Portland's best hotels, the Northern Pacific and Southern Pacific railway ticket offices, the Shahan department store, the Masonic Temple, and the Chamber of Commerce. During the exposition from June 1 through October 15, the Dekum lay on the favored route from hotels to fair grounds, reflecting the glitter of gay throngs nightly.

Sweeny negotiated from New York City through the real estate brokers, Rountree and Diamond, to purchase the Dekum Building and the old Dekum homestead, the latter occupying a full block bounded by Thirteenth and Fourteenth and Morrison and Yamhill. He paid $350,000 for the building and $75,000 for the homesite, the last assets of the estate of Frank Dekum on which there was a $149,000 mortgage. With the forecasts of falling land values, the Dekum heirs probably thought themselves well rid of the indebted property. Dekum's four sons and three daughters accepted 1,250 shares of preferred stock in the Federal Mining and Smelting Company in partial payment, which reduced Sweeny's cash commitment to them by one-fourth. Federal was selling at $90 on the New York market, and the Dekums agreed that Sweeny might repurchase the stock within three years.[23]

Sweeny had no immediate plans for the Dekum Building, telling the Portland *Oregonian* that it "is a paying investment and nothing will be done to it." To this he added, "I am not altogether a stranger in Portland. I lived here from 1877 to 1882, working most of that time for Knapp, Burrell and Company, later organizing the Merchants' Exchange. Afterwards I went to Spokane but I have been in the habit of coming to Portland several times a year." [24]

For a time Sweeny talked of erecting a hotel on the Dekum homestead because the Portland Hotel, the city's favorite, had been overcrowded for years. He offered to buy the Portland but regarded the asking price of $150 a share for its stock as too high. At Sweeny's request a New York architect drew plans for a $750,000 steel-framed hotel, eight stories high, with electric lights and gas heat, hot and cold baths, and room telephones. Sweeny displayed his rolled blueprints grandly about the city. But the project languished six years, delayed by an Oregon statute prohibiting the sale of liquor in a hotel within four hundred feet of a school building. Then Sweeny considered erecting a $200,000 opera house, five stories tall, to be the largest on the Pacific Coast, seating three thousand spectators.[25] He discussed its management with the veteran theater operator, John F. Cordray. Nothing came of either scheme for the Dekum homestead. Finally an automobile repair garage and small shops rose on the site.

Sweeny's purchases in Portland did not stop with the Dekum estate. In May, 1905, he obtained undeveloped ground at Seventh and Morrison for $100,000, and the Washington Block at Fourth and

Washington (near the Dekum Building) for $200,000. In June he paid the Catholic Archbishop of Portland $125,000 for two lots on the northeast corner of Third and Stark, within a block of the Dekum, causing the *Oregonian* to comment that since Sweeny had begun buying real estate in Portland, the prices of downtown property had doubled.[26] By the end of June, 1905, Sweeny had spent $850,000 in Portland in ten months.

On the property at Third and Stark, Sweeny razed a one-story frame to erect a $130,000 building as the Portland branch of a Spokane furniture company, Tull and Gibbs. Then in October, 1906, he bought the annex to the Dekum Building, also occupied by Lipman, Wolfe and Company, lying between the Dekum and Washington blocks. It gave Sweeny, said the *Oregonian*, "control of more than half a block of the most valuable property in the heart of the city's business district."[27] The annex was his last sizable real estate acquisition.

The *Oregonian* printed a box listing each of Sweeny's properties, what he had paid for it, and its estimated value after less than two years, calculating that the ground and buildings had cost him $1,146,120 and had appreciated to $1,730,000.

While his agents, Rountree and Diamond, and the attorney, John M. Gearin, were selecting the ground, Sweeny spent much of his time in New York or London. It seems unlikely that his Portland investments were the result of a personal assessment of land values.

To manage the various properties he and Emeline had accumulated, Sweeny formed the Sweeny Investment Company on May 27, 1905, with a capitalization of $2,500,000 to trade in real estate, securities, and stocks in Washington and Oregon. The officers were Sweeny, Emeline, and their son-in-law, Francis J. Finucane. All the stock was held by these three in a manner designed to give each officer a vote equal to each other: Sweeny held one share, Emeline one, and Finucane one, Sweeny and Finucane together 12,498 shares, and Emeline and Finucane jointly 12,499 shares.[28] Sweeny established a trust in 1906 to distribute his stock to his heirs. Emeline, Finucane, and the Sweeny children were to share in this trust. Although Finucane served as president of the investment company until April 10, 1907, its operation was entrusted largely to managers: Bruce Clendening in Spokane, and Robert E. M. Strickland in Portland. When he returned home from Notre Dame University, one Sweeny son, Frank, was elected an officer and after his father's death was to manage the company briefly.

Charles Sweeny's span as a buyer and seller of real estate lasted ten years, from 1896 to 1906. His land was always secondary in interest to his mines. In those ten years he had helped centralize the chief commercial properties in Spokane along Riverside Avenue, and had participated in maintaining the importance of the million-dollar corner by purchases which enhanced its influence.[29] Much of his property in Portland and Spokane was to decline in value as skylines changed, but future vicissitudes could not alter the fact that after his split with F. Lewis Clark, Charles Sweeny remained a commanding figure in real estate in two cities. He had closed out the Dutch on Riverside Avenue in Spokane and had turned aside depression in Portland.

# VIII

## PROSPECTING BY PRECEDENT

LTHOUGH the romance of mining deals with gold rushes and discoveries, a good share of Charles Sweeny's mining took place in the dreary routine of courtrooms. Assertive and opportunistic, Sweeny was fated to legal disputation almost from the day he bought the ground of Eagle City. In mid-1884, as we have seen, he was named by A. J. and Catherine Prichard as a defendant, with Wyatt Earp, John Earp, Henry White, and others, in a lawsuit by which the Prichards sought to recover mining claims and ten-thousand-dollar damages.[1] Prichard was attempting to hold title to claims he had located in others' names. Although the jury agreed that he was legally right, it awarded him no locations and no damages. From this encounter Sweeny and the Earps emerged as local heroes because their action was regarded as a test of the legitimacy of a number of claims staked on behalf of absentees.

Twelve years after his first lawsuit in the district, when Sweeny and F. Lewis Clark owned the Last Chance outright, Charles Sweeny would understand the law intimately from monotonous weeks cooped in courtrooms. In the fall of 1901 his attorney, Weldon B. Heyburn, summarized no less than thirty-six Sweeny cases scheduled in various courts, and on a single day in January, 1906, the United States Supreme Court ruled on three.

Not only did Sweeny's cases parade some of the foremost courtroom talent of his time and clarify legal precedent, but for years his trials afforded some of the best entertainment in the Coeur d'Alenes, a continuing drama played by consummate actors for high stakes.[2] Sometimes the plot would be agonizing, sometimes hilarious. When the courtroom scene lay outside the district, the Coeur d'Alenes followed testimony in the newspapers like serialized novels.

Broadly speaking, Charles Sweeny's lawsuits can be divided into two categories: one, an extended battle against the Bunker Hill company for control of Wardner's commercial mineralization, and two, Sweeny's impingement of others' claims, notably the Skookum and the Ella.

The most complicated of his scores of lawsuits pivoted on exact interpretations—"construction," the lawyers call it—of statute and precedent, but even Sweeny's simpler cases demand some understanding of mining law as it had developed in the last years of the nineteenth century. In many early mining regions, the common miner occupied the position of elite citizen, the storekeeper that of necessary evil, and the attorney, of unwelcome parasite. Some Colorado districts barred attorneys from miners' courts.[3] This does not seem to have been true of the Coeur d'Alenes, where a covey of barristers followed the first gold rush and others arrived virtually overnight when labor disputes offered them opportunities to find clients. A number of attorneys prospected or hired as hands until they could establish practices, as Heyburn had done. Others, like Frank Ganahl, invested in mines. In 1885 Ganahl bonded, among his acquisitions, the Fanny lode claim from Sweeny for twenty-five thousand dollars. Still others accepted shares of mining stock as payment for their legal services.

As it stood, mining law was compounded of custom and regulation. The earlier American miners in Colorado, California, Nevada, and Montana had established simple rules eventually sanctioned by courts, so it is not surprising that the men of Eagle City, Idaho, gathered in the town street on June 3, 1884, to adopt their own code, based on customs in Montana or earlier diggings.[4] What is perhaps surprising, in view of the usual disdain for lawyers, is that the Eagle City code was framed by an attorney, Albert Allen, who acted as chairman of the meeting. Without doubt the town's erstwhile proprietor, Charles Sweeny, was among those who voted to accept Allen's proposed regulations.

Most of the Eagle City code related to placer mining, although within two years lode mining absorbed the prospectors so wholly that placers seemed incidental. (Placer mining consists of washing mineral, usually gold, from the earth with water; lode or vein mining, of digging mineral or ore-bearing rock.) The Eagle City regulations stipulated, however, that lode locations must conform to the Federal Act of May 10, 1872—and that act required a miner to find a piece of land on which a mineral vein actually appeared, and to stake his claim over an area running lengthwise in the direction of the vein's course, surveyed with parallel end lines.

Even though Eagle City wrote its own mining regulations, the Coeur d'Alenes were not without law, for in addition to the Idaho territorial code of 1864, the district was subject to the federal courts. On formation of the territory in 1863, Idaho had been divided into three federal judicial districts; Shoshone, Nez Perce, and Idaho counties—then comprising all of northern Idaho—had been lumped into district one. Intended as temporary, the Eagle City mining code was short-lived, indeed, and no miners' court sat as in earlier Montana camps. When Sweeny and the Earp brothers challenged Prichard's claims in 1884, their case went before the bench as Shoshone County civil case number twenty-four.

As a matter of expediency, Idaho Territory had copied California and Nevada's mining laws in 1864, including the significant provision for lode miners that the locator of the vein at the place where it rose nearest the earth's surface (its apex) possessed certain rights to follow its plane downward even outside the vertical boundaries he had staked.[5] Consequently, in the Coeur d'Alenes, the salient provisions of territorial and federal law were those stating the idea of pursuit downward, the extralateral concept. The miners called this the "apex law," and it was to be the mine owners' bane and the lawyers' bonanza. Much of Sweeny's litigation with the Bunker Hill involved this apex law—the right of an owner to follow his vein downward on its dip beyond the vertical bounds of his claim between extended parallel end lines.

The great struggles over the apex law in the Coeur d'Alenes stemmed from the textbook language describing a model vein in the Federal Act of 1872, which the courts tried to clarify, and from the fact that Phil O'Rourke, Noah Kellogg, and Con Sullivan had all guessed wrong about the direction of the vein they staked, so that the Bunker Hill, the Sullivan, and subsequent claims near them straddled the course of the vein rather than following it as required in the statute. It was to take a good deal of underground work before anyone recognized this error.[6]

Moreover, in their rush to stake ground near the Bunker Hill, the prospectors often forgot which claim had been posted before another, so that buyers later were to be hard put to establish priority of their ground. A question of prior right arose as early as April 19, 1887, when the Portland owners of the Tyler claim applied to the land office at Coeur d'Alene City for a patent—that is, a title to public land. When the Tyler's application was publicized, the next-door Emma and Last Chance Mining Company (consisting of Charles Sweeny, John M. Burke, and Robert J. Linden) challenged the Tyler claim in the circuit court. This challenge was known as "adversing" the claim. Through Heyburn, Sweeny and his partners contended that the Last Chance lines had been staked first. The evidence bore them out, so that 1.474 acres of the area offered for patent by the Tyler actually belonged to the Last Chance.[7]

Two separate juries could not induce themselves to award a decision to the Last Chance, however, and the contest seemed deadlocked until the Tyler withdrew without offering any reason. The court thereupon gave the Last Chance the disputed portion, sliced from the Tyler's east end. Evidently the Tyler's attorneys, John McBride and Joseph N. Dolph, believed that pushing the case further might endanger the whole Tyler ground because, as the clearly prior location, the Last Chance now claimed that it could pursue ore into the Tyler boundaries.

The Tyler, consequently, was patented as a claim 600 by roughly 1,071.5 feet. Its owners, J. A. and W. B. Honeyman and William B. Ladd, all of Portland, let it be known that the property was for sale. This was at the time that Sweeny, Burke, and Linden attracted financing from F. Rockwood Moore and his cronies, Sweeny conceived the idea for his giant tunnel, and Sweeny, Moore, Cyrus Burns, and John Chapman formed the Idaho Mining Company, which claimed additional ground west of the Tyler. The combination of adit and expanded claims for the Last Chance apparently convinced the Tyler's new owners, also Portland men, that their property was threatened by encirclement. The Tyler began digging a short, inclined shaft to intercept the Sweeny Tunnel, breaking into it in August,

1891. Back to court: the Tyler sued for its mineral, for damages, and for an injunction to stop the Last Chance's boring into alleged Tyler ground.

This was the beginning of nearly six years of litigation between the Last Chance and the Tyler. Their dispute was to reach the Supreme Court of the United States where the justices would comment on the inadequacy of mining law. Although the Tyler was neither Sweeny's most significant nor his longest case, it offers an instructive introduction to the vagaries of mining law.

Quite evidently, even at this early stage of development in 1891, the Last Chance and the Tyler were working the same vein, which apparently apexed in both claims with conflicting extralateral rights. Heyburn's first retort to the Tyler suit was to challenge the Tyler's validity as a mining claim on the plea that, after losing its snip of ground to the Last Chance, the Tyler had become five-sided whereas the federal statute provided only for four-sided claims with parallel endlines.

During the sixty-five months that followed this first argument, the lives of the leading performers and the fortunes of the Coeur d'Alene district, itself, changed. Through the Last Chance, the Republican, and the Idaho Mining companies, Sweeny acquired irregular surface claims named the Last Chance Fraction, the Republican Fraction, and the Skookum Fraction, southeast of the Tyler, which the Tyler characterized as "outposts for the protection of the Last Chance claim." By the time the long contest ended, the Tyler was but one of many petitioners occupying Sweeny's attention.

The immediate result of the Tyler's complaint in 1891 was that the circuit court enjoined the Last Chance from extracting mineral from contested ground until it considered the case, and then decreed that, because the Last Chance was prior, its right to pursue the vein overrode that of the Tyler, a verdict the Tyler carried to the Ninth Circuit Court of Appeals in San Francisco, where the Tyler won an order for a new trial in a decision dated January, 1893. During the months between these verdicts, the injunction was raised and the Last Chance's development accelerated—but with the appellate court's order, the Last Chance again was enjoined from taking ore from outside its vertical boundaries and in March, 1893, the mine was placed in the custody of Frank R. Culbertson as agent of the court.

The court of appeals ruled that the Tyler had not abandoned its total claim by forfeiting part of it in 1887, brushed aside Heyburn's argument of the five-sided shape, and issued this fruitless appeal for compromise: "Litigation is expensive. Compromises are favored. Agreement to withdraw from litigation to save expense should be sanctioned and encouraged." What the court did not consider was that Charles Sweeny regarded the Last Chance as his key to the ore bodies around it and that compromise might seal off these from his big tunnel.

The appellate court also expressed its opinion that while "the mining laws of the United States were passed upon the theory that the lodes and veins of mineral-bearing rock in their general course could be readily ascertained by their locators," the natural occurrence of lodes obeyed no such neat pattern, necessitating locations "in various shapes and forms, varying from a plain parallelogram, which is required by law." Although they remarked acidly on the shortcomings of federal statutes, the appellate justices ruled in favor of the Tyler on its plea that the lower court should not have considered testimony proving the Last Chance the prior location, as that question had been settled when the Tyler withdrew from its patent suit in 1887.

At the direction of the San Francisco court, the case went back to Boise where the district court heard the testimony over again, excluding evidence of prior location; this time the Tyler won and the Last Chance appealed to the Ninth Circuit Court which upheld the verdict for the Tyler. After the ruling the Tyler owners threw a victory party. Sweeny, boarding the special Last Chance train to Spokane, muttered to a reporter, "It's only horse and horse," meaning that this decision was no more final than previous ones. Sweeny's growl proved prophetic, for the Last Chance went to the Supreme Court, asking a review of the appellate decision. On April 15, 1895, the highest bench declared that proof of prior location was the "pivotal" evidence in the contest, because the disputed ore lay within the extralateral rights of both companies so that only the prior locator could be permitted to follow the vein's dip. As for the Tyler's withdrawal from that adverse suit in 1887, on which its attorneys based their present demand that prior location not be considered, the Supreme Court spoke scathingly, asking if the Tyler "sought to walk away from the case, to say that the judgment amounts to nothing? We are of the opinion that this cannot be tolerated." The court conceded that "our conclusions . . . obviate the necessity of considering another very interesting and somewhat difficult question presented by counsel," that of extralateral rights to the vein that entered the Tyler at an endline and passed out its sidelines—a situation not covered by federal statutes. As the Last Chance had hoped, the Supreme Court ordered a new trial.[8]

By this time, the *Spokesman-Review* was calling the Tyler–Last Chance contest "one of the most noted mining cases in the history of the country," estimating the disputed vein worth five hundred thousand dollars and adding to this the two-hundred-thousand-dollar damages sought by the Tyler to assert that nearly three-quarters of a million dollars was at stake.

The case went to trial in Boise for a third time in spring, 1895, and once more the locators of the Last Chance and the Tyler told their stories to ascertain prior location.[9] Heyburn called as a witness C. E. Tyler, locator of the Tyler, who now worked as a carpenter in Maine, and Tyler retold his version: he and S. R. (Sandy) Divine had located the Tyler on September 20, 1885, after looking over the Bunker Hill and Stemwinder claims. Tyler had paced off the ground while Divine tacked up a location notice.

Then Michael Carlin testified, as he had previously, that he and John Flaherty had located the Emma and the Last Chance on September 17, 1885, after finding whitish ore "plain to be seen" protruding from the ground, an outcrop of mineral as long as a box Carlin pointed out in a corner of the courtroom. Carlin and Flaherty had been prospecting with Jack Smith and the same Divine who later helped stake the Tyler. Despite attempts in cross-examination to shake his memory, Carlin held to his story: Flaherty had named the Emma, and he, Carlin, the Last Chance, and both were older than the Tyler by three days. When his turn on the stand came, Sweeny disclosed that he had bonded the Tyler, Emma, and Last Chance claims in April, 1886, later gave up the Tyler, but bought the others in June, 1887. He believed that up to 1895 his company had spent as much as $700,000 developing the Last Chance.

With the Supreme Court's mandate to consider prior location "pivotal," the Boise court this third time ruled in favor of the Last Chance. The Tyler's appeal resulted in affirmation of the decision. The Last Chance had not asked damages, however, and was awarded none, but it claimed $14,000 in costs which the court reduced to $9,418 and ordered the Tyler to pay. Even the award of costs was appealed but the appellate court in October, 1898, directed that the costs would stand against the Tyler. The Last Chance had long since obtained an order to lift the injunction on underground operations when the Tyler failed to appear to contest it on June 25, 1895. Thus closed the case of the Tyler versus the Last Chance, with the Last Chance in possession of mineral that, in the years that had passed during the trials, had been proved scattered and low grade.

Sweeny's unremitting battle to control the vein that coursed through the Last Chance claim was part of his struggle to maintain access to ore that could be tapped through the Sweeny Tunnel. Whereas the Tyler–Last Chance litigation had hinged on prior location, in 1895 Sweeny entered an extended contest to protect a claim staked not above, but beneath, the ground surface. A separate company was organized to exploit this orebody, the Shoshone Mining Company—the one that Frank Moore had offered in his last days, as security for his debts, to the creditors of the First National Bank. The Shoshone occasioned the first public breach between Sweeny and the Bunker Hill ownership, setting off a chain of legal skirmishes that ended only when the Last Chance ceased to be useful.

As a result of probing from the Sweeny Tunnel, a plane of ore was discovered about twelve hundred feet underground, which was named the Shoshone. It extended outside Sweeny's vertical boundaries but, as Heyburn was to explain, "It either would have passed out to be owned or located by anybody, or else it was necessary to locate it where it was found." Sweeny therefore claimed that his men had staked the Shoshone underground and by calculation extended the lines upward to the surface simply as information about what lay below.[10]

In the resultant suit for possession, underground locating was not the only novel prospect. The Shoshone emerged on unposted land almost immediately swallowed by a resurvey of the Kirby and Wardner claims owned by Bunker Hill people. Then the Shoshone was demonstrated to be the third claim with similar boundaries, the case was to reach the Supreme Court not on its merit but as a result of challenges to the jurisdiction of lower courts, and in the span of more than five years of hearings, the case was to lose its identity among other suits involving the same litigants and the same vein—for all were working the ledge that passed through the Bunker Hill, the Stemwinder, the Emma, the Last Chance, the Tyler, the San Carlos, and others. In fact, by 1903 Sweeny had added fourteen other locations to the operating mines strung like the tail of a kite to the Bunker Hill.

The Shoshone case was relatively simple, as mining cases go. Once the claim was discovered, Sweeny applied for his patent on August 21, 1895. Three days later, after their hurried resurvey of the Kirby, the Kirby's owners adversed the Shoshone application in the circuit court, asserting that the ground and whatever lay beneath it belonged to them. They filed a second suit to protect their property adjacent to the Kirby. The Kirby's owners of record were Royal L. Rutter and Frederick W. Bradley, the latter manager of the Bunker Hill and Sullivan. There can be little doubt that they intended to use the Kirby to confine Sweeny and extend the Bunker Hill.

One facet of Heyburn's defense concerned the original location of the Kirby. Jacob Johns, one of its discoverers, explained that he had paced off the Edith on July 10, 1886, and "located another claim right over it—right on top of the Edith." This "claim right over it" was, of course, the Kirby, which included two hundred feet more ground than the Edith. Both were recorded, and when Rutter and Bradley bought the Kirby, Johns told them about the Edith. The Kirby was no more than an expanded location and a name change, but in court Heyburn made much of it, claiming that the Kirby could not be valid if the Edith were. He also claimed that Johns had not seen mineral as required by statute, although the evidence (which the court acknowledged "conflicted") indicated that seams two or three inches wide had been found by adit.

In the meantime Sweeny sued the Kirby in the state court to protect his title to the Shoshone. When Federal Judge James H. Beatty dismissed the Kirby's case in Boise as out of his jurisdiction, he remarked that the Shoshone seemed a valid claim, inquiring rhetorically where one might be expected to post notice of an underground claim if not on the surface. The state court ruled for the Kirby, so that by the end of 1896, both Sweeny and the Kirby had lost their cases—in different courts—and both appealed.[11] The Ninth Circuit Court combined the two appeals, ruling that Boise had had jurisdiction and that the Kirby had been a valid location, giving it prior right over the Shoshone. Sweeny appealed this decision to the Supreme Court of the United States which declared on April 30, 1900, that the circuit court at Boise had not had jurisdiction so that after five years of trials, "The matter stands as if no proceedings were ever had." All those five years Sweeny's companies had been taking ore from the Shoshone Mine and since the litigation had begun, the Shoshone company had been absorbed by the Empire State–Idaho, Sweeny had recruited new allies and new money, and the Bunker Hill had concluded that it must await another occasion to stop Charles Sweeny.

As Sweeny, now spending Toronto and New York money, under-took the consolidations that were to bring much of the Coeur d'Alenes under his command, the mining towns heard from courtrooms some incidents of his spurt to power. Not all of Sweeny's many trials in-volved mining law, for what the newspapers were to label "one of the most celebrated cases in the history of the Coeur d'Alenes" was launched to regain a stolen deed. It was instituted by a one-time Sweeny partner to recover his share of the Skookum, one of a group of claims west of the Last Chance—a group that included the Viola, San Carlos, Likely, Cuba Fraction, and Jersey Fraction—from which Sweeny extracted most of his profitable ore after April, 1898.[12]

Sometime in 1897 the Last Chance tunnel, Sweeny's undulating adit probing in various directions, penetrated the Skookum and sev-eral lesser claims owned in part by a small investor, Kennedy J. Hanley. Hanley accepted 125,000 shares of Chemung stock for his claims although Clark, who handled the negotiations, told him the Skookum was "of no value" and said that he and Sweeny wanted to buy it "not because it was of any value for its ore, but because it was surrounded by other claims which were of value and would be useful to them for combining . . . for working purposes . . . and give breadth, bulk, and character to their plan to put the consolidated land on the market." [13]

Hanley previously had brushed with Clark and Sweeny over a one-third share of the Skookum owned by the estate of David Mc-Kelvey. Partly to end their differences Clark suggested that he and Sweeny buy out Hanley, who was "anxious to close out his interests and avoid all further business complications or dealings with them," as his attorney phrased his view. Hanley agreed to sell his stock and two deeds, one for the controversial McKelvey one-third which he continued to contest by appeals to the courts, and a second for his undisputed one-eighth of the Skookum, all for twenty-eight thousand dollars. Clark and Sweeny met Hanley in the Exchange National Bank in Spokane and paid down two thousand dollars. Hanley showed them two envelopes, one containing his 125,000 shares of Chemung, and the other, the two deeds, to be deposited in escrow until Hanley received his final payment. He was called momentarily to another section of the bank, and before he returned, Charles Sweeny switched the deed to Hanley's one-eighth interest in the Skookum to the envelope containing the Chemung stock. Consequently when Clark paid over sixteen thousand dollars on the following September 1, enough to release the stock envelope, he withdrew this envelope from escrow, receiving not only the stock but Hanley's uncontested one-eighth deed.[14]

When the Idaho supreme court ruled against his appeal for the McKelvey deed, Hanley was left with nothing—his one-third revoked by court order, his one-eighth with his Chemung stock in Clark's strong box. Hiring John McBride, the solicitor who also represented Rutter and Bradley, Hanley sued in the district court for the return of his one-eighth, for an accounting of ore taken from the Skookum, and for a receiver to operate the Skookum until Hanley got what he asked. On January 9, 1899, Judge A. E. Mayhew found in favor of Hanley and appointed a receiver.

Twenty-one days later, however, the Idaho supreme court decreed that Judge Mayhew had not had authority to put the Skookum into receivership and reversed Mayhew's decision, saying that Hanley's complaint was "fully met and overcome by both allegation and proof," and that his story of switching deeds was "unreasonable and inconsistent with usual business methods." Hanley had implored justice "apparently with unclean hands," observed the supreme court, while Clark and Sweeny produced witnesses from the bank who swore to their version that Hanley had agreed to sell both stock and deed for the eighteen thousand dollars he received.

Hanley's attorney, McBride, simply moved his case into federal court. By now the year 1900 was well spent, the Empire State–Idaho had thrust its Arizona Tunnel into Skookum ground, and Hanley faced the spreading thicket of Sweeny's affairs. As the engineer, J. M. Porter, explained: "I know that said [Empire State–Idaho] company is the defendant in several suits which involve hundreds of thousands of dollars, as well as the title to certain properties of said company, and the affairs of said company are thereby becoming involved in such a way that the said company's ability to respond to a decree for accounting is decreasing."[15] Moreover, said Porter, Sweeny's firm had recently absorbed another (the Buffalo Hump Mining Company) "and the difficulty of securing an accurate estimate [of ore] . . . ex-

tracted from the said Skookum mine . . . is becoming more difficult." This was two years after Sweeny had switched Hanley's deed—
but Hanley was to spend ten more years in court in his quest for an
accounting. Not allowed to look inside the Skookum, he was stigma-
tized by Sweeny's people as a ne'er-do-well harassing a successful
mine promoter. Hanley went doggedly ahead in court. There was
nothing else he could do, for he was losing money in business and at
the gaming tables, holding to his hope that when he finally cornered
Sweeny, his one-eighth of the Skookum would pay his debts.

While Hanley fought in court, Sweeny continued to work in the
Skookum and the claims around it. In 1900–1 the Empire State–Idaho,
in its general manager's estimation, produced about one-eighth of the
domestic lead of the United States. More than half of the company's
Wardner ore came from the Skookum.[16]

The federal court at Boise now ruled that Hanley had been de-
frauded. The circuit court of appeals affirmed this verdict and refused
Sweeny's appeal for a reversal, and Hanley apparently had recovered
his one-eighth of the Skookum. He had no accounting, however, and
reckoned by February, 1902, that Sweeny owed him $315,000 for
mineral taken from the mine.[17] At this point, Heyburn offered the
ingenious argument that Hanley, as a former stockholder in the
Chemung, had merely held his one-eighth Skookum in trust for the
Chemung. Heyburn asked that a receiver be named to take any money
awarded Hanley and pay the Chemung's outstanding accounts.

Further exploration in the Wardner area, Heyburn added, now
revealed that the Skookum lode apexed in the San Carlos claim,
owned by Sweeny, and ore was being lawfully extracted by Sweeny in
accordance with his right to pursue the plane from its San Carlos apex.
Judge Beatty accepted Heyburn's dialectics but the circuit court of
appeals would not, ruling that Heyburn could not bring up new matter
to overturn its previous decision. As Sweeny continued to work the
Skookum, Hanley demanded an injunction, which was denied. Instead
the court directed Sweeny to deposit Hanley's share of profit in the
First National Bank at Wallace. Three months later Sweeny and
Hanley still were arguing about Hanley's proper share. On May 18,
1902, the court consequently enjoined Sweeny from taking more ore
from the Skookum.

The injunction hampered the Sweeny camp at a time when it strove
to maintain a good profit record to show its stockholders. E. J. Rob-

erts, Sweeny's general manager during 1901–5, urged Heyburn to
press for early decisions on his appeals on the Skookum and another
rival claim, the Stemwinder, "owing to the limited amount of ore
developed outside the ground covered by the Skookum and Stemwinder injunctions." [18] W. Clayton Miller wrote Sweeny on September 27, 1902, that his Wardner ore bodies were "gradually but surely
lessening in value," and outside his enjoined property, "there is no
first-class ore in sight." Not only was Miller dubious of Sweeny's
ability to continue producing ore at Wardner, he was appalled at
Heyburn's eagerness to go into court. Miller complained that Heyburn
now wanted to try all of the more than thirty suits involving the
Empire State–Idaho in the fall terms of various courts, although
Miller "pled with him for days to postpone everything except those
now in hand, as we have nothing to gain." [19]

Judge Beatty's injunction stood until November 17, 1902, when
he reiterated that Hanley owned one-eighth of the Skookum and
ordered that he be paid $175,867.02 as his share of the net profit to
date. From then on Sweeny deposited one-eighth of the Skookum's
income in the bank as a hedge against its eventual loss to Hanley and
hired a bonding company to indemnify him. To sustain his dividend
rate, Sweeny then resumed taking ore from the Skookum in March,
1903, on Heyburn's assurance that he could protect this action in
court. Hanley again sought an injunction, Beatty denied it, and the
Ninth Circuit Court of Appeals also turned down Hanley with the
explanation that the majority owner ought to have the right to continue mining "in the absence of any showing of wrong-doing."

Hanley resorted to paying the editors of a Spokane weekly newspaper, *The Outburst,* to attack Clark and Sweeny, raking over the
failure of the First National, the partners' acquisition of the Last
Chance, the switched Skookum deed, and other matters. Perhaps the
articles were also intended to prick Sweeny's inflating ambitions for
political office. The stories stirred enough concern that for a time
Spokane city and county commissioners mulled action to seek repay-
ment of funds lost by local governments in the collapse of the First
National, but when the county commissioners refused to appropriate
money to pursue a suit, nothing further was done. [20] Hanley then won
a judgment against the American Bonding Company of Baltimore,
which had indemnified Sweeny, but delivery of the bond was delayed

by further court maneuvers. Bruce Clendening wrote the American's officers: "We beg to inform you that we are advised by counsel that the judgment in favor of Mr. Hanley . . . is not a final judgment. . . . We now inform you that Kennedy J. Hanley, the plaintiff in the case, is irresponsible financially, and that any monies paid to him in satisfaction of said judgment will be lost should the said judgment be reversed or set aside by the circuit court of appeals or by the supreme court of the United States." [21]

Thus Kennedy Hanley's suit against Charles Sweeny to retrieve a switched deed dragged through various courts, and no matter how often Hanley seemed to win, he never received any money. The *Engineering and Mining Journal* observed on June 16, 1904, that "the Skookum case has been three times to the Supreme Court and eight times to the court of appeals." In 1910, twelve years after he had instituted his first suit for his share of the Skookum, Hanley lost his property at a sale to satisfy his debts. Although M. W. Bacon, Hanley's creditor in the amount of $51,856, acquired Hanley's share of the Skookum, Sweeny's successors in its management denied Bacon entry to the mine to ascertain whether his share was actually worth the money.[22]

Sweeny's affairs in court reached their comic climax in the case of the Ella, similar to the Skookum suit in its allegations that Sweeny found ore by exploring beyond his ground and buncoed its owner. In this case, Sweeny challenged no down-on-his-luck miner but the redoubtable Patrick (Patsy) Clark, a successful operator who had started in Butte and made money in the Rossland and Coeur d'Alene camps. In the view of the *Spokesman-Review*, the Ella loomed as "a battle of the giants," when the newspaper broke the story on June 12, 1901, that Clark and three others had filed suit in district court charging Sweeny and F. R. Culbertson with swindling them out of claims worth a million dollars.

Clark, his brother James, B. C. Kingsbury, and James P. Harvey charged that in 1899 Sweeny had used diamond drills to explore the Ella Mine at a depth of twelve hundred feet through an adit running eastward into it from the adjoining Poorman. Sweeny's Buffalo Hump Mining Company had purchased the Poorman only a few months previously from a syndicate represented by Patsy Clark, and this sale (of the Consolidated Tiger-Poorman) was renegotiated with suspicious Butte stockholders who believed Sweeny had bought the property too cheaply, although the Tiger-Poorman was supposed to be worked out.[23]

This was the same Patsy Clark who had stolen Bunker Hill ore on a night in 1887 for Simeon G. Reed so that Reed could assay it before buying the Bunker Hill and Sullivan. Patsy Clark and Charles Sweeny both lived by the code: Let my adversary beware. Consequently, a shout of laughter rose from the mining towns when they learned that Clark charged that Sweeny, after finding "half a million dollars worth of ore" in the Ella, had talked Clark into selling the Ella and Missing Link fractional claims for four thousand dollars with a tale that Kennedy Hanley would have recognized: the locations were "no good and had no value as mining claims," but Sweeny's Buffalo Hump company, which owned one-fifth of the Ella, wanted all of it "for the basis of forming a new corporation and making a big showing in the shape of surface ground." [24]

The trial was transcontinental, Sweeny testifying in New York, Culbertson in San Francisco, and the other witnesses in Idaho or Spokane. Testimony showed that Joseph MacDonald, a reputable consulting engineer who had since been appointed general manager of the Alaska Treadwell Gold Mining Company, had recommended that Sweeny explore southward from an abandoned adit which Clark himself had previously driven from the Poorman into the Ella. Sweeny hired C. W. Butler, a diamond drill operator, who found good ore in each hole he bored. The Sweeny crews during October, 1899, made a 47-foot crosscut, struck the vein, and followed it 144 feet in Ella ground with a width of 4 feet of paying ore all the way. After that, Sweeny allowed no one at the 1,200-foot level but "men he could swear by." Culbertson was induced to sell his one-fifth of the Ella and Missing Link to Sweeny, and with this in hand, Sweeny persuaded Clark to sell him the rest. He bought the Ella and Missing Link for four thousand dollars and half the adjoining Sheridan for another three thousand.

Clark did not learn of Sweeny's rich strike in the Ella until four months after the sale, and then went leisurely to see it—out of curiosity rather than outrage—but did not enter the mine because he was told there had been a lift accident. In answer to a question from Clark, Sweeny declared that the ore lay in the O'Neill, another claim in the cluster that included the Poorman, Ella, Missing Link, Sheridan, and others. Thus Clark did not discover the true location or value of the ore until yet another brother, Thomas, slipped through the workings to remove a chunk for assay. Then two Clark hirelings, J. C. Ralston and Joseph Dolan, disguised themselves as common miners, crept through the timber station of the Poorman, signaled the engineer to lower the cage, and explored. They estimated the size of the hole and value of the ore. Using this report, Clark concluded Sweeny had extracted mineral worth $450,000.

Not only had Sweeny used Clark's own adit and concealed the value of his mine, but as a crowning indignity, he subverted Clark's spy. Culbertson, to whom Clark gave one-fifth of the Ella for spying on Sweeny, abetted Sweeny's duplicity. In cumbersome legal terms, the miffed Clark complained that he "conveyed to F. R. Culbertson the undivided one-fifth interest in the Ella and Missing Link lode mining claims for the sole purpose of compensating Culbertson for his services in watching the claims; and in the event that in the workings of the Poorman mine any ore bodies should be struck so near the Ella line as to be probable that the same extended into and through the Ella, he should advise your orator [Clark] of the fact." [25]

During the trial, Sweeny's attorney, Heyburn, asked Patrick Clark if he himself had not known of ore in the Ella. Clark's memory wandered. Neither could he produce his company's records although Heyburn pressed him continually for a month. Finally Clark belatedly unearthed the books showing that while he managed the Poorman, he took 283 tons of ore worth $16,524.78 from the Ella.

Clark's evasiveness lent no credence to his plaint against Sweeny and Culbertson; his payment of Culbertson to spy on Sweeny besmirched his protests. The district court ruled against Clark and his associates, refusing to restore them the Ella or to enjoin Sweeny as they had petitioned. Clark naturally appealed to the Ninth Circuit Court in San Francisco where he earned only a tongue-lashing from the judges, who declared him not "legally or morally entitled" to any information that Culbertson might gain as Sweeny's employee, and added, "A court of equity will not undertake to balance frauds between complainants and defendants, but shuts its doors against those who come without clean hands asking for its aid." When Clark's appeal for a review was denied by the United States Supreme Court in October, 1903, the *Spokesman-Review* declared that Sweeny had won "the famed million-dollar suit," as indeed he had.

His erstwhile opponents notwithstanding, Charles Sweeny's principal adversary in the Coeur d'Alenes was the Bunker Hill and Sullivan, which hired able attorneys to fight him.

Although the Bunker Hill's first probings of Sweeny's legal ground seemed to discourage them, in the Kirby case they found seed for future action. Of this, F. Lewis Clark, who sensed the danger, wrote the comptroller on May 22, 1897, that the Bunker Hill and Sullivan had purchased the Stemwinder, immediately south of the Emma and Last Chance. Clark warned, "The supreme court's recent refusal . . . to grant the Last Chance a writ of certiorari [in the Kirby case] on the apex question would make it likely that the Bunker Hill people will endeavor to sweep all the country west from the Stemwinder and south of the Last Chance by means of the Stemwinder claim." Clark mentioned that he was spending a thousand dollars a week for lawyers.[26]

Before asserting its right in the Stemwinder claim, the Bunker Hill undertook a diversion, locating "the only unappropriated piece of surface ground in the vicinity" as the King claim on June 22, 1898. The King, a triangular scrap between the Tyler and Sweeny's Viola and San Carlos claims, was staked as a parallelogram with its end lines aimed deliberately toward Sweeny's ores beneath the San Carlos, Skookum, Likely, and Cuba claims, the last two located only weeks before the King. By asserting that the mutual vein apexed in the King, the Bunker Hill sought to pursue its dip inside Sweeny's boundaries, using the King to attack from the north the region the Stemwinder would assault from the east.[27]

In a nonjury trial, the district court upheld the validity of the King location. Clayton Miller mailed a certified copy of this decision to Sweeny in New York with the comment, "You will notice that the decision is sweeping and is a complete victory for the Bunker Hill, giving them everything they asked for, including, as I read it, the ore under the San Carlos. . . . It means that we have lost, temporarily, at least one-half of the ore developed." [28]

Before Sweeny's appeal to San Francisco could be heard, the Bunker Hill tried to draw its noose tighter about him, using the Stemwinder, another of those claims between the Last Chance and the Bunker Hill staked by Divine, Smith, and Tyler in a few days in 1885. Fred Bradley acquired the Stemwinder for $107,499 on November 26,

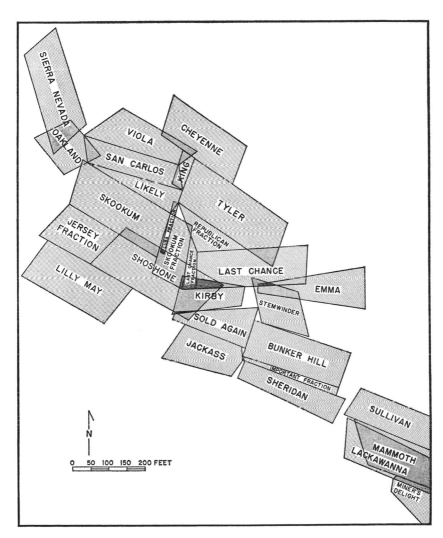

MAP 3. Diagram of surface claims in disputed areas (based on exhibits submitted in court cases)

1897, at a sheriff's sale, and deeded it to the Bunker Hill. Behind the Bunker Hill's purchase of the Stemwinder lay not only the company's improved understanding of the complex geology of its vein, but its scheme to bore the nine-thousand-foot Kellogg Tunnel to probe the mountains, like the Sweeny Tunnel. The Bunker Hill began planning this adit in 1896, and spent $200,000 driving it in 1899, with the intention of penetrating ores in the extralateral claims of the Bunker Hill Mine no later than the end of 1901. Using its knowledge of Sweeny's holdings gained from the Kirby case, and pressing the Stemwinder's prior location and apex as superceding any rights of the Last Chance, the Bunker Hill meant to invade Sweeny's ore.

Sweeny countered this dire threat to his entire Wardner structure with two suits brought simultaneously in 1900 against the Bunker Hill, one charging trespass via the Kellogg Tunnel, and the other asking an injunction to prevent use of the tunnel. He contended that the ore the adit was to strike apexed in the Last Chance or San Carlos and Viola and, moreover, would siphon the Last Chance's water supply. These two petitions to the district court signaled the advent of ten years of costly litigation that, in sum, delivered neither contender a definitive victory.

Judge Beatty stopped Kellogg Tunnel construction immediately. When the trespass case came before him in May, 1900, for trial, he did his best to determine the Stemwinder's merit based on prior location and boundary lines. Witnesses were asked to reconstruct, hour by hour, their activities of fifteen years earlier, those insoucient days of 1885 when the land lay open and miners were agreeable to sealing compromise with a handshake. Among the witnesses, all of whom tended to digress, was Sandy Divine, who had staked the Stemwinder and remembered that he had not finished his corner posts on the first day. "I put up three stakes on the east end; that is, I blazed them," he told the court. "I had a small ax. . . . On the west end I blazed two trees, and did not put up my southwest corner stake that day. I put them all up but one that day." [29] Divine had squared small trees where they grew as his corner posts. He had run the Stemwinder's north line onto Emma property but when J. I. Smith, the Emma's locator, challenged him, Divine agreed that the south line of the Emma would be the north boundary of his Stemwinder, and piled a stone monument to mark it. This testimony, Judge Beatty concluded, demonstrated that the Emma had been located first, the Stemwinder second, and the Last Chance third, on the same day, September 17, 1885.

Although the judge remarked that "all circumstances considered, there is reason for doubt," he ruled the Stemwinder's title prior to that of the Last Chance, restricted the extralateral pursuit of the Stemwinder to the extended south line of the Emma, and modified his injunction to permit continued construction of the Kellogg Tunnel as long as these boundaries were observed. As he recited his verdict, Judge Beatty commented on the inadequate federal precedent and expressed hope that a reviewing court might untangle it better than he: "It is often most painful to enforce such a law, but, as it is, it must be followed until changed. It is remarkable that there seems to have been no effort made for its improvement, which might so easily be done." [30]

Judge Beatty's decision granted less than the Bunker Hill wanted but more than Sweeny could concede. Both appealed, and the Ninth Circuit Court of Appeals overturned Beatty, holding that the Last Chance held prior right to the disputed ore because the Stemwinder, under its earlier Portland ownership, had failed to adverse the Last Chance patent. In addition, the court noted, the Stemwinder's petition was based on an amended location in which the Stemwinder's lines were redrawn to conform with federal requirements for parallel endlines, but angled, at the same time, to conflict with the Emma's extralateral rights. Of this appellate decision, Roberts wrote Sweeny, "The present decision will release all of our Jersey ore bodies. . . . The amount gained on this decision from the claimed rights of the Stemwinder is nearly nine acres of mineral-bearing ground containing our known shoots." [31]

As a result of this rebuff by the appellate court, the Bunker Hill sought compromise (partly because its owners seriously considered selling) while Heyburn mounted an assertive campaign to contain the Bunker Hill within its vertical lines. When the Bunker Hill proposed mediation to Clayton Miller, he deferred to Sweeny, who wrote Frederick Burbidge, the Bunker Hill and Sullivan manager, "Referring to your letters of the 6th and 11th inst. addressed to Mr. W. Clayton Miller . . . in reference to a compromise which you propose between the two companies in the matter of the trespass case involving the Tyler, Emma, and Last Chance claims . . . while I do not care about making a compromise of this particular case . . . if you will come down here and go over these matters with me I think that you and I can arrange a settlement, not only of these two cases but of several others over which we are in litigation." [32]

Despite this conciliatory letter, no agreement came of the talk between Sweeny and Burbidge. Heyburn soon was chortling that "in a casual conference yesterday with the attorneys for the Bunker Hill" he had refused them "a stipulation that would enable them to avoid electing . . . whether or not they would claim the ore bodies . . . under the Bunker Hill, and leave out any claim on behalf of the Tyler, Stemwinder, or King. . . . They are in quite a dilemma over it. They realize they are up to that point where they either have to assert their right on behalf of the Tyler to jump over the plane of the Last Chance, or forever hold their peace." [33]

Thus the ritual of negotiation ended; the truculent duel resumed in court. Sweeny possessed a momentary advantage because, as the Bunker Hill's new manager, Stanly Easton, complained in 1903, for more than four years the Bunker Hill's plan to develop ore within the extended lines of the Bunker Hill and Stemwinder claims had been deterred by various injunctions granted Sweeny. During those years the Bunker Hill's unchallenged ores were depleted, half its labor force was dismissed, and its Tacoma smelter gasped for ore. [34]

The contest between Sweeny and the Bunker Hill flared in half a dozen bitter skirmishes. When Sweeny filed for patents on his Likely and Cuba Fraction lode claims, the Bunker Hill adversed them. Miller adversed patent applications by the Bunker Hill for its New Era and Wheelbarrow claims. The Bunker Hill sued for $49,000 allegedly lost by Sweeny's unlawful extraction of ore from the Summit Mine, next to the Shoshone. Sweeny sued the Bunker Hill for $75,000 worth of ore allegedly taken from Emma ground. Each tied the other with injunctions. So suit begot countersuit, charge drew countercharge, while Roberts fumed that Heyburn "was getting fat on these legal scraps." [35]

The major campaign now concerned the Bunker Hill's suits to obtain title to ores within the extralateral rights of the Stemwinder's endlines extended eastward into Sweeny ground. The King had been denied; the Tyler was hardly worth resurrecting. But the Stemwinder, lying adjacent to the Bunker Hill Mine itself and nearly as old, provided the axis of dispute. Heyburn challenged the right of the Bunker Hill and Sullivan to pursue ore beyond the vertical boundaries of the original Bunker Hill claim because O'Rourke had mistaken the course of the vein and laid his endlines where his sidelines should have been under federal law. Neither had O'Rourke filed notice of his Bunker Hill claim within the fifteen days required by Idaho statute, but the court pointed out that the state law provided no penalty for late filing. Moreover, O'Rourke did not erect stakes on the west end of his claim until after the Emma and Last Chance claims were located. None of Heyburn's assertions did more than obfuscate the issue. Finally he demanded that the Bunker Hill and Sullivan company disclose all its claims to Sweeny ore and that the court quiet Sweeny's titles to disputed ground. With these opening shots began the series of battles that mining law textbooks would call the Second Stemwinder Case.[36]

For the most part the second Stemwinder case was like the first. But there was, in addition, a singular aspect. The Bunker Hill and Sullivan's attorneys, although they did not deny the rights of the Emma and Last Chance to pursue their planes of ore, insisted that the Stemwinder's extralateral right allowed it to cross over the plane pursued by the Emma and Last Chance and to continue to follow ore on the other side. The Stemwinder's pursuit did not end where it met the Emma and Last Chance—the right was merely intersected. This argument was without precedent in mining law.

As the trial began, each day revealed new complexities. Five Sweeny claims—the Viola, San Carlos, Skookum, Caribou, and Jersey Fraction—had been located lawfully between the dates of the original and the amended Stemwinder boundaries. Three of these Sweeny claims were patented with rights to pursue ore in four other Sweeny claims, the Lily May, Butte, Good Luck, and Number Four, all directly in the path of the Stemwinder's asserted cross-over rights. Both the Bunker Hill and Sweeny admittedly worked the same vein, which could be shown to apex in several claims. As geologists and engineers took their turns in the witness chair, their theories about the course and width of the vein revealed grave discrepancies. "No one has been able to set definite limits to the ledge," the court remarked, "and that it has no distinct hanging wall cannot be doubted. Its one distinct and persistent feature is its footwall . . . the axis of action." In simple terms, everyone knew where the ore ended, but few could agree on how wide it was.

It should be noted that by the time the second Stemwinder case reached the district court, Heyburn had been elected United States

Senator from Idaho for a six-year term. While Heyburn was not entirely out of the case, Sweeny's principal attorney was Frank T. Post. Post faced Curtis Lindley, whose textbook on mining law had gone through its second printing, John McBride, and M. A. Folsom for the Bunker Hill.

This case moved as slowly as other Sweeny lawsuits, for it was to drag through the courts for six years. Even before the first witness spoke, Sweeny's mines were absorbed by a new company so that the corporate names in the trial record were anachronisms. The attorneys resorted to gargantuan demonstration: Post constructed a collapsible wooden mock-up of the Wardner mines underground, and hired two Columbia University geologists to provide a painstaking plaster relief map of the surface. Like the exhibits, the arguments were elaborate. Simplicity was impossible, for Sweeny held eighteen claims involved in some manner, and the Bunker Hill and Sullivan, nine.

The Bunker Hill and Sullivan people testified that they had been shocked to learn in 1903 that at one point Sweeny's adits approached within four hundred feet of their own. After the Bunker Hill acquired the Tyler, which could be reached through the Sweeny Tunnel, a door was installed at the intersection of the two mines. The Empire State–Idaho owned the door and kept it locked. Only the superintendents of the two mines carried keys. By 1908 the Sweeny and Bunker Hill workings were to meet at several points as the labyrinth of adit and stope sought the vagrant lode.

Thus as the miners struggled underground to find and extract ore, the attorneys fought above ground to hold their discoveries. After June, 1904, an element of delay became discernable in Sweeny's repeated demands on the courts, for in that month the Ninth Circuit Court of Appeals ruled that the Stemwinder could follow the plane of ore within its extended endlines and cross over the intersecting Sweeny rights of pursuit. Moreover the Bunker Hill and Sullivan's Kellogg Tunnel, now eleven hundred feet long, penetrated the main ore bodies during 1904, after its attorneys succeeded on July 3, 1903, in lifting the last Sweeny injunction against the great project. The discovery of ore in the Kellogg Tunnel initiated a shift of population from Wardner, where the Sweeny Tunnel began, to Kellogg, the portal of the Kellogg Tunnel.

The Sweeny companies were now contained in the Federal Mining and Smelting Company with top-rank eastern financing. Roberts resigned the management in 1905; Sweeny spent most of his days in New York City, sending depositions to court rather than testifying in person, and relying on Clayton Miller, Post, Clendening, and others in Idaho for his information about events at the mines. By 1905 Charles Sweeny was essaying the role of financier with a swagger.

Still the lawsuits crept on. The Wardner ore bodies to which Sweeny possessed lawful titles were playing out; Canyon Creek now provided his principal ores. As the contest with the Bunker Hill continued, Federal and the Bunker Hill and Sullivan took ore from whatever ground they held by the latest court decision.

Finally in 1908 Sweeny determined one final thrust against the Bunker Hill and Sullivan. He would use a suit to quiet his title to the Republican Fraction claim to challenge again the Bunker Hill and Sullivan's rights to the long-disputed vein. Miller, however, counseled delay, saying that many citizens of the Coeur d'Alenes believed the mining companies controlled elections and judges. He felt that Sweeny should wait until after the elections so that the new lawsuit would not appear to be merely political in its intent. As his letter demonstrates, the mine owners united in political activities while they fought in court. He wrote Sweeny:

> Political conditions are so complicated in this country and a loss of the election would be such a detriment to our Company, as well as to the mining interests in general, that we have concluded not to bring this suit so as to give them a nail on which to hang the claim that State officials or County officials could be affected, as we have already stated there is no suit in the State Court. . . .
>
> The Bunker Hill people are taking a more active interest in the election, and their shift bosses have been working as we hoped they would do. With their aid, or not particularly active opposition, we hope to win a majority of the offices for the Republican party in this county.[37]

Shoshone County in 1908 voted for a Republican president and governor, and although Heyburn lost in the county to the attorney A. G. Kerns, he was strong enough elsewhere in Idaho to be returned to the United States Senate for his second term (which was terminated by his death on October 19, 1912.)

Once the election was tabulated, Miller reopened the legal battle as Sweeny directed by handing the sheriff of Shoshone County a court order on January 16, 1909, to remove all Bunker Hill and Sullivan stakes, monuments, and markings that conflicted with those of the

Federal company. For its part, the Bunker Hill and Sullivan prepared its most massive assault on the courts with maps, models, and charts to fight again all the old issues.

But this titanic confrontation never came to trial. Not only was Federal's ore playing out at Wardner but the cost of prosecuting its tenuous suit might have wiped out its profits. Sweeny retired as president of Federal in January, 1909, and—lacking Sweeny's personal antagonism against the Bunker Hill and Sullivan—his successor proved conciliatory.

On April 29, 1910, the Federal and Bunker Hill and Sullivan compromised. Federal accepted 27,000 shares of Bunker Hill and Sullivan stock, adding to this 1,000 shares previously purchased by Sweeny, and agreed that when the various properties in the old Last Chance complex failed to show a profit in any five consecutive months, the claims and the Sweeny mill were to become the property of the Bunker Hill. To effect the transfer of stock, the Bunker Hill and Sullivan increased its total from 300,000 to 327,000 outstanding shares at ten dollars par value. Federal retained the privilege of exhausting the ores of its mines above the level of the Kellogg Tunnel.[38]

In 1916, when the net earnings of the Federal properties at Wardner amounted to no more than $95,494 despite inflated wartime prices, the embattled Last Chance finally was dug out. Federal abandoned nothing to the Bunker Hill and Sullivan but the echoing shells of their mines, for, as the Idaho mines inspector observed in his annual report, the Last Chance had "been exhausted to its converging litigation limits at the Kellogg level of the Bunker Hill and Sullivan and worked back to the surface for the recovery of old fills and low-grade remnants."

The Bunker Hill and Sullivan announced its acquisition of the old Sweeny mines and mill in May, 1917, at a time when the Bunker Hill itself was completing a new mill a mile below Kellogg at a siding to be called Bradley. The years of litigation at Wardner were finally at an end, thirty years after the Tyler's patent application had been adversed by the owners of the Emma and Last Chance.

A number of decisions and clarifications in Sweeny's lawsuits continue to be cited as precedents in mining trials although they may impress the layman as finicking detail. In Sweeny's time the judicial restatement of federal statutes that allowed sidelines to become endlines to establish extralateral rights was a momentous definition. The

Tyler case produced the ruling that a locator who abandoned part of his claim did not give up all of it. The same case restated the old California codes' principle that the miner's lode is his important possession and his surface incidental. The Stemwinder case affirmed that a junior locator may lay his vertical boundaries across those of the senior to establish extralateral rights, defined the shape of a legal claim, and posed the question of a miner's right to follow the plane of his ore on the other side of an intersecting right.

No one can reckon how much Sweeny's lawsuits cost. Outside the law books, few mention the names once awesome in the district's courtrooms: Skookum, Shoshone, Stemwinder, Last Chance, Empire State–Idaho, and all the others. Nothing in the massive permanence of the Bunker Hill smelter at Kellogg today suggests that for a dozen years, the Bunker Hill and Sullivan fought to survive the challenge of Charles Sweeny.

# IX

# MERGING THE MINES

$B$y the year 1901 most of the mines in the Coeur d'Alenes belonged to big companies. The prospector and his partner had given way to the manager and his stockholders, as the prospector had given way throughout the West.

Some of the men who had located claims in earlier days still worked them, and some of the early investors remained—men like Charles Sweeny, John Finch, Amasa Campbell, Patrick Clark, and others among the Coeur d'Alene district's pioneers. But there were also investors who, in diversifying their commitments, bet some money on the district: Darius O. Mills, the unsmiling California banker who had exiled himself to New York to engage in philanthropies; Cyrus McCormick and James L. Houghteling of Chicago; William H. Crocker, president of the Woolworth-Crocker Bank in San Francisco; John Hays Hammond, the globe-trotting engineer; and others. Even the old-timers looked outside the district for financial support: Sweeny's money flowed from New York and Toronto, Clark's from Montana, and Finch's and Campbell's from Youngstown, Ohio.

In 1901 the Empire State–Idaho employed about 350 persons, owned seventy mineral claims, operated fifty power drills, and produced 41,000,000 pounds of lead and 870,000 ounces of silver. Thus Charles Sweeny's empire thrived.

Because their long war with the mining unions had—if their differences at the bar of justice had not—impressed the mine owners with the strength of unity, they joined forces to try to improve their smelter

170

contracts with the American Smelting and Refining Company, the one significant customer for their product. The Bunker Hill and Sullivan, which operated its own smelter at Tacoma, and the Hercules stood back. The Mine Owners Association sent a delegation of Sweeny, Culbertson, and Richard Wilson of the Mammoth to New York to entreat American, the "smelter trust," to buy no ore or concentrates from new companies for the next five years. This would assure the older companies of their market; it "would give them the exclusive right to put ore on the market and no one else could sell unless to them," complained Mrs. Harry L. Day, the wife of the Hercules manager. The Hercules had just begun to produce.[1] For the older companies, the agreement Sweeny and the other representatives sought would have the effect of enlarging the production quotas imposed by American.

The key to American's domination of the smelting industry lay in the fact that no other smelting company possessed the capacity to treat the output of the Coeur d'Alenes. As Sweeny was to explain, "The general run of the contracts in those days was a stipulated tonnage contract. There was no smelting company large enough to take all the ore from any one big mine . . . so they [American] stipulated that you might sell them so much per month. . . . And that, of course, had the effect of keeping the companies' ability to extend their operations down."[2] With the trust's strength, it did not need a compact of the kind the Coeur d'Alene owners wanted. Sweeny, Culbertson, and Wilson returned from their quest "disgusted," without the exclusive arrangement they desired.

The trust amounted to a virtual monopoly. Organized from eighteen concerns by J. P. Morgan and Company on behalf of H. H. Rogers, John D. Rockefeller, Jr., and Leonard Lewisohn in 1899, it quickly acquired most of the important lead smelters in the United States. The trust owned plants at Pueblo, Leadville, and Durango, Colorado; East Helena and Great Falls, Montana; at Omaha, Denver, Kansas City, Chicago, and Salt Lake City. When the trust in 1901 absorbed M. Guggenheim's Sons, it paid so handsomely in stock for the Guggenheim properties that the five Guggenheim sons achieved control of the trust.[3]

The term "trust" was then applied to any monopoly. The newspapers bruited constantly of trusts—the meat trust, the tin plate trust, the steel wire trust—and demanded that political candidates declare their stands on trusts. The courts dissolved Rockefeller's Standard Oil trust in 1892. Editors consequently represented trusts to their readers as nefarious, to be regarded with suspicion.

Few smelters operated outside the Guggenheim trust. Excepting the Hercules' shipments to the Selby smelter at San Francisco and the Balbach at Newark, New Jersey, the Bunker Hill and Sullivan's to the Pennsylvania Company at Carnegie and its own plant at Tacoma, and the Hecla's to the Ohio and Colorado at Salida, Colorado, the ore of the Coeur d'Alenes went to trust smelters. The Empire State–Idaho shipped to trust plants at Pueblo, Leadville, and East Helena. To protect themselves against careless assaying and weighing, the Mine Owners Association established the Northwestern Sampling and Milling Company, generally called the Wallace sampling works, to assay and weigh shipments before dispatching them to smelters.

Coeur d'Alene producers dealing with the trust operated under six-month contracts with individual smelters, were paid uniformly three and one-half cents a pound for lead, and were limited as a group to approximately eight thousand tons monthly. Of this, the Empire State –Idaho's quota often approached twenty-six hundred tons. There existed also an understanding between the railroads and the trust on ore-hauling rates. Therefore in the first years of the twentieth century, the Coeur d'Alene mining companies no more controlled their destinies than they had in the last years of the nineteenth; then they were limited by the unions, now by the trust.

One attraction of the trust's contracts was steady price. Before American's formation, as Sweeny recalled the situation, "There was a great deal of instability in the price of lead. . . . [The price] was made by a firm of brokers in the City of New York called Behr and Steiner, and they made what was known as the Western Union Quotation for lead. They quoted lead to the Western Union Telegraph Company and it was known as Western Union. It was really made by these brokers who were at that time under control of the smelting companies." [4] Contract payment rates based on these quotations often varied widely from actual lead prices but the mining companies, said Sweeny, had "no way of getting the real facts." At one time, the mine owners considered appealing to the courts to require accurate price reporting, and Sweeny offered to seek "evidence" while visiting New York.

With each passing year, the Coeur d'Alene district grew more important as a source of lead. In 1890 the district dug roughly 24,000 tons of lead, about 16 percent of the total production of the United States. By 1901 the Coeur d'Alenes—at half capacity due to the trust's quotas—produced 81,275 tons, approximately 29 percent of the national output.[5]

The trust maintained a delicate balance between national production and consumption. It promised to furnish lead to its own customers at a fixed price for one year to relieve lead buyers of the necessity of stockpiling, and could not change production rates or prices without reneging on this pledge. Moreover, the trust intended to command the entire lead industry of the United States—and this plan included domain over the mines of the Coeur d'Alene district. In this immense design, Charles Sweeny was to play a considerable role.

Sweeny's 1901 trip to New York with Culbertson and Wilson was only one attempt by the owners to improve their position by confronting the smelter trust. They were spurred by statistics: in 1900 the Coeur d'Alene mines produced concentrates and ores worth ten million dollars, and although 1901 should have been more profitable, the trust squeezed the district's gross in that year down to eight and one-half million.[6] Near the end of 1901, however, the lead market expanded and the trust allowed its smelters to accept two-thirds of the Coeur d'Alene district's capacity. In July, 1902, the district's limitation was raised to 80 percent of its potential, but the trust refused to alter its price of three and one-half cents (although the quoted price stood at four and one-eighth cents a pound) or to countenance a reduction in railway shipping or smelter processing rates.

Despite its firm grip on the lead industry, the trust seemed to regard seriously the possibility that the mining companies, might, as they occasionally threatened, build their own smelters. To protect itself, American Smelting and Refining now signed long-term contracts with pig lead buyers that would hinder new smelters from finding markets. The trust also expanded its holdings in the Missouri-Kansas lead fields, and negotiated to buy the Selby and Tacoma smelters.

Blocked from full production, bound by arbitrary prices and rates, the Coeur d'Alene district mine owners fought against domination. Since talks failed, the mine owners resorted to their ultimate strategy: they closed their mines. The Empire State–Idaho sent a notice to its stockholders on August 14, 1902, which read:

All the mining operators in the Coeur d'Alene mining district, Idaho
. . . have decided, for business reasons, to close the entire district on September first next, and until they resume they will, by agreement, suspend
dividends. This is a united action of all the companies and is done for the
purpose of bettering the market conditions for the product, and is in no
way caused by any change in the physical condition of the mines, nor does
it affect the value of the properties.[7]

On September 1, 1902, all the mines that had contracts with the
trust suspended their shipments. The Mine Owners Association again
sent a delegation of Sweeny, Campbell, and Peter Larson to Chicago
to demand higher production quotas and lowered railroad and
smelter charges. This deputation returned after presenting its arguments, leaving behind David H. Hyman of New York, representing
the Frisco Consolidated. Hyman eventually worked out an agreement
with the trust that provided for a reduction in railroad rates of approximately two dollars a ton, smelter charges one dollar a ton lower,
and higher district quotas which would aggregate twelve thousand
tons monthly, very near capacity. This compact, known as the seven
companies contract, resulted in reopening the mines. E. J. Roberts,
general manager of the Empire State–Idaho, summarized the contract
in his annual report for the year ending April 30, 1903: "A concession
of three dollars was granted, resulting in all the mines entering into a
contract with the American Smelting and Refining Company for the
term of one year from September 1, 1902, on a greatly increased
production, at a price of $3\frac{1}{2}$ cents a pound for lead, and the ruling
price for silver, with the usual smelter deductions." [8]

It was estimated that the lower railway and smelter costs would
increase the district's aggregate profits by $100,000 a month. Sweeny,
for one, said his Empire State–Idaho company could hire a one-
third larger work force as a result of the contract. For their part the
Guggenheims remarked that the one-year smelting agreement precluded the construction of competitive plants by mine owners.

During this time, while he cooperated with the other owners,
Charles Sweeny also quietly played his own private game for stakes
higher than a few hundred tons of production or a concession in railway rates. Sweeny had in mind the splendid scheme of organizing a
monopoly of his own that would take in all the bigger mines of the
Coeur d'Alene district.

Merging the mines of the Coeur d'Alenes was not a new idea. James

F. Wardner wrote a letter proposing it as early as 1888 to Samuel T. Hauser; James B. Grant, general manager of the smelter trust, told a congressional committee in 1901 that one company could buy all the Idaho mines, limit their output, and make money at it; the *Engineering and Mining Journal* of October 28, 1899, reported negotiations well advanced for a consolidation that "will control all—or nearly all —of the output of the Coeur d'Alenes." Sweeny had been asked about the merger rumors, but denied knowledge, saying, "The trust, nor none of its representatives, has spoken to me about buying up the Coeur d'Alene mines. There was some talk the other day about a syndicate being organized for the purpose of buying them up, but I don't think there's any truth in the report." [9]

Apparently the consolidation of the Coeur d'Alene district under his management was first seriously proposed to Sweeny by E. J. Roberts, who joined Sweeny in 1901 with the impression that Sweeny, spending much of his time in the East, "wanted somebody to cuss in Spokane when things didn't go right." [10] What Sweeny demanded was vigilant management of his mines, and soon after he hired Roberts he wrote out his requirements: "Until we can get more tonnage [from the trust], you and Miller will have to figure on making a higher grade concentrate although you will lose a little more lead in the mill. You will have to get the average up to about sixty-two percent for both mines. You will also cut off every corner so that the two mines will make a net profit of $30,000 per month and pay a monthly dividend of $25,000." [11]

Three months after he became assistant general manager of the Empire State–Idaho, Roberts went to San Francisco as a witness before the Ninth Circuit Court of Appeals. On his return to Wallace, where he had opened an office rather than conducting business in saloons as Miller had done, Roberts occupied several days in compiling the costs of Sweeny's various lawsuits. He was appalled. His sums demonstrated that, fantastic as it seemed, Sweeny might save money if he bought contending mines rather than fighting in court.

When Roberts presented his figures and suggested merging the mines, Sweeny was first dubious. The more he thought of it, however, the more the climactic gesture enchanted him. Not only might he save money—but consider the mighty stroke: all the mines of the Coeur d'Alenes under his direction! And so Sweeny and Roberts hatched their plan. They would buy every important mine in the Coeur d'Alenes—the Bunker Hill and Sullivan, the Mammoth, the Standard, the Hercules, and all the others.

To accomplish his design, Sweeny first needed money, and second, someone to negotiate his purchases. Sweeny could not openly buy in his own name because, in Roberts' words, "The mine owners thought him a sharper. They didn't like his bragging." Some owners, like the Day family, openly despised Sweeny.

The scheme required many millions of dollars. How much was hard to guess until preliminary bargaining began, but Sweeny obviously needed unstinting funds. To preserve his own interest, his financing must come from someone outside the Guggenheims' reach. Characteristically, Sweeny chose the biggest name he could think of: John D. Rockefeller, the richest man in the world, who twenty years earlier had sent Sweeny home penniless with his refusal to buy options on Seattle and Portland waterfront property. Rockefeller had retired from active participation in business in 1895, as a matter of fact, leaving the guidance of his wealth to his son, John D. Rockefeller, Jr., and Frederick T. Gates, who gave much of their attention to distributing the Rockefeller fortune to various philanthropies.

Once he had chosen the unsuspecting Rockefeller, Sweeny enlisted as his negotiator with the mine owners that annealed veteran of a thousand political skirmishes and courtroom ambushes, United States Senator George W. Turner, now rich from his share of the Le Roi Mine in Rossland, which had sold for five million in cash. Turner's wide acquaintance, his mining experience, and his political eminence might imply that he was optioning mines for eastern buyers; he might escape detection as an agent for Sweeny. Turner would be discreet, and if Sweeny, himself, could keep his secret, he could hide behind Turner until the moment he stepped forward as the surprise buyer of the district's mines. But before Turner came the Rockefeller money.

Sweeny went to New York to beard Rockefeller, camping on the doorstep at 26 Broadway for ten days before gaining an audience with Gates in the Rockefeller offices with their massive rolltop desks, mustard-colored carpets, bare walls, and battered furniture, with the telegraph key in another room rattling messages between Cleveland and New York on a private wire.[12] When finally he talked with Gates, Sweeny bared an ingenious plan: not only did he propose merging the important mines of the Coeur d'Alenes but his new corporation was to include Rockefeller's Puget Sound Reduction Company at

Everett, Washington, and the Monte Cristo Mine about sixty miles east of Everett.

The smelter company, capitalized for nine hundred thousand dollars, had erected its plant in 1892 to process custom ores from the Slocan and Kootenay districts of British Columbia and from United States mines, but based its prospect primarily on the Monte Cristo, which soon played out, in contradiction to an engineer's report that it contained a rich lead vein "running entirely through a mountain." Smelter and mine were white elephants. For a few years, ironically, the Monte Cristo produced most of the domestic arsenic consumed in the United States, amounting to perhaps 500 short tons annually worth thirty thousand dollars. The 240-ton smelter, opened July 1, 1893, struggled to profit from the scant ore supply available, a shortage made more acute by the Guggenheim's aquisition of the smelting trust. The Everett smelter's able manager, William C. Butler, was beset both by competition and by the erratic United States metals market.[13]

Rockefeller was drawn into these and other Puget Sound investments by two enthusiastic fellow Baptists, Charles L. Colby and Colgate Hoyt, who observed the headlong contest between the Northern Pacific and the Great Northern to construct the shorter route across Washington State.[14] As members of the Great Northern's executive committee, they appeared to have inside information and founded a town where they expected the Great Northern to touch water first. They named their town Everett, for Colby's son, and visualized it as an important future shipping and commercial center with a prosperous domestic and Oriental trade.

Their artless enthusiasm—and the fact that they risked their own money—encouraged Rockefeller to support them. Consequently they platted Everett in 1890–91 and began selling lots, established a nail mill and a paper mill, erected a shipyard, and, hearing reports of rich mineral deposits in the mountains, added their smelter and a two-million dollar railway, the Everett and Monte Cristo, to the hamlet of Monte Cristo and its mines. Before the Monte Cristo shipped its first ore perhaps six hundred thousand dollars was spent in its development. The financial crash of 1893 shattered Everett's rosy prospects. Colby, Hoyt, and their friends were quickly wiped out and, little by little, recalled the younger Rockefeller, "Father found himself carrying the load for all of them; the others getting out. Eventually he owned as much as eighty percent" of the various enterprises, all losing him thousands of dollars a month. A flood in 1897 smashed the railway to Monte Cristo.

One of Gates's first endeavors as overseer of Rockefeller's empire, was to liquidate the Colby–Hoyt investments without the "expense and humiliation of bankruptcy," as Rockefeller phrased it. For six or seven years, Gates struggled to revive or sell various Puget Sound enterprises. Then Charles Sweeny approached him. Sweeny's proposal to form a strong new company that would enhance the value of the smelter and the feeble lead mines, in addition to exploiting the Coeur d'Alene district, struck Gates as an attractive solution to his Everett predicament, as Sweeny had surmised. Gates agreed to put Rockefeller money behind Sweeny's grand scheme to buy the major mines in the Coeur d'Alenes.

Rockefeller patronage meant Gould money, too, for shy, amiable, polo-loving George J. Gould, manager of his father's seventy-three-million-dollar fortune, had joined Rockefeller in a number of investments after breaking with the Morgans at the outset of his business career.

Sweeny's new company possessed no name and no officers—except that Sweeny naturally conceived of himself as its leader—but it had the significant asset of F. T. Gates's promise of Rockefeller support. With this, George Turner set about obtaining options on the major mines of the Coeur d'Alene district. In 1902 these included Sweeny's Empire State–Idaho, the Bunker Hill and Sullivan, the Standard, the Mammoth, the Morning, and the Hercules, most of which were for sale. Finch and Campbell owned the Standard and three-eights of the Mammoth. The Standard had been acquired in 1891 for $26,000 by sales of stock mainly among friends in Youngstown, Ohio. Their share of the Mammoth was purchased in 1899 for $375,000 from the widow of an owner. By the end of 1902 the Mammoth had paid back its price in dividends.

The Morning, located in 1887, had passed through several ownerships and in 1902 belonged to two Montanans, Peter Larson, a railroad contractor, and Thomas Greenough. There were months when the Morning's production rivaled that of the Bunker Hill and Sullivan.

The Hercules offered Sweeny a special challenge, for it had been discovered and developed by amateurs who struck rich ore in 1901, and was not for sale at any price. Located in 1889 by a Wardner storekeeper's son, Harry L. Day, and his partner, Fred Harper, it was worked by the owners who sold stock to a dairyman, his herdsman, a railway engineer, and others like them, who also paid for their shares by contributing manual labor on the claim. From the instant the Day family realized the worth of their claim, they headed family letters with the slogan, "Mum's the word!" [15]

Turner sounded Finch and Campbell in 1902, found them willing to sell their share of the Mammoth and the Standard, and then bargained with Richard Wilson, Walter MacKay, James and W. R. Leonard, and A. L. Schofield for their five-eighths interest in the Mammoth. At a total price of $1,500,000, Turner obtained an option on the two mines until August 18, 1903.

Sweeny personally approached the Bunker Hill and Sullivan. There could be no disclosure of his intrigue by a forthright offer as an adversary to buy the company, and Sweeny had a personal score goading him. "They have taken the very meanest advantage all the time," he told Roberts, "encouraged everything that would injure us, even when there was no benefit to be derived through it. I feel very bitter toward the entire Bunker Hill crowd." [16] Sweeny's attorney, Post, later expressed the same feeling in his letter to the comptroller on February 22, 1906: "The Bunker Hill company and the mining company in which Mr. Sweeny is interested have been in continuous litigation for many years and there is no friendship or friendliness between them. It is a well known fact that they have for many years had spies in each other's camps; that is to say, that each has had men working underground for the other who would report the condition and situation of the other company's properties." [17] There could be nothing surprising in Sweeny's willingness to buy properties adjacent to his own, or in his apparent desire to end the lawsuits by buying out his competitor.

To Sweeny's gratification, the Bunker Hill and Sullivan seemed eager to consider selling. "I am still negotiating for the Bunker Hill," he wrote Roberts on January 22, 1902, "and it looks more favorable now than at any time. . . . I have stipulated that all legal proceedings stop and all injunctions be released, and all proceeds of the Bunker Hill apply on the purchase price and if I have just a little luck, the Bunker Hill will be in our reach before long." [18]

Roberts talked with F. W. Bradley in San Francisco, the former manager and since 1897 president of the Bunker Hill and Sullivan, learning that a group of owners believed the company's reserves were giving out. The company's $318,000 operating profit for the period June, 1900, to May, 1901, was its lowest since 1896–97; the year 1902 improved profit only $19,000; and the first months of 1903 failed to keep pace with the two previous years.[19]

Bradley told Roberts that since his friends had invested three million dollars in the Bunker Hill and Sullivan, he "couldn't let them down," and would take three million for the company.[20] Roberts suggested to Sweeny that he bid $2,500,000 for the Bunker Hill and Sullivan—and there the negotiations dangled for weeks on a variance of $500,000. Its dividends over twenty-four months in good ore would pay the difference; until the company suspended payments in 1902, ostensibly to rebuild the Tacoma smelter, the Bunker Hill and Sullivan paid its stockholders $21,000 nearly every month.

There were other bidders for the Bunker Hill and Sullivan, to whom Bradley quoted the identical price of three million dollars. One was Fred Burbidge, acting with David Hyman of New York (the same man who had negotiated the seven companies contract) on behalf of the Guggenheim sons, but the Guggenheims suddenly withdrew from bargaining without an explanation. Perhaps they accepted Bradley's impression that the ore was depleting at Wardner or perhaps they reached an understanding with Sweeny, as many in the Coeur d'Alenes suspected.

One of the Days mentioned in a letter that the "Bunker Hill people were badly frightened . . . even to the extent of giving Mr. Sweeny an option on their property at $3,000,000." Anything that happened to Sweeny concerned the Days, for when he had learned that they would not sell him the Hercules, Sweeny began an unsuccessful campaign to drive the Days into bankruptcy by blocking their access to railroads and electric power, refusing them rights of way, and buying claims intended to encircle the Days' Hercules.

Sweeny and Roberts secured permission from Bradley to examine the Bunker Hill and Sullivan workings. In January, 1903, Bradley sent Easton a telegram directing him to clean up the mines for inspection. The inspectors proved to be Roberts, W. Clayton Miller, Dave Rees, and W. Gus Smith, all Sweeny men, whom Easton regarded as "seasoned engineers and miners." They snooped for three days, finding little showing of ore and few men working, and finally asked Easton if he "could not show them something worthwhile," jibing that the "operation was near its end." [21]

Underground the Bunker Hill, like other mines, was humid and gloomy, lighted at intervals by clear incandescent bulbs that cast black shadows behind the hewn fir timbering. The Bunker Hill had timbered with seven-foot clear-sets, however, that allowed a man to walk upright. Most other Coeur d'Alene mines used six-foot clear-sets, forcing men to stoop as they walked. The Bunker Hill was working from two main adits: the upper, the Reed; and the lower, the Kellogg. Stopes of the Bunker Hill intercepted the Last Chance tunnels at several points.

Roberts concluded, he wrote Sweeny on February 1, 1903, "They evidently have not got the reserves they claim to have. . . . As the property stands now, the price they ask is double what it is worth." [22] The Bunker Hill and Sullivan's usefulness in expanding the Empire State–Idaho was another matter. Roberts and Miller had "figured considerable on the value to us, and our conclusion is that its acquisition would double the value of our Wardner properties." Roberts urged Sweeny to show John Hays Hammond both Miller's report and the proceedings of the Shoshone County commissioners on the valuation of the Bunker Hill for taxes, in the hope that they might "possibly get a reduction in price if he knew the truth regarding the present state of the property."

Roberts believed that by working the Last Chance and Bunker Hill jointly—including all their associated claims—Sweeny could earn a profit of sixty-five thousand dollars a month under terms of his current smelter contracts, and increase this within six months if the Empire State–Idaho developed the mines as a single unit. Miller thought there must be ore that the Bunker Hill people had missed. And Roberts had earlier suggested that with his own smelter, Sweeny could improve his estimated profits considerably. [23]

Sweeny carried these reports and recommendations to Gates, embroidering Miller's hunch that rich deposits remained hidden in the Bunker Hill properties. Roberts gathered later that Sweeny "in his blustery way" so extolled their outlook to Gates that a story circulated in New York that the Bunker Hill "was within half a mile of its biggest strike." Moreover, the Ninth Circuit Court of Appeals on July 3, 1903, allowed the Bunker Hill and Sullivan to continue exploration by means of the Kellogg Tunnel. The Bunker Hill and Sullivan broke off negotiations and refused to discuss further a possible sale. "Once Sweeny's story got out," Roberts was to recall wryly, "you couldn't have bought the Bunker Hill for ten million."

With the end of his hazard at the Bunker Hill, Sweeny also lost his chance to buy the renovated Tacoma smelter, jointly owned since 1898 by several of Darius Mills's companies, the Bunker Hill and Sullivan, the Alaska Treadwell, the Alaska Mexican, and the Alaska United gold mining companies. Roberts casually met William R. Rust, the smelter manager, on a train, and Rust, not connecting Roberts with the offer to buy his smelter, freely admitted that without Bunker Hill ore the Tacoma smelter would be badly crippled. On Roberts' advice after this conversation, Sweeny offered $500,000 for the ten-year-old plant, but Rust opposed a sale and succeeded in deferring negotiations until the Bunker Hill and Sullivan suspended its bargaining with Sweeny. Two years later, Bernard Baruch was to pay $5,500,000 for the Tacoma smelter, buying it for the Guggenheims to prevent its falling into Rockefeller hands.[24]

Excepting the Bunker Hill and the Hercules, Sweeny's plan to merge the Coeur d'Alene mines progressed well. Turner extended his options on the Standard and Mammoth to September 1; he also secured options that were never to be taken up on the Cleveland, Kerns, and Olympia groups, and the Basin and Ambergris companies.[25]

With bargaining completed, the venture was organized on June 24, 1903, as the Federal Mining and Smelting Company, perpetually chartered in Delaware, and authorized to issue $30,000,000 in capital stock at $100 par. Three men, Horace J. Knowles of Wilmington, and Richard H. Stewart and Thomas Jewett Hallowell of New York, subscribed $3,900 to establish the Federal. Of 300,000 authorized shares, 200,000 preferred would draw 7 percent annual dividends, and 100,000 common, 6 percent. Cash purchasers of the original issue paid 90 percent of face value.[26]

Spokane first heard of Federal when Amasa Campbell mentioned that he and John Finch were selling to Charles Sweeny who was backed by Rockefeller and Gould money. Exposed, Sweeny told his story in expansive detail. It was now mid-August, two weeks short of the expiration of his options. Sweeny was ready to talk.

In the last week of August, the man the newspapers called "moralist, Sunday school teacher, financier, and son of the wealthiest man in the world," John D. Rockefeller, Jr., arrived in Spokane enroute to see the Coeur d'Alenes from Gould's private railway car, "Atalanta," accompanied by Sweeny, Miss Gertrude Sweeny, Roberts, and Miller. According to the newspaper reporters who trailed him, Rockefeller sat in the train while it switched in the Great Northern yards, then strode back and forth on the station platform, wearing a dark suit with a white tie sparkling with a horseshoe stickpin of diamonds. John Finch boarded the car for lunch; he and Rockefeller ate bread and milk.

Finch was an important shareholder in the new Federal, of course, for it had been formed from Finch's and Campbell's Standard, from the Mammoth, and from Sweeny's Empire State–Idaho. Sweeny, who held Empire State Idaho stock worth approximately $1,000,000, sold his Wardner mines to Federal for $3,000,000 in preferred stock and a bonus of $1,500,000 common. For Sweeny's Burke mines, Federal paid $2,100,000 in preferred, with a bonus of $1,050,000 common. No cash changed hands.

Finch and Campbell sold their Standard for $2,250,000, half in preferred stock with a bonus of $562,000 common, and half in cash. The various owners of the Mammoth received $1,500,000, half in preferred stock with a bonus of $375,000 common, and half in cash.[27] The sale of the Standard represented undiluted profit to Finch, Campbell, and their Youngstown stockholders, for the company had been organized by selling stock at ten cents a share. A nine-cent assessment per share provided operating capital. The mine was so productive that not only had the Standard paid $2,910,000 in dividends, but its stock rose to a market price of $4.50 a share.

The Puget Sound Reduction Company at Everett and the Monte Cristo Mine also went to Federal for $600,000 cash, with no stock involved, thus allowing Gates to jettison the properties with no book loss. Some of the Monte Cristo land holdings had previously been sold to lumber companies for their timber.

The Federal's officers included Sweeny as president at $25,000 a year; Edwin Packard, who had been president of the Empire State–Idaho, as first vice president; Finch, second vice president; Roberts and Miller, general manager and assistant; Bruce Clendening, treasurer; and E. V. Carey of New York, secretary and assistant treasurer.

Among Federal's directorate glittered the names of Gates; Rockefeller; Gould; George W. Young, president of the United States

Mortgage and Trust Company, New York; Charles D. Warren, president of the Traders Bank of Toronto; E. J. Barney, president of the Barney and Smith Car Company, Dayton, Ohio; and Peter Bradley, vice president of the Agricultural Chemical Company, New York. The board also included William Butler, manager of the Everett smelter, Richard Wilson of the Mammoth, and Knowles, one of those who put up $3,900 to midwife the Federal.

To purchase its various properties, Federal issued $10,500,000 worth of preferred stock and $5,250,000 common, approximately half its authorized paper. As his promoter's reward, Sweeny received 7,250 shares of preferred and 3,625 common, which together were worth more than $1,000,000 at their par value of $100 a share.[28]

With its publication of the Coeur d'Alene mines' merger, the *Spokesman-Review* declared, "Charles Sweeny is now the dominant power in the Coeur d'Alenes."

Sweeny seemed to have ascended to the eminence and wealth he had so long sought. Goodbye to the flaming Belcher, wool bales in Portland, storekeeping, grubbing in the rock-strewn earth of mining claims, unflinching promotion of mining stock, and a thousand hours in courtrooms. Without challenge, Charles Sweeny was now indeed the dominant power in the Coeur d'Alenes.

# X

## SWEENY AS PRESIDENT OF FEDERAL

CHARLES SWEENY served as president of the Federal Mining and Smelting Company for five years and four months. During this time Federal matured, expanded, paid regular 7 percent dividends on its preferred stock, fought some of Sweeny's old fights, and encountered new vexations. If Sweeny brought to Federal certain ripe rivalries and prejudices, he also contributed experienced management that proved wiser than his guidance of his personal fortunes.

In 1903 Federal was bright with promise. Befitting his new eminence, Sweeny enlarged and redecorated his offices on the second floor of the Exchange National Bank Building in Spokane. As Idaho offices for Federal he bought a former bank building dug partly into a hillside at Wallace, a brick structure with a guard's porthole inside its entrance, using as his own a room with two fireplaces, lighted by windows that afforded him a view of the river valley. The foot of the mountain behind his building sloped to his casements.

In contrast to raw early Wardner, Wallace was soon to be described in *Overland* magazine as "a veritable little jewel of a city, set snugly in its beautiful velvet case of green-clad hills . . . clean, bright, wide-awake . . . only about a dozen blocks long and half as wide." [1] Its streets, paved with rolled tailings from the mills, *Overland* estimated, "would run something like four or five dollars per ton in lead and silver if carefully treated."

Sweeny spent little time there, however, preferring New York City to Wallace or Spokane. In New York Federal was one of many small companies among those with multimillions of resources. Nonetheless Sweeny's ambition for Federal was "to command such a large amount of output of ores that we could not only dictate terms to the railroad companies but to the smelting companies." [2] This design required increased production in Idaho as well as Sweeny's hand on the financial machinery. As a demonstration of its glittering prospects, Sweeny wanted Federal to declare a dividend as soon as possible. Moreover, some of his personal investment in Federal had been loaned Sweeny by Rockefeller. He hoped to discharge this debt speedily, goading Roberts to increase the earnings of the company's Wardner and Burke mines.

Roberts' task was not easy. The Mammoth and the old Last Chance properties yielded low-grade ores, as he explained to Sweeny: "We tried to make up the Wardner shortages by shipping several hundred tons more first class at extra expense. We will push things hard until you are free from your obligation to Rockefeller on the stock proposition. Then we can let up a little and get the mines on a more uniform basis of production." [3] Roberts also recognized that "it was of great importance to have the first quarter show as good profits as possible," to impress Federal's shareholders. Consequently he, Miller, and the others in Idaho bent to enhance production as they might, in face of the triple restraints of smelter quotas, low-grade ores, and a glutted market.

On the first day of September, 1903, the Federal had taken physical possession of its mining companies in the Coeur d'Alenes with a theatrical flourish. John A. Finch went to New York to sign over his and Campbell's claims, but rather than wait until payments were due on October 1, Sweeny ceremoniously handed Finch $1,145,000 cash and a like amount in Federal stock in a neatly ribboned package. Finch telegraphed Campbell that "Federal discounted the payments . . . and cleaned up the whole deal" in minutes. In Wallace, Roberts and Miller stalked into the mine offices to seat themselves at desks signifying command, as company employees boggled uneasily.

While Roberts continued to apprise him of low quality ores, Sweeny swaggered through New York. He refused to sign a Federal contract with American Smelting and Refining without a guarantee of stable prices and fees for four years, allowed himself to be quoted in newspapers and mining magazines as saying that Federal had "not decided whether to smelt its own ores or have them treated by American," and then finally signed a six-year contract with the trust. Printed reports —unfounded—circulated that Federal proposed to consolidate the silver-lead mines near Park City, Utah, called the Daly, the Daly-West, and the Silver King, to extend Federal's share of the nation's crude lead.[4]

Sweeny had considered erecting smelters to treat his own ore before he organized the Federal company, and after preliminary scouting for funds wrote Roberts in 1902 that "the smelting company is an assured fact on a much larger scale than we expected, with a smelter at Denver and Spokane, and we have $3,500,000 already raised for it. But not a word must be said to anyone about it." [5] James J. Hill was agreeable to a partnership with Sweeny in smelting, promising a rate of $5.00 a ton for coke and a $2,500,000 railroad between Spokane and the Coeur d'Alenes. Further inspection of the mining districts concentered on Spokane, however, convinced Sweeny that "it was impossible to get the quantities of dry ores that would make it possible for us to smelt the lead ores . . . of the Empire State–Idaho Company profitably," and he abandoned the plan.[6]

With the formation of Federal and the acquisition of the Everett smelter, Sweeny revived his intention to smelt his own ores. His engineers reckoned construction costs and ore supplies for plants at Denver, Pueblo, Salt Lake City, and Omaha, which implied that before the expiration of Federal's six-year contract with Asarco in 1909, Federal would embark into competition with the trust. George Gould, who envisioned Federal smelters as captive to his railroads, eagerly pressed the scheme. It would cost at least twenty million, but Sweeny later was to assert, "Our people were willing to go ahead with the smelting proposition." [7]

Were they? In future years, Roberts was to conclude that Sweeny's smelter blueprints were his chief weapon against the trust's hard bargaining; another acquaintance heard Sweeny disclose that his smelter inquiry was designed to inflate the price of Federal stock toward its sale to the Guggenheim sons. Under oath Sweeny testified that his smelters were not built because "after a good deal of investigation, I finally thought that it would be better for me, getting along in years and pretty well tired out, anyhow, working pretty hard, if I could sell out. It would be a better proposition than taking the responsibilities of the smelting proposition on my shoulders." [8]

American Smelting and Refining Company's gambit to block

Sweeny's threatened entry into smelting was to buy the Puget Sound Refining Company at Everett and its companion mine, the Monte Cristo, at their book value of six hundred thousand dollars on November 15, 1903. The erection cost of the Everett smelter was $200,000, but it was carried on Federal's books at six hundred thousand dollars—the price the Guggenheims paid. In the bargain, Federal acquired from American the Wallace sampling works at half price. Thus Sweeny relieved Gates of his encumbrance at Everett without loss, and added to Federal's domain the assaying center of the Coeur d'Alenes.

Before long, Sweeny's sale of the Everett smelter produced another advantage. Lead had been plentiful in 1903, but almost immediately after buying the Puget Sound plant, American Smelting and Refining found itself short of ores, and wholly lifted its limitations on the Coeur d'Alene district output. "It is doubtless for the purpose of developing a lead ore supply for the Everett smelter that the trust is now raking this district with a fine tooth comb," observed Harry Day of the Hercules. In December the railroads lowered their ore-hauling rates.

As Federal's president, Sweeny undertook consolidations of various separate mines to eliminate duplicated operating costs. On February 1, 1904, he merged the Mammoth and Standard, which worked the same vein, renamed these the Mace Mine, connected the adits of the old Standard to those of the Mammoth a half-mile distant, retimbered the main shaft (without stopping work during construction), and dictated exploitation of the properties.

The Tiger-Poorman, renamed the Burke Mine, occupied a vein parallel to that of the Mace. One of the few early claims developed by shaft, the Burke by 1904 was 1,700 feet deep, producing 600 tons daily, concentrated in its own mill. The Mace disgorged 1,050 tons daily, processed at the two Mace mills near Wallace. To this, the Last Chance, Skookum, and other Wardner mines added 450 to 500 tons each day, concentrated at the Sweeny Mill on the Coeur d'Alene River below Kellogg. Thus Federal operated major mines and four mills in the Coeur d'Alenes with a payroll of not less than nine hundred men. On August 19, 1904, Federal acquired a 51 percent interest in the Page Mining Company and the adjacent Blackhawk Mining and Developing Company, in the Wardner area, for eighty thousand dollars consolidating these into a single enterprise although the separate company names were preserved until 1910.[9]

Of Sweeny's formidable realm, E. J. Roberts wrote privately to an old friend, "I am still pegging away trying to run the largest mining concern in this country. . . . It is now backed by the Gould and Rockefeller crowd and is making net earnings of about $125,000 a month." [10] Federal, in 1904, produced 43 percent of the lead of the Coeur d'Alenes, or 21 percent of the domestic lead of the United States. It reported to the Shoshone County Assessor $1,169,036 in net earnings for fiscal 1903–4 (a quarter-million more than the Bunker Hill and Sullivan), paid its anticipated 7 percent on preferred, and 4½ on its common stock. But despite an acceptable record in its truncated first year, Federal's quotations lagged on the New York market: common closed 1904 at $64 a share, preferred at $78. Common had risen from the $30 a share paid June 13 when its first one hundred shares were offered to the public, but preferred was down from the $90 it brought Sweeny when he had sold five thousand shares on June 10.[11] The fluctuating bids for Federal reflected the fact that it was a comparatively small issue, so that relatively few shares bought or sold could affect its prices quickly.

As 1905 neared, Sweeny renewed his consideration of a chain of Federal smelters. Now his engineers studied Asarco plants, themselves, on the pretext of duplicating them, while Bernard Baruch, a trusted friend of the Guggenheim sons, noted that acquisition of either the Selby at San Francisco or the Bunker Hill smelter at Tacoma "would have made the Standard Oil Group serious competitors of the Guggenheims on both the Pacific Coast and Alaska." [12] Baruch volunteered to buy these smelters for Asarco and, grasping his opportunity when Darius Mills, the major shareholder in the Tacoma plant, declared he would not treat with Rockefeller, Baruch purchased the Tacoma smelter for the Guggenheims in January, 1905. Both buys —at San Francisco and Tacoma—educed such precarious dickering that Baruch afterward gave the smelter managers $300,000 apiece for their aid in closing the contracts.

While Sweeny's talk of smelters again attracted attention, a general speculative rise in stocks in 1905 drove Federal higher than its 1904 quotations. By February 16 common stood at $98 and preferred reached $93 a share. In his later years Charles Sweeny liked to boast that he had inflated Federal's stock by his maneuvers; he doubtless did puff it by his high-blown confidence in a Federal smelting empire and by judicious purchases at the right moments. Sweeny claimed he forced Federal quotations upward with his smelter ruse while he cautioned Rockefeller and Gould to keep their mouths shut—an incident which, if it occurred, probably produced inward smiles for the financial giants of the company Sweeny called his own.

At any event, Federal stock increased in value. When preferred reached $85 a share, Finch and Campbell sold the shares they had taken as half payment, throwing in their common stock as a bonus. Finch's and Campbell's friends in Ohio sold, too. The buyer was Charles Sweeny. In mid-February, 1905, George Turner sold his five hundred preferred, bestowed for arranging options on the Standard and Mammoth, handing over his common as a bonus. Turner's stock brought him $140 a share from an undisclosed buyer, probably Daniel Guggenheim or his agent.[13]

Sweeny, meanwhile, quietly advised the men closest to him to sell their Federal stock when the price seemed attractive. The Rockefeller group now was ready to let the Guggenheims have the merged mines of the Coeur d'Alenes—at Rockefeller's price. Clendening and Roberts, who did not immediately apprehend Sweeny's deliberate antic, held their shares with the explanation, "We did not think it would look well for us to throw our holdings on the market at the first movement. It would indicate lack of faith in the properties." [14] Set straight by Sweeny, both soon sold. As Federal quotations strengthened and various minor shareholders took their profits, Roberts protested to Sweeny that the Mace mines had been closed by cold weather and that Federal would be pinched to pay the 10 percent dividend Sweeny now had promised. To no avail: Sweeny talked on, and Federal continued upward.

On February 18, 1905, Roberts resigned as general manager to rejoin D. C. Corbin, his former employer, in constructing a railroad between Spokane and the Canadian Pacific Railway. His resignation drew from Sweeny a letter of vain remonstrance: "There is twice as much money to be made with my crowd," wrote Sweeny. "They will own the Bunker Hill, Morning, and Hecla before very long. . . . A little piece of railroad a couple of hundred miles long is not to be compared at all. . . . I am very likely to take the presidency of the Amalgamated Copper Company, settle the Heinze business and buy the Calumet and Hecla, increase the capital of the Amalgamated to $225,000,000. Men who are with me will have the great future." [15] Unswayed, Roberts was succeeded by W. Clayton Miller.

Federal's spurt on the market in the general upsurge and the threat of Rockefeller competition in smelting, among other considerations, impelled the Guggenheims to a decision that they had deliberated for many months—one which Rockefeller and Gates must have anticipated. As early as 1901, M. Guggenheim's sons had concluded that they must buy mines to assure steady ore supplies for their smelting trust; now in 1905 they formed the American Smelters Securities Company and with its capital stock bought mines. Federal Mining and Smelting was one of the first mining companies acquired by the smelting trust in 1905, and in Charles Sweeny's opinion Federal's proposal to compete in smelting "was the real cause of the American . . . buying out the Federal company." [16]

Federal's 1905 annual meeting was scheduled for March 20 in New York City. Before that date, most of the 52,500 shares issued as common stock disappeared from trading. Common alone carried voting power (except on stock increases). On March 16 Charles Sweeny delivered more than half the common, 28,105 shares, to Daniel Guggenheim, who purchased them at $120 each from Sweeny, Rockefeller, Gates, and the attorney, George W. Murray. Of this block, 8,450 belonged personally to Sweeny, some of it recently acquired from Finch, Campbell, and others eager to take an early profit. [17] With more than half the voting stock in their possession, the Guggenheims controlled Federal. They had borrowed $2,000,000 from Rockefeller, Jr., to buy Federal common.

Although Sweeny agreed as a stipulation of his stock sale that he would "no longer operate in the Coeur d'Alenes," he was re-elected president of Federal at the 1905 meeting. He read a statement at the meeting that said, in part, "The majority of common stock . . . has been bought by Daniel Guggenheim from John D. Rockefeller, George Gould, Charles Sweeny, and others, in March, 1905. The price paid for this stock was $120, and Mr. Guggenheim bought all the stock offered to him at that price." [18] Sweeny continued to direct the management of the company; Daniel Guggenheim transferred his stock to the American Smelters Security Company and he and his brothers contented themselves, for the time being, with seating a majority of their people on the Federal board of directors.

Sweeny told newspapermen that the sale of Federal brought him $2,660,000, although his later statements under oath suggest that the amount was nearer $1,014,000 for his common stock alone, because he continued to hold his preferred. The *Spokesman-Review* estimated that "it would take three boxcars loaded to their limits to bring Mr. Sweeny's $2,660,000 back to Spokane should it be dished out to him in silver." [19]

The smelter trust doubtless would have purchased Federal Mining and Smelting without Sweeny's bumptious talk about building his own smelters. Without Sweeny, Asarco probably would have bought Federal more cheaply. The Rockefellers, Gates, and Gould—who may have simply seen an opportunity in organizing Federal to make some money at the smelter trust's expense—accepted their best opportunity to dispose of their investment at a profit. To Rockefeller, Sr., Federal was surely one of those enterprises whose name he merely recognized without taking part in its management.

Almost immediately after Federal's sale to the Guggenheim brothers, Sweeny rebought Federal shares, and was to hold as many as four thousand common on occasion, selling or buying as the market dictated.

Within days of its acquisition of a majority of Federal stock, the trust consummated a twenty-five-year smelting contract with the Bunker Hill and Sullivan company. Asarco had not, indeed, abandoned its efforts to gain control of the Bunker Hill, too, by stock purchase. Operating under his shorter contract, due to expire in 1909, Sweeny foresaw possible future difficulties for Federal in selling its ore. There had been an oversupply of lead in 1903 and if another were to occur in 1909, the Federal company, as Sweeny explained, "might have found themselves in a place where they could not contract for their ores at all. If 1909 should prove to be a year [of abundant lead] . . . the smelting company would have . . . enough lead ores to answer their purpose without taking the ores of the Federal company." [20]

As a consequence, with the approval of Federal's directors, Sweeny negotiated during the summer of 1905 with American Smelting and Refining to secure a twenty-five-year contract for Federal. On October 13, 1905, he was able to sign an extension of his earlier contract to 1930, containing terms similar to those of the Bunker Hill company. Sweeny managed to extend the price for ore in his 1903 contract, $4.10 per hundred pounds for lead, a peak price that had not been reached in ten years before 1903. Eminently pleased, Sweeny regarded the terms as favorable to Federal, and the compact as securing his company's market for a quarter of a century.

Moreover Federal continued negotiating to buy the Bunker Hill, the Hecla, and the Morning mines in the Coeur d'Alenes, even though Sweeny's earlier designs on the Bunker Hill had failed. The plan was outlined in a letter Sweeny wrote Packard on July 13, 1905: "In order to avoid litigation with the Bunker Hill, it is proposed for the Federal Company to buy the Bunker Hill mines and also add to the Federal Company properties of the Utah Copper Company, which is earning $3,500,000 per annum. . . . It is proposed to issue $10,000,000 of preferred stock . . . and we are accordingly arranging to call a special meeting of the preferred and common stockholders on July 20 for this purpose." [21] Sweeny revealed that Daniel Guggenheim had met George Turner in San Francisco, where the head offices of the Bunker Hill were located, "to straighten up Bunker Hill matters if they can."

At the special meeting, the increased stock issue was approved, only to be rescinded on October 21 after the Bunker Hill directors refused to sell.

Before Roberts left the Federal, Sweeny wrote him that "Turner has seen Campbell respecting the Hecla. Mace [Amasa Campbell] expressed himself as being confident to whip his people into line if he is given a little time to work on them." Sweeny's correspondence confidently asserted that the Hecla would soon belong to Federal, but in 1906 this proposed purchase also fell through. Sweeny told Clayton Miller on February 20, 1906, that after J. B. Smith, manager of the Hecla, "had arranged with Mr. Guggenheim for us to make an examination on the basis of a price, he backed out; and I rather incline to believe the reason being that the mine would not stand the examination for the price asked. For the present the whole matter is off." [22]

Peter Larson and Thomas L. Greenough, owners of the Morning, agreed to sell, however, asking $3,000,000, and Sweeny undertook to raise the money. With the twenty-five-year smelting contract as gilded assurance of his company's stability, Sweeny arranged in London, England, for the banking house of Benson and Company to buy $3,000,000 worth of Federal stock for cash to enable Federal to pay for the Morning. But a week later, the London firm withdrew from the deal, leaving Sweeny with a commitment to buy and no money to pay.

The Federal directors on October 16, 1905, had authorized the purchase of "the Morning and You Like group of mines and the Defiance lode" for $3,200,000. When Benson and Company withdrew, the directors met again on October 21 to approve a new Federal issue of $2,000,000 preferred and $1,000,000 common. On October 23, Federal bought the Morning and You Like, historic producers of the Coeur d'Alenes. To pay for the mines, the company used cash supplied at the last moment by John D. Rockefeller, Jr., who took the titles to the Morning and You Like as his security. The stock issue approved October 21 was sold the next month to repay Rockefeller. Federal's shareholders, given first opportunity to buy the new shares, took approximately $1,333,330 preferred and $666,667 common, and the remaining $1,000,000 worth was subscribed by an underwriting syndicate organized by Sweeny.[23]

In applying on November 18 to list its new issue with the New York Stock Exchange, Federal again publicized its twenty-five-year smelting contract as an inducement to investors. Previous Federal paper had been admitted to the Exchange list on November 9, 1904.[24]

In this manner, Federal gained the Morning and its sister You Like. Larson and Greenough were willing to sell principally because their mines faced costly development to extract deep ores below the upper five levels that were considered worked out. At the sixth level, a crosscut was being driven fourteen hundred feet toward the You Like, and the ore scavenged from the depleted upper workings and from the You Like was shipped to the trust's East Helena smelter.[25]

The Morning operated a 110-ton concentrator by waterpower which Federal largely dismantled, installing in its place a fine-grinding flotation process that was revolutionary in 1905. The Morning was again to be a prodigious producer, one of the deepest silver-lead mines in the world. By 1950 it had yielded no less than $54,000,000 worth of ore.

The one consequential mining company that would entertain no overtures from Sweeny was the Hercules. Sweeny harassed its owners by attempting to cut them off from transportation and power. On one occasion Harry Day of the Hercules wrote his attorney, William E. Borah, that after he negotiated with Finch and Campbell for the old Union Mine's tramway as a thoroughfare to the lower end of

Burke, he was "dumbfounded to learn that Sweeny had quietly acquired control . . . and his agents absolutely refused to acquiesce in the deed to ourselves, remarking that we would never get an outlet in a thousand years." [26] Thwarting the Hercules cost Sweeny, in this instance, only $359.40 for 5,990 shares of Hidden Treasure stock to control this approach to the Day properties.

The end of fiscal 1904–5 found the Federal Mining and Smelting Company the largest individual producer of raw lead in the United States, paying dividends as high as 17 percent on its common stock, 7 percent on preferred, and recording a net profit of $1,242,698. The chief mines of the Coeur d'Alenes, except the Hercules, were now in the hands of corporations, their destinies determined by directors in distant cities. Labor acceded to conditions established by the owners. As if to emphasize the altered relationships between employed and employer, in February, 1905, the Federal, Morning, and Hecla adopted an insurance association for their miners, providing a relief fund toward which workers contributed one dollar and the companies, fifty cents per man each month. Wages and hours had not changed since 1900 but steady improvements had occurred in mining and milling methods. These conditions would have increased profits, had not lead prices declined sharply. The mining companies temporarily relied on silver to provide their margins of return. Consequently, Federal meticulously searched its ores for higher silver content, and succeeded in raising its average ounces of silver per ton of crude ore from 4.05 in 1905 to 4.48 the following year, although the proportion was to decline to 4.15 in 1907. The lead content of Federal's ores diminished during the same period, throwing the whole burden of paying operating costs on silver.[27]

The narrow margin of profit possible under these circumstances precluded setting aside funds for other purposes, as Miller was to observe in his letter summarizing the period 1903–8: "Operating costs, which include betterments for this period, averaged slightly more than two and one-half cents per pound of lead paid for. This includes nothing for interest on the investment, nor a sinking fund or amortization fund to absorb capital by the time the mines are worked out. On the average life of a mine, fifteen percent should be provided to take care of those two items, assuming the average profitable life of a lead mine in this district to be twelve and one-half years." [28]

In fiscal 1905–6 Federal increased its net profit to $2,685,300 and paid higher total dividends, while the Idaho mines inspector declared that Federal's output "doubtless constitutes the largest tonnage of lead mineral ever raised to the surface in one year under the management of one man," referring to Miller. Opening the new Number Six level of the Morning disclosed rich ore, and 1906–7, despite the decreased silver content in its crude ore, returned Federal $2,532,250 in net profit and allowed even more generous dividend payments. Common paid 14.5 percent; preferred, its regular 7 percent for a fourth consecutive year.[29]

But 1907, marred by a stock market decline in March and a gale-force financial panic in October, ended what Clayton Miller wistfully would recall as Federal's "bonanza" years. Lead prices ebbed to 2.5 cents a pound delivered at New York, and fluttered into 1908. Silver also fell. Many of the Coeur d'Alene district mines curtailed production, dismissed workers, and decreed stringent economies.

To stem the flow of profitless ore, Sweeny said, he "tried to cut down the production of lead, not only of our own mines but the Coeur d'Alene mines, but I was up against the Sherman anti-trust law and was cautioned by my lawyer, [George W.] Murray, that I had better be very careful about talking about this restraint of trade." [30]

At Rockefeller's insistence, in December, 1907, Federal closed the Morning, which had been shipping thirty-five hundred tons of concentrates each month, then locked the Tiger-Poorman, the Last Chance, and finally all of its properties in the Coeur d'Alenes except the Mace mines—the Standard and the Mammoth. With Missouri competition driving lead prices even lower, Rockefeller argued that it "was better to shut down than to sell cheaply," Miller told Sweeny. "I closed up the Empire State to mollify Mr. Rockefeller's people. They wanted the Standard closed also." [31]

Finch and Campbell buttoned their Hecla. The stoppages threw a thousand men out of work until June, 1908, when the mines slowly reopened as a result of an advance in lead prices. Then Federal experienced trouble in hiring machine men, for many veteran mine workers had deserted the hushed district. Despite the panic, Federal distributed its usual 7 percent dividend on preferred stock during 1907–8, but for the first time, common paid nothing. The company's net was calculated at more than one million dollars below that of 1906–7. Moreover, Charles Sweeny suffered the severest personal reverses of his life in 1907 when the stock market crashed.

As if financial panic were not enough, the mines encountered the abrasiveness of nascent bureaucracy. Certain Federal properties on the western end of the Wardner mineral zone, located ten to twenty years earlier, fell within newly reserved federal forest areas. When Federal applied for patents, reported *Engineering and Mining Journal* for October 12, 1907, "The department sent an inexperienced kid to pass on the matter. He looked over the ground and proposed to the general manager of the Federal Company that if the claims were really held in good faith as mineral claims, the work, instead of being confined to a shaft and crosscuts and drifts from it, should be scattered on each of the claims of the group!" The forestry service also challenged Federal's removal of trees for timbering its stopes, a "departure from the free and easy methods of the past," observed the magazine. Federal, the largest timber user in the district, complained lustily.

Next, the State of Idaho began enforcing a new law in 1907 that required corporations to pay a fee to obtain a state license, although the attorney general ruled that this applied only to paying mining properties.

Offsetting these irritations, one problem was solved in 1908 when the Ninth Circuit Court of Appeals in San Francisco ruled in favor of Federal, the Bunker Hill and Sullivan, and other mining companies, in their defense of their use of the south fork of the Coeur d'Alene River for dumping. A group of farmers had sued the mining companies in November, 1904, with the complaint that waste from the concentrators was filling the channel and poisoning the stream for agriculture. Productive little hay and dairy farms thrived in the meadowlands along the river as it approached its outlet into Lake Coeur d'Alene. The farmers alleged that the intent of the Mine Owners Association "was to prevent the complainants . . . and others similarly situated, from securing any redress." [32]

The association, in fact, had erected a dam at Osburn in 1901 to contain tailings and other waste, and had purchased approximately two thousand acres below Kellogg for a dump. In 1902 a second dam was erected at Pine Creek, two miles below the Federal (Sweeny) mill, to catch mine and mill waste. In their defense, the mining companies claimed to produce among them 40 percent of the nation's lead and to employ 2,654 men at an aggregate payroll of $8,872 a day. Both the Idaho district and the appellate court refused to enjoin the mining companies, judging that because mining and farming both were "lawful business," the court was compelled to consider comparative injury and could not destroy a greater enterprise for a lesser. The farmers' case was vitiated, to a degree, by unusually good crops along the Coeur d'Alene in the year after they filed suit.

Legal disputation between the mining companies, quiescent during the panic, returned with better times. First, Federal defended its Sierra Nevada Mining Company against an apex claim of Senator Jonathan Bourne of Oregon. *Engineering and Mining Journal* remarked, "By many, it is believed that Senator Bourne's interest has really passed to the Bunker Hill and Sullivan Company, and that this litigation is a renewal of the long fight between the Bunker Hill and Sullivan and the interests of President Charles Sweeny of the Federal Company." [33]

Pope Yeatman, chief consulting engineer for the Guggenheim brothers, arrived in the Coeur d'Alenes from New York to determine for himself if legal contention need continue. His attempts at compromise with the Bunker Hill and Sullivan miscarried, to be followed by a flurry of Federal complaints—three lawsuits filed in three days— among them, a petition for rights to ore within the Republican Fraction lines and a cash judgment of $7,300,000. This lawsuit, entered in the district court by the January Mining Company, organized by Frank T. Post, the Federal company attorney in Spokane, revived the controversy about the course of the Wardner vein through the Bunker Hill claim, the Stemwinder, the Emma, the Last Chance, and even the Tyler. [34]

But dismay at apex litigation, decried in the Coeur d'Alenes as expensive and enervating, paled when Sweeny announced the permanent closure of the venerable Tiger-Poorman after the mine had lost money for two years, $106,028 in 1907–8 alone. [35] The mine had been developed by a vertical shaft to a depth of twenty-two hundred feet. Now its pumps were dismantled and moved to the Standard, and the Tiger-Poorman was allowed to fill with water. It was the first major mine in the Coeur d'Alenes quitted because its accessible ore had been exhausted, although commercial mineral was known to lie at greater depth in a quantity not explored due to the high costs of reaching it.

Little in the first decade of the twentieth century stunned the Coeur d'Alenes as did the throttling of the Tiger-Poorman. Until the demise of the old mine, the Coeur d'Alene district had ignored contemplation of its life span. Now each moribund stope was searched for signs of lassitude and each man breathed less securely, sobered by the gurgle of seeping water in the empty depths of the Tiger-Poorman.

Shuttering the Tiger-Poorman in the fall of 1908 was among Charles Sweeny's last duties as president of Federal. His health had failed in the Panic of 1907. In the face of new legal trials, an urgent need to find and develop new properties to sustain the company, and Emeline's importuning that he rest, Sweeny decided near the end of 1908 that he would retire from Federal. He was to remark that he was "getting along in years and pretty well tired out, anyhow, working pretty hard." To entice her husband from his mines, Emeline proposed an auto trip through Europe or a voyage around the world. Federal's directors probably encouraged Sweeny to step aside, pointing out that with his successor in office the company might compromise its fruitless lawsuits in the Wardner area and liquidate its obligation in the Sullivan Group Mining Company, a Canadian venture advocated by Sweeny.

Sweeny's resignation was accepted on January 29, 1909, at the annual stockholders' meeting. The Everett attorney, Francis H. Brownell, was chosen the new president because, said the minutes, "It seems to the Board of Directors judicious and necessary that there be elected to the presidency a gentleman learned in the law, who will devote a large amount of time to . . . legal controversies." The directors intended that their new president "be freed from responsibility for the actual operation of the company's mining properties." Brownell accepted on condition he receive a two-year contract.[36]

Charles Sweeny left to his stockholders one of the signal lead-and-silver mining companies of his time. In the contrary year that was Sweeny's last as president, Federal earned a net of $882,371. The company managed to pay only 1½ percent on its common stock—a dividend declared thirteen days before Sweeny's retirement—but on its preferred paid its habitual 7 percent. In Sweeny's years as president, Federal distributed to its holders of $6,000,000 worth of common stock a total of $2,643,750, and to those who held its $12,000,000 in preferred, a total of $3,934,250.[37]

In Sweeny's own Coeur d'Alene district, Federal dominated. Its principal rivals at Sweeny's retirement were the Bunker Hill and Sullivan and the obdurate Hercules. Federal's properties included its Wardner group of forty claims extending more than seven thousand feet along the Wardner lode, its Burke array of ten claims, its Mace holdings of sixteen claims, and the Morning, of thirty-two locations. Federal operated four mills: the Sweeny, which it valued at $170,000; the Burke, $195,000; the Mace, $338,000; and the Morning, $200,000. Federal also owned the district's sampling works and the only equipment in the region for reproducing blueprints. Whenever a mining company ordered blueprints duplicated, Federal made copies for its own files, which contained detailed sketches of its workings and those of its competitors.[38]

Sweeny remained a director of Federal, and his son, Frank, served briefly as the company's secretary in 1910. Within a year of Sweeny's retirement, a series of disasters befell the Federal company in Idaho: In January, 1910, fire destroyed ore bins and equipment at Mace; in February, a snowslide at Mace killed forty workmen including the mine superintendent; and in August, the Coeur d'Alenes were swept by a forest fire that endangered the entire district and razed much of the town of Wallace. Luckily, Federal's major loss in the holocaust was $15,000 worth of flumes. Next, the Morning Mine's concentrator was judged inefficient, and Federal experimented with a series of advisors and novel processes in the hope of extracting higher proportions of lead and silver. Timber awards amounting to $100,604 were levied against Federal under the conservation policies of the federal government, although the company settled for $17,091. As a consequence of these events, common stock paid no dividends in fiscal 1909–10.[39]

Federal recovered from depression and natural catastrophe to influence American mining for nearly half a century more. On April 30, 1953, it was merged with the American Smelting and Refining Company. In its fifty years Federal recorded net earnings of $66,435,359.[40] In 1926 and again in 1937 it paid all dividends in arrears, and when plans were made to retire preferred stock in 1939, Federal would have distributed $22,222,800.58 on it. Except for a dividend in 1927, however, no dividends were declared on common stock until 1937. Federal operated not only in the Coeur d'Alenes but in the tri-state district of Missouri, Oklahoma, and Kansas. Its Morning Mine in Idaho was the deepest lead producer in the world, its ore persisting beneath the level where geologists had predicted the great mine would bottom out.

Although he remained a director, Charles Sweeny's chief function on Federal's behalf after 1909 was to answer lawsuits that concerned the period of his management. Among the most notable was that attacking his twenty-five-year smelting contract, brought in the New York state courts in February, 1913, by Sidney Norman of Spokane and other stockholders who comprised .024 percent of Federal's common and .0048 percent of its preferred stock.[41] Norman had canvased Federal stockholders by mail before instituting his suit but elicited little response. He and his small band asserted that Sweeny had worked in the best interests of the smelter trust, rather than Federal, when Sweeny wrote the long smelting contract, and that "dummy directors" had ratified the agreement.

Norman, a newspaperman and mining broker, heard his complaint dismissed by the lower court, and lost his appeal to the New York Supreme Court, which read its unanimous decision on December 7, 1917. The bench said, "An effort is made to attack the independence of action and good faith of Charles Sweeny. . . . But the proof establishes that he was never in any way connected with the smelting company, either officially or financially. He was an experienced mining man. . . . He appears upon this record to have intelligently and honestly represented the Federal Company in its contractual relationship with the Smelting Company."

With this vindication ended Charles Sweeny's durable embrace of the Coeur d'Alenes.

# XI

## LAST DAYS

*C*HARLES SWEENY'S career entered its climax in the formative years of the Federal Mining and Smelting Company. Sweeny was nine days beyond sixty in 1909 when he resigned as the company's president. He recognized the time that followed as his declining years. His vigor and his compulsion spent, he passed his days after Federal toying with his trappings of fortune. He owned yachts, rented expensive apartments, dallied with the stock market, promoted oil land, and guided his heirs toward their independence from him. Together his companies and his children drifted from the stream of his life into channels of their own.

Sweeny dawdled in his last years because his activities no longer affected the destinies of men or mines. For the first time in two decades, he lived a comparatively private life. Unaccustomed to rest, and unwilling to recede entirely from public attention, he found leisure forced upon him nonetheless, as his influence and notoriety eroded. Sweeny dabbled in the stock market; he had begun to bet on the board before leaving Federal, but in these last months of his life he simply sought a shimmer of his spangled days. His crotchety forays into the market suited the pattern of his final seven years, for after 1909 he was unable to settle long in one place or give his attention to one plan.

In the midst of organizing Federal, Sweeny had grasped randomly at what might have been his major achievement as a promoter, and this occupied him briefly after he resigned from Federal's presidency.

His chance acquisition was the Sullivan Group of three mining claims in the Fort Steele district of British Columbia. A number of Coeur d'Alene district veterans recognized these vast low-grade lead-zinc ore deposits as potentially valuable but feared that the mineral could not be recovered profitably. Colonel Ridpath and George Turner, with other Spokane investors, formed a company and sold a good deal of stock in the East, using as a salesman the natty acting assistant door-keeper of the United States Senate, Bernard W. Layton. The money they raised began development, but smelter returns were unsatisfactory, and some smelters rejected the Sullivan Group ore because of its high zinc content and their inability to separate the ore.[1]

The company determined to build its own smelter, floated a bond issue for this purpose, and put up a plant at Marysville, British Columbia.[2] By an odd mischance, they hired the brother of the engineer they intended to retain, and the smelter construction was bungled. Its erection and initial operation was further complicated by frequent changes in resident managers. The company fell $140,000 into debt—without a suitable means of producing metal.[3]

When Sweeny engaged Turner to arrange options for him on Coeur d'Alene mining properties, Turner persuaded Sweeny in turn to take control of the Sullivan Group, averring that the enterprise needed only a workable smelter to produce a fortune for its stockholders. Both Clayton Miller and E. J. Roberts inspected the Sullivan Group, and both reported favorably. As a consequence, Sweeny committed Federal to buy the Sullivan Group, over the objection of Rockefeller's lieutenant, Gates.[4] On May 21, 1904, Sweeny assumed control of the Sullivan Group. Within a week, he rebonded the properties for $204,000 to build a new smelter on the foundation of the old, a renovation that Roberts directed.

Then started a series of disappointments. The company could not devise a satisfactory method for processing its huge reserves of complex ore. Early in 1905 Roberts realized that the Sullivan Group was doomed to a second smelter disaster, but Sweeny resolutely pushed development, resorting to having the ore sorted by hand for smelting to increase the yield per ton.[5]

When the Guggenheims bought control of the Federal company, they showed little patience with the floundering Sullivan Group, and ordered it sold. Sweeny reluctantly concurred, although he blamed the failures on Turner.[6]

Shortly after Sweeny resigned from Federal, the new president, Brownell, reorganized the Sullivan Group as the Fort Steele Mining and Smelting Company, shouldering aside Turner in the process. The Fort Steele bought the Sullivan Group at a sheriff's sale in 1909 for $13,500, and soon thereafter negotiated its lease to the Consolidated Mining and Smelting Company of Canada, which later exercised an option to purchase the claims.[7] With relief, Federal's directors concluded that four years of operating the Sullivan Group lost them only $56,000.

After scores of attempts to separate the Sullivan Group's ores economically, Consolidated developed differential flotation in 1920.[8] This proved to be the key that had been sought by Sweeny, Roberts, Miller, and the others in the defunct Sullivan Group company. In 1923, nineteen years after Charles Sweeny had bought the Sullivan Group, the three-thousand-ton Sullivan concentrator rose at Kimberley, and exactly a quarter of a century after Sweeny had bought into the Sullivan, it was acclaimed as the world's largest producer of lead and zinc. Had he been able to solve the riddle of treating its ores, it might have been Sweeny's greatest achievement as a promoter.

Except for lawsuits which spilled over from earlier years, the sale of the Sullivan Group ended Sweeny's active participation in mining. Since his loss of money and health in 1907, Emeline had urged him to take life easier, proposing a cruise around the world to ease him out of the financial steeplechase. Perhaps with such a trip in mind, Sweeny bought the 144-foot yacht *Czarina* shortly before Christmas, 1906, and presented it to Emeline.[9] On December 26 the vessel was rechristened *Emeline*. It was a 206-ton, two-masted steam-screw ship, launched three years earlier at Elizabeth, New Jersey, the first of two yachts Sweeny was to own.

Despite outfitting the *Emeline*, the Sweenys did not—as did the F. Lewis Clarks—participate in the various competitions for yachts that delighted seaboard society. Sweeny evidently considered the *Emeline* a trophy; his entertaining continued to mix with business.

After incorporating the Federal, Sweeny had centered his activities in New York and his boyhood home of Paterson. He complained to Miller, of the Sullivan Group failure, that he "was not out there at all." This was virtually true; Sweeny had spent little time in the West after the senatorial election of 1905. He retained his downtown real estate in Portland and Spokane, but shed his other investments, leaving the management of his real estate to the Sweeny Investment Company.

It was in 1908, however, that Sweeny moved permanently from Spokane to New York and sold his great gray granite home overlooking the city to the railroad contractor, Patrick Welch, for a reported eighty thousand dollars.[10] The three-story house had been designed twenty years earlier by the ambitious young architect, Kirtland K. Cutter, and was first owned by the Father of Spokane, James N. Glover, who spent one hundred thousand dollars to build and furnish it. In 1888 the location had been remote. One of Glover's few neighbors remarked that his wife had been frightened by passing Indians.

Although specially designed woodwork was ordered from Minneapolis mills or hand-carved, the granite stones for the home's exterior were quarried within ten miles of Spokane. Glover mortgaged his showy house, lost it to Dutch lenders in 1893, and two other owners occupied it briefly before the Dutch sold the house in 1898 to the attorney, Frank H. Graves. Graves, his wife, Maud, and their two sons lived there six years, and then sold the place on the next-to-last day of July, 1904, to Charles and Emeline Sweeny for fifty thousand dollars—ten thousand dollars in cash, the Sweenys' home at Pacific and Chestnut as a twenty-thousand-dollar payment, and the Sweenys' assumption of a twenty-thousand-dollar mortgage to the Hypotheekbank. The *Spokane Daily Chronicle* reported the sale as the largest of a private residence in the city's history.[11]

The Glover—now Sweeny—lawns covered two and one-half large city lots in an area intersected by basalt outcroppings and steep inclines. In November, 1904, the Sweenys bought the lot and one-half next west of their property for eleven thousand dollars from Graves's brother, Jay P. Graves, where the Sweenys were to erect a handsome brick house for their daughter, Mary Gertrude, when she married Francis J. Finucane.

Glover's old house contained a hall two stories high with a wood-carved balcony overlooking it from the master suite, in the style of an English manor. Its walls were hung with blue tapestry, and lions' heads grinned from a marble fireplace. Throughout, the house was opulent; even the windows in its pantry were leaded. But what people talked about when Glover built the place was its three indoor bathrooms. Later tenants added six more.

During the residence of the Charles Sweeny family, the huge

house dazzled Spokane with parties. Glover had entertained scarcely at all, the Graves rarely, but the Sweenys staged elaborate and frequent parties that scattered shafts of gaeity across the city in the valley below. One gathering arranged by the son, Charles, was the talk of the town for months, for an orchestra played on the mezzanine while dancers swirled in the high room, and a lavish dinner was served at midnight.

Sweeny doubtless was proud of his house but not often in residence, while Emeline and the children made it their own. They were accustomed to settling quickly in a new home because the family had moved often; they had lived on Second Avenue, west of Post Street, when Sweeny first brought them to Spokane, then on East Riverside, next in Wardner, Coeur d'Alene City, again in Wardner, and thence to Spokane where they occupied a house at 2107 West Pacific Avenue, one of the city's better districts. Sweeny was said to have won the home from Jay P. Graves in a poker game. They were in this house that chips bought when Sweeny traded with Frank Graves for the Glover mansion on the hill.

When Sweeny saw a chance to get his money, he sold the granite house promptly. The wealthy Welches continued the social display of the baronial home. Moreover, by 1908 a row of millionaires' mansions were strung along the heights west of the house. One rarely saw a wandering Indian.

Sweeny may have sold the house to put his hands on cash after the Panic of 1907, for he also sold his stock in the Exchange National Bank in November, 1908, to a local syndicate formed among E. T. Coman, a Colfax banker, Coman's associate William Huntley, who already owned 400 and 365 shares respectively, and Lillis F. Smith of Endicott, Washington, popularly known as the "wheat king of the Palouse." Harry Day, Sweeny's erstwhile foe in the Coeur d'Alene mines, was revealed as a major shareholder in the bank's reorganization and increase of capital the following January.

The Exchange had been organized in May, 1889. It was one of Spokane's old, stable banks, one of three to survive the Panic of 1893, and in February, 1898, the city's first to record more than $1,000,000 in deposits. In their sprint toward fortune, Clark and Sweeny had acquired more than half the bank's 2,500 capital shares by paying Colonel Isaac N. Peyton $196,000 for 1,400 shares in May, 1899. When he and Clark split in the next year, Sweeny arranged to take Clark's stock in the Exchange, and in 1902 bought the six-story bank building.

The Exchange bank paid frequent dividends and when its authorized stock was tripled to 7,500 shares in January, 1907, Sweeny retained 3,843 of the 7,241 issued, holding the shares in his name and that of the Sweeny Investment Company. Under Sweeny's aegis, the Exchange was the only Spokane bank directed by one family. But in 1907, when Sweeny sold Coman 400 shares, he relinquished his absolute majority, keeping 1,340 shares for himself and 2,103 for his investment company. Sweeny also sold the Exchange building to the bank in 1907 for $375,000 in anticipation of the purchase by Coman, Huntley, Smith, and Day of 3,300 bank shares from him at $180 each. To deliver 3,300, Sweeny had acquired a few small holdings in the months before the sale—a deliberation that discounts the possibility that he sold merely to recoup his losses in the 1907 market crash. Counting Huntley's and Coman's personal stock, the bank's new owners held 4,075 shares and—although their purchase from Sweeny cost them $594,000—the bank was healthy enough to declare another dividend and increase capitalization to $1,000,000 within two months after Sweeny sold out.

With the sale of his home and his bank, Charles Sweeny left Spokane. From 1908 onward, he considered himself a resident of New York, notwithstanding a sojourn of a year in Greenwich, Connecticut. He and Emeline moved from Spokane to the Ansonia in New York, a palatial apartment house frequented by celebrities, then to Greenwich, but within twelve months returned to New York to make their home thereafter at the massive Apthorp Apartments, a twelve-story structure surrounding a court, built by the Astors, and one of the largest apartment houses in the world.[12] Both Sweenys visited Spokane, staying with their son, Frank, or daughter, Gertrude, and each arrival evoked rounds of parties. The Sweeny real estate was entrusted to managers, Finucane in Spokane, and the popular bachelor, Robert E. M. Strickland, in Portland.

With his move to New York, Charles Sweeny completed a circular pathway that had led him from his youthful home in New Jersey to war in the South, westward to California and Nevada, northward to Oregon and thence to Idaho, and finally back to the Atlantic seaboard. Probably Sweeny never reviewed his career this way. But as he grew older, his memories and his talk dwelt more on his experiences in the war and in Idaho's mines than on the years of yearning

in California and Oregon. Thus in 1910 he petitioned the War Department to change the fictitious name, James McNulty, on his service
record, writing on his application form as his occupation, "Retired—
doing nothing." Then he was entitled to wear the service medal
authorized in 1905 by the Congress, and Emeline, eligible for a
widow's pension of twenty-five dollars a month.

Despite his retirement, Sweeny was not actually doing nothing. He
was playing the stock market, speculating in oil properties, signing
occasional depositions for long-standing lawsuits, and fanfaronading
his cronies.

By 1910, his market risks were circumspect. He had been a plunger
when he first acquired substantial money, precisely the kind of investor that Rockefeller, Jr., disapproved when he termed speculating in
stocks "a pastime in which a man who has no scruples against
gambling may indulge with funds he does not need."

Evidently Rockefeller admonished Sweeny more than once about
speculating—but Sweeny liked to follow his hunches. In 1907 friends
said that Rockefeller warned Sweeny to sell before securities prices
fell in mid-March, which Sweeny did promptly, avoiding losses. Then
the board rallied and Sweeny, assuming the difficulty past, bought
again. When the crash followed suspension of the Knickerbocker
Trust Company on November 4, some estimated that Sweeny lost half
his fortune. Sweeny never revealed publicly what the panic had cost
him. The shock broke his health, and he remembered six years afterward that "when things were worst on earth," Rockefeller bought five
hundred shares of Federal from Sweeny to tide him over.[13] Possibly
Sweeny's losses shadowed those of George Gould, who lost half his
father's substantial estate, plunged his railroads into receivership,
and was never to be decisive again in financial affairs.

As business rallied, Charles Sweeny returned to the market, much
as he had returned to the mines after his burns in the Belcher, and near
the end of 1909 canceled one of his princely holidays in Spokane to
remain in New York during a manipulation of Rock Island Railroad
stock. Reported to have purchased twenty-five thousand shares at
thirty-five dollars, Sweeny realized a quick profit when Rock Island
leaped thirty-one points in a single day.[14]

Shortly before the Panic of 1907, Sweeny had trifled with active
promotion by forming the Globe Exploration Company, organized in
1906 as a Delaware corporation to lease oil lands in Kern County,

California. Globe was capitalized for ten million dollars although no stock was issued, no capital paid in, and its annual reports invariably recited, "Company's business not begun as yet." [15]

Sweeny and Edwin Packard were the principals in Globe. While it conducted no business of record (its annual reports stated its purpose as "exploration work and mining"), Globe leased oil land in the Midway-Sunset district of Kern County, joined the Independent Oil Producers' Agency, and waited for the impetus of new development to usher it to prosperity. Despite insecure titles in some sections, the region had yielded commercial petroleum as early as 1894, and by 1904 Midway-Sunset had become the principal gas field in California, its products moving by rail and pipelines.

Sweeny may have regarded the Globe as an enterprise for his sons, for in 1910 Frank and Robert were appointed its secretary and treasurer, and Frank spent some weeks in California attending the company's business. Later that year, without having operated a well, Globe sold to its neighbor, General Petroleum Company of California. Frank returned to Spokane to organize a grocery chain while Robert, who had not budged from New York, honed his golf game.

Sweeny's interest also turned to another yacht. In 1910 he sold the *Emeline* to purchase a larger, more famous vessel, the *Katomba*, in 1911. As the *Rivera*, she had belonged to Pliny Fisk, son of the noted New York banker, Harvey Fisk, and then as *Katomba* to Frederic Gallatin, grandson of Albert Gallatin. Sweeny rechristened his second yacht, too, the *Emeline*. She was a two-deck, twin-screw, schooner-rigged ship, 196 feet long, launched in December, 1898, at Troon, Scotland.[16]

While Sweeny thus frittered, the citadels of his day slowly crumbled. The Bunker Hill and the Last Chance settled their disputes, J. J. O'Connor's death in 1912 ended his juridical effort to collect from Clark and Sweeny, and Clark stepped from life. Widely known as an international yachtsman, Clark's eerie passing attracted newspaper notice. On the night of January 16, 1914, Clark saw his wife aboard her railway car at Santa Barbara, California, told his chauffer he would walk the quarter-mile back to his hotel—and was never seen again. His hat was found on the sea shore. One year later his will was admitted to probate on the assumption that he had drowned in the Pacific Ocean.

No matter how capricious his investments, Sweeny tried to provide his family the means to maintain what he had gained. As early as 1906 he had established a trust by which his wife, his son, Charles, and his son-in-law, Francis Finucane, divided 12,499 shares of the Sweeny Investment Company. This was one share less than half. The remainder was to be apportioned among his heirs. In this division, Emeline apparently acquired 7,500 shares, Charles 2,500, and Finucane 2,499.[17]

Six of Charles and Emeline's children—Emeline, Sheridan, Richard, and the triplets, Louis, Florence, and Sarah—had died as infants in various towns of the West, and six had survived.[18] There were four living sons and two daughters, as well as Lillian, the daughter of Sweeny and Maggie Swords, whom Emeline accepted as her own.

Of the Sweeny children, Charles, born in San Francisco in 1882, was to become famous as a soldier-of-fortune. Cut to his father's pattern, young Charles enlisted at sixteen for infantry service in the Spanish-American War, entered West Point military academy at the end of fighting, but resigned in his second year to serve Francisco Madero against the Mexican dictator, Diaz, and in 1911 was enrolled as a student in the French military school, St. Cyr, after a recess from battle at his father's home. When the First World War erupted and Sweeny enlisted in the French Foreign Legion, the United States stripped him of citizenship. He was the first American in the French army promoted to officer rank for gallantry. After severe wounds at Verdun, Sweeny was transferred to the tank corps, then designated one of four French officers sent to Washington, D.C., as a military advisory committee.

By this time he was a national hero. Citizenship restored, Sweeny was commissioned a major in the 318th U.S. Infantry. Slight, mild in manner, Charles Sweeny missed no war worth the name for the next quarter of a century. He fought the Bolsheviks in Poland in 1919, aided Ataturk in the Turkish revolution, then signed a contract as a correspondent for the New York *World* in Morocco. When he reached the front, however, he quit to organize fifteen American aviators to fly against Abd el Krim. For this, the United States again denoted him a noncitizen. The *Literary Digest* of August 1, 1925, pictured Sweeny in the uniform of a French colonel, thin-lipped, severe, wearing round black-rimmed spectacles, over the caption, "A Fighting Irishman."

Sweeny next served the Loyalists in Spain, and before the United

States entered the Second World War, organized the Eagle Squadron of American aviators to battle the German air force. This was his last war. For some years after, Sweeny lectured and wrote a book and magazine articles. He died in Murray, Utah, in 1963—his father's first son and the last to die.

A second son, Robert, enjoyed international notoriety during the twenties as a talented amateur golfer of mysterious but considerable means. Robert's finances were tangled, indeed, but not really secret. He had joined his father's partner, Packard, in several promotional ventures, one of which, the Maxim Munitions Company, was forced into bankruptcy in 1919.[19] Robert spent the next eleven years evading the judgment against him as Maxim's major shareholder, eventually fleeing to London in 1930 where he was sued by Maxim's creditors. He left the United States owing Packard twenty thousand dollars secured by the worthless stock of a Canadian pulp and paper company.

In one of his attempts to divest himself of garnishable assets, Robert sold his 2,581 shares of the Sweeny Investment Company back to the company for $60,022 with an understanding that he might rebuy at the same price within three years. Seven years later, having neglected to repurchase the stock, Robert sued for $175,000 as the securities' true value, but lost his case. He lived thereafter in England, where he died in 1945. His son, also named Robert, was noted as a flier in the Eagle Squadron, a golfer, and in 1940 as a gay bachelor engaged momentarily to the heiress, Barbara Hutton.

Of the Charles Sweeny sons, only one worked in his father's business enterprises. This was Frank Rockwood Sweeny, born in Spokane in 1887 and named for Frank Rockwood Moore. After graduating from Notre Dame University, Frank returned to Spokane in 1907 to enter the Exchange National Bank as a teller. In 1910 he bought the Spokane Pottery Company at Clayton, Washington, then went to Kern County for a few months to represent Globe Exploration, dipped into real estate, returned to Spokane, and in 1915 was one of three organizers of a grocery chain, Economy Stores.

While Charles and Emeline Sweeny lived, they usually stayed at Frank's home when they visited Spokane, but after the elder Sweenys were gone, Frank moved to England to seek opportunity as an investment broker, and died there in 1932 of a ruptured appendix.

The fourth and youngest adult Sweeny son, Joseph Sarsfield, born in 1895 at Coeur d'Alene, was barely out of Yale when he fell at

Verdun in October, 1918, serving as a captain in the regiment commanded by his brother Charles. Sarsfield left a widow and infant son in Baltimore, Maryland.

The Sweeny daughters were Mary Gertrude, born in 1880, and Emeline Agnes, ten years younger. When she was twenty-four, Gertrude married Finucane, who had come to Spokane in 1900 as manager of the Spokane branch of the Bank of Montreal. They were wed with a papal benediction at St. Charles Borromeo Church in Brooklyn, New York. Born in England, the son of a naval officer, Finucane had been educated in a naval academy, and then migrated to Canada with a brother. He had been assigned to various western branches of the Bank of Montreal as American prospectors opened mining districts in southern British Columbia, and when he arrived in Spokane was considered young, at thirty-three, to be a branch manager. Finucane enjoyed his father-in-law's confidence, and was an able businessman as well, assuming the presidency of the Northwestern Power and Light Company in 1903 (which furnished electricity for the Northport smelter) and in 1907 buying a major share of Holley-Mason-Marks Hardware Company which operated branches throughout the region tributary to Spokane. It was for Gertrude and Francis Finucane that the Sweenys built the three-story Tudor manor on property next to their own. The graceful home had rooms connected by flowing arches that opened on landscaped lawns, and stood at the top of Washington Street, looking into the heart of the city.

Gertrude and her husband traveled frequently and entertained often. After Gertrude died in 1934, Finucane sold the home. At her death, Gertrude was wealthy beyond her father's legacy. She had distributed among her family her stock in the Sweeny Investment Company and left $478,531 more, principally in securities.

Shortly after her debut in New York City, when she was twenty, the younger daughter, Emeline, married Clifford Lee Corbin, a career army officer. She was to follow her husband around the world to his various stations, including appointment as military attaché to Chile, while he rose to be director of procurement for the Quartermaster Corps by 1942. He retired four years later, a major general. Less than two months after the Corbins observed their golden wedding anniversary, Emeline died of a heart ailment and was buried at Arlington.

Lillian, the daughter of Maggie Swords, married Clarence K.

Edwards and lived quietly in Oakland, California, visiting the Sweenys in Spokane occasionally.

These were the children of Charles Sweeny. All had witnessed their father's rise to wealth. Sarsfield, the youngest, was perhaps five when Sweeny began to flaunt his expanding affluence, and eight when Federal Mining and Smelting was formed. He could remember wearing the castoff clothing of his older brothers. Charles, the oldest son, had left his father's home to fight in Cuba about the time Sweeny organized the Empire State–Idaho.

Not only was he generous with his family, but within his means, Sweeny was generous to his Church. Born a Catholic, he died in his faith. Most of his contributions appear to have been spontaneous, and his charity was the one activity for which Sweeny sought no publicity.

The Reverend Charles Mackin, a Jesuit who undertook construction of St. Aloysius parish church in Spokane, wrote in his memoirs of a trip to the Coeur d'Alene mining district before 1900 when, after visiting the sick, he called on the Sweenys at Wardner. The two oldest children were said to be boarding at a Catholic school but the others were home. Reluctantly the priest descended into the Last Chance Mine because Sweeny insisted, and although Father Mackin maintains he did not discuss an orphan asylum he was trying to establish in Spokane, Sweeny shortly mailed him a check for one hundred dollars with a note, "I'll send you another hundred before Christmas." [20]

After Sweeny had grown rich, Father Mackin recorded a number of contributions. Sweeny "used to come and give to the poor although he lived in another parish," the priest recalled, and he named Sweeny as one of four men who paid a three-thousand-dollar debt incurred when a damaged Hillyard church was remodeled as St. Patrick's school.

After eleven years of fund-raising, Father Mackin's "orphan asylum" was erected in 1901 as St. Joseph's Children's Home. Not only had Charles and Emeline Sweeny provided its chapel but when unpaid construction bills totaled $38,000, Sweeny wrote his personal check to satisfy the entire amount. [21] The Sweenys had financed more than half of the four-story pressed-brick building. A good share of the rest of its cost was contributed by Mrs. James Monaghan, who did her own housekeeping and gave the orphanage the money she would have paid servants.

Father Mackin also told about his attempt to establish an adequate home and school for wayward girls, to be staffed by Sisters of the Good Shepherd who were conducting their classes in a rented house. The priest struggled to raise $6,500, the price of a desirable forty-acre site, but could count only $1,500. Sweeny had been in New York. On his return to Spokane, he offered the priest $5,500, the deed to the selected property was made out to Emeline, and she in turn deeded it to the Home of the Good Shepherd. A new building was opened three days after Christmas in 1906. The Monaghan's Spokane Cab Company moved the nuns and girls without charge.

At that time, Sweeny whispered to Father Mackin that he had set aside fifty thousand dollars for him, adding apologetically that Bishop Edward J. O'Dea of Seattle had come to his home and wheedled twenty thousand dollars of it. Mackin said he refused the remainder with the words, "It would be wrong, Charlie, because the people would come and say that's a Sweeny building and it would take their interest away as a charitable institution."

Few charities of Charles and Emeline Sweeny have been written in record books. They contributed to Sacred Heart Hospital, and in 1907 gave five thousand dollars toward an infirmary for Gonzaga University. It was declared that Emeline gave the land for Our Lady of Lourdes Cathedral in Spokane, completed in 1908 and in 1931 the sixth Roman Catholic cathedral in the United States to be consecrated. She was also generous to other parishes, and Bishop O'Dea, who may have been referring to the twenty thousand dollars asserted that Sweeny "gave liberally" toward constructing the cathedral at Seattle. Doubtless this is true, but there stand no monuments raised to the charity of Charles Sweeny.

Sweeny was contemplating his days in 1914, for by then he was a frequent hospital patient. The state of his health worried him enough that he wrote his last testament in February of that year. It appears that from 1906 on, he had been transferring title to his holdings to his heirs. Out of his bed, he continued to play in the stock market, dealing in both foreign and domestic paper, investing comparatively small amounts in stable securities: $7,002 in Baltimore and Ohio, $23,175 in Union Pacific, and $7,400 in Westinghouse, as examples. Each was bought or sold as minor fluctuations changed the market. Between November, 1914, and February, 1916, Sweeny's transactions through Raymond, Pynchon and Company of New York amounted to a few pennies more than $252,565—which could have represented

$10,000 committed twenty-five times. Sweeny was merely diverting himself.[22]

He was rudderless. His health permitted no forays after fortune; he had withdrawn from active association with companies that continued to list his name on letterheads. Late in 1915 Sweeny entered Portland Surgical Hospital for observation, was released, then suffered a stroke, and returned to the hospital on February 1, 1916. Emeline moved to Portland to be near him. He rallied slightly in March and April, and then began to lose strength. For a week near the end of May his passing was expected at any moment, and at 3:45 on the morning of May 31, 1916, Charles Sweeny died.

Six years earlier his opinions had been headlines in newspapers. Now his obituaries were brief. The *New York Times* listed his demise in agate type among the expired clerks. The Portland *Oregonian* spared him three paragraphs, summing him up as "a Spokane capitalist and mining man . . . for years associated in a business way with the development and upbuilding of Portland." At his death, indeed, he was best known as the father of that dashing American in French uniform, Charles Sweeny.

Sweeny's estate had been willed to Emeline, his widow and his executrix. (In his will his address, written "Spokane," had been lined out and "New York" inserted.) He left no real or personal property of value. Except for unmarketable stock in the Buffalo Hump Mining Company and the New River Collieries of New Jersey, Sweeny left simply clothing and trinkets and bills to two brokerage houses for $31,033.

O'Connor had called Sweeny a fraud, Patsy Clark had called him a conniver, Hanley, a thief, Norman, a pawn, but the last words spoken in the mortal presence of Charles Sweeny were compassionate. Bishop O'Dea eulogized him at a Requiem Mass in the Spokane cathedral Sweeny had helped build, saying, "To the members of this congregation, in particular, I say you would be very ungrateful should you forget him. He was your best friend. To him, more than to any other benefactor, you owe this beautiful church."

While many who might have remembered Sweeny had preceded him in death—and some living did not mourn him—his honorary pallbearers formed a phalanx of the past. Sam Piles, whom Sweeny had sent to the Senate; Charles Hopkins, a compatriot of Coxey days and the senatorial campaign; F. H. Brownell, Sweeny's successor as president of Federal; Harry L. Day, who had followed Brownell as Federal's president and who, in an earlier day, would have leaped to bury Charles Sweeny; and Frank Post, his attorney. Among the active pallbearers from mining days were Bruce Clendening, Robert Strickland, and Frank Culbertson.

Sweeny was laid at temporary rest until a private mausoleum was erected in May, 1918, of Barre, Vermont, granite at Spokane's Fairmont Memorial Park among the private vaults of other families— Clark, Kellett, and Leonard.

Emeline Sweeny pined for her husband. She spent much of her time with Frank in his home on the basalt cliff above the old Glover mansion. Her friends believed that she had not recovered from Charles's death when Sarsfield fell in France. On January 3, 1919, Emeline's heart failed and she was buried, as her husband had been, from Our Lady of Lourdes Cathedral.

In death, as in life, the Sweenys could not avoid attorneys. Emeline's estate was taxed both in Washington and in Oregon after a series of hearings on its value, primarily to determine the worth of her seventy-five hundred shares in the Sweeny Investment Company. Oregon first appraised her stock at $374,955 and then reconsidered, setting its value at an even $750,000. The Portland attorney, John M. Gearin, cautioned Frank Sweeny, his mother's executor, against challenging the decision, writing, "There is a feeling, you know, in favor of inheritance taxes and it is a difficult feeling to combat." [23] Eventually the taxes and outstanding notes against Emeline's estate amounted to $70,702.

In addition to her shares in the Sweeny company, Emeline left $73,125 in other securities, including $2,000 worth of San Francisco Remedial Loan bonds and $5,000 in bonds of the Portland Commercial Club.

Emeline's will, written December 9, 1918, dispensed her cherished personal belongings: to Emeline Corbin, her ermine-lined Russian sable of fourteen skins; to the son, Charles, a painting by Merle entitled, "Mother and Child"; to Frank, a ring in which an emerald was surrounded by diamonds; and to others of the family, various items of sentimental ornament.

The children carted off $8,500 worth of Emeline's household and personal goods, leaving a pathetic inventory in their wake: an ironing board worth fifty cents; a rug, and leather sofa, sixty-five dollars each; a Columbia talking machine valued at seventy-five dollars; and a barrel of books worth five. Sifting through this miscellany, R. E. Dodds of Tull and Gibbs store in Spokane estimated that the remaining worldly possessions of Emeline Sweeny, who once had been given a yacht for Christmas, would sell for $808.50.

# NOTES

$M$UCH of the information for this study of Charles Sweeny came from raw files—documents of all descriptions crated for half a century. Oral history shaped some of the story, and the National Archives disclosed some of it. The gaps were filled from newspapers and magazine accounts, court records, informal talks with members of pioneer families, and general reading. Each source presents its own challenge in annotation.

The notes are long, chiefly because much of the information in them will be new to accounts of the Idaho mines. The notes acknowledge, report sources, or amplify the text. In the first note for each chapter, I have attempted to identify useful reading when it exists or to comment on sources.

Each note that cites archival or raw material tells its location. The following abbreviations indicate locations that occur frequently.

Asarco: the storehouse of records of the American Smelting and Refining Company, crated or filed in an old brick substation at Wallace Mills, near Wallace, Idaho. These records represent the companies absorbed by Asarco. Except for labels painted on the crates or file cabinets, these are not identified or catalogued. Through the courtesy of R. Worth Vaughan, vice-president and general counsel for Asarco, I was allowed to search these records at my pleasure. The crates contain whatever the companies thought worth saving when they closed business—and doubtless do not contain what they thought worth hiding.

Magnuson: the personal collection of pioneer lawyers' briefs and an index of early mining district newspapers compiled by Richard G. Magnuson of Wallace, Idaho. The newspapers themselves have been given to the University of Idaho.

NA: the National Archives of the United States.

Roberts: letterbooks of the late Edward J. Roberts in possession of the Roberts family.

Sweeny: a small packet of deeds, memorandums, and miscellaneous records in the safe and basement storeroom of the Sweeny Investment Company, Spokane, to which the author was given unrestricted access through the courtesy of Charles C. Finucane.

UI: The University of Idaho archives. In addition to Magnuson's newspaper files and a superb collection of photographs of the Coeur d'Alenes in the Barnard-Stockbridge collection, the archives contain the Weldon B. Heyburn papers, 1893–1910, consisting of three letterbooks, letter files of unbound incoming correspondence, a scrapbook of newspaper clippings, printed briefs from various cases, and a political pamphlet. The Heyburn papers are chiefly useful to a scholar with a detailed knowledge of the region and times, and do not provide a continuous story in themselves.

Although I do not abbreviate an identification of the Washington Water Power Company, Spokane, I extracted a good deal of material from the records, letterbooks, reports, contracts, and other documents that are held by the company and remain to be processed. Most of the miscellaneous records and letterbooks lay, until 1960, in boxes stacked in unused powerhouse vaults, and were opened on a selective basis by Kimball I. Jack for his inquiry into the company's history.

Oral history has been shown in individual footnotes. Roberts told me a great deal about Charles Sweeny, and later inquiry confirmed Roberts' recollections. Roberts' version is generally accepted as accurate when there is a conflict in sources or a lack of information from another source. Interviews with Roberts cover approximately thirty pages of handwritten notes. Roberts' notebooks, maps, and miscellaneous records, in the manuscript collection of the Eastern Washington State Historical Society, Spokane, provide valuable background information although they are not cited here.

The late Walter L. Nichols was briefly Sweeny's protégé when Nichols was a young man entering the stock brokerage business. During their travels together, Sweeny recalled for Nichols many stories of his career in mining, including his relationships with the Rockefellers. Interviews with Nichols fill seven typewritten pages.

Annotation presented the same general problem encountered in the text: that of simplifying Sweeny's story without sacrificing accuracy. The compromise reached, in most cases, was to simplify the text and allow complexities in the footnotes.

## I. SOLDIER, MINER, MERCHANT CHIEF

1. Sweeny's military career was taken from the McNulty-Sweeny service record, including his Volunteer Enlistment, in Records Group 49, NA, and from statements on file with the Bureau of Pensions, Department of the Interior, Certificate No. 838380, which includes extracts from his service record, his certificate of marriage, and a copy of the Family Record from the John Sweeny family Bible. Sweeny's service record was checked against the actions of the Third New Jersey recorded in *War of the Rebellion* (Washington, D.C., 1891), Series I, volumes XXXIII, XXXVI, XL, LIII, and XLVI, which reproduce dispatches of officers involved in the engagements. Direct quotations from dispatches are from this source. The general activities of Sweeny's early years are based on a newspaper biography by Conner Malott which was purported to originate in personal interviews with Sweeny over a period of years. Entitled "From Grocer's Clerk to Millionaire Mining Man, Charles Sweeny's Career Reads like a Fable," this appeared in the *Spokesman-Review* (Spokane), July 23, 1916, and has been checked against city directories, Sweeny's sworn testimony in trials, and other sources wherever practical. The parts of this chapter dealing with Sweeny's buying and selling of mining claims came from careful reading of the indexes to deeds in Shoshone County, Idaho, and each deed with Sweeny's name attached to it.

2. Sweeny's Mexican adventure from Malott, "From Grocer's Clerk to Millionaire." A search of the *San Francisco Daily Morning Call, Daily Alta California,* and *San Francisco Evening Bulletin* for May–June, 1866, which printed dispatches from the Mexican war, did not disclose any mention of this American Legion. A letter in the *Bulletin,* May 11, 1866, speaks of the U.S. warship *Saranac* lying in Acapulco Bay with marines formed on deck. B. S. Obson, comp., *Handbook of the U.S. Navy, 1861–64* (New York, 1864), describes the *Saranac* as a 1,446-ton side-wheeler with thirteen guns, and confirms that the vessel was attached to the Pacific squadon as early as 1861. Because it would be hard to concoct this kind of detail, the presence of the *Saranac* at Acapulco seems to the author to substantiate Sweeny's story.

3. Sweeny's residences came from San Francisco city directories, and the facts of his father's family from the family Bible. His marriage to Maggie Swords is reported in both his pension certificate (NA) and his marriage certificate attached to it. A perusal of the marriages and deaths listed in the *San Francisco Daily Examiner* for 1870–72 failed to turn up a mention of Maggie. There are two Swords families in the San Francisco directories as early as 1868. Newspapers and directories were used because the city's records were destroyed in the fire and earthquake of 1906.

4. From "Pen and Scissors," *Territorial Enterprise* (Virginia City, Nev.), July 17, 1873.

5. Sweeny's relationship with Mackay based on Malott, "From Grocer's Clerk to Millionaire." His Grass Valley work is mentioned in his testimony in the case of the Tyler v. Sweeny, Ninth Circuit Court of Appeals, October, 1892 (Asarco). Sweeny's recollections of his career, reflected in testimony over a period of years, tend to vary with regard to places and dates. The author has chosen what seem the most likely of conflicting statements. A search of the *Territorial Enterprise* reveals no report of an offer of one thousand dollars for timbering the Consolidated Virginia. Neither is Sweeny mentioned in reputable histories of the Comstock. Development of timbering in Comstock mines is generally credited to Philip Deidesheimer who, on the evidence of letters in the Hauser papers held by the Montana State Historical Society, appears to have worked in Montana before going to California.

6. Reports of the fire appear in the *Territorial Enterprise*, October 31, 1874, and in William Wright [Dan DeQuille], *History of the Big Bonanza*, p. 191.

7. Sweeny described himself to Malott as an officer in the California militia, but he is not listed among the captains or organizers in *San Francisco Daily Examiner* stories of July 26, 27, and 31, 1877, which deal in detail with several hundred "veterans of the late war" who organized as a Veterans Guard and, in armed squads of ten to twenty-five men, were posted in the city. Various citizen companies also formed, but Sweeny is not mentioned in newspaper stories about their leaders. The San Francisco newspapers did not reveal Sweeny's role in the sandlot riots, or trace him from the Belcher fire to Portland. Possibly during this interim he went to Grass Valley. H. H. Bancroft, *California, 1860 1890*, pp. 688 89, mentions a depression in San Francisco resulting from the riots, drought, silver mine reversals, and slowed immigration, which may have prompted Sweeny, like others, to move northward.

8. For various early accounts of the exchange organization, see the *Oregonian*, November 24, December 8, 10, and 18, 1879. Articles of incorporation of the Merchants' Exchange Association of Portland, dated December 6, 1879, are file 241-A, Multnomah County, Ore. Items dealing with the history of the Exchange appeared in the *Oregonian* for December 8, 1929, and September 19, 1951. Details on various aspects of Portland commerce are from the *Oregonian*, August 15, 1878, which records shipments of wheat to the United Kingdom during 1873–77 and mentions competition with San Francisco, and Liverpool complaints. The *Oregonian*, November 19, 1880, reports that the total amount of Oregon and Washington wheat shipped from Portland in 1880 was 4,600,426 tons. A biography of R. B. Knapp, in [Lewis and Dryden,] *Oregonian Souvenier*, p. 97, in-

cludes a discussion of Knapp, Burrell and Company. Alfred L. Lomax, "Pioneer Woolen Mills in Oregon," *Oregon Historical Quarterly*, XXX (1929), 238–58, mentions Knapp, Burrell and Company's role in developing the wool industry, saying (p. 257) that the company "had connections in New York." Charles Henry Carey, *History of Oregon*, reports the first shipment of wool to the East (p. 796), and the first cargo of Oregon wheat to a foreign port (pp. 915–16). An obituary for Burrell appears in the *Oregonian*, April 13, 1885. To give some idea of the Exchange's facilities, it should be noted that John McCracken, with William Ladd, had been one of the organizers of the Oregon Telegraph Company in 1862, and became its superintendent in 1879. The firm had completed its line to California in March, 1864, to Seattle later the same year, to The Dalles in 1868, and to Boise, Idaho, in 1869. McCracken was also president of the Portland Board of Trade. Thus the Exchange had access to telegraph facilities and included Portland's influential merchants. Ladd was a pioneer banker, and Steel, his brother-in-law, cashier of the First National Bank of Portland.

9. The story of Sweeny's waterfront options was told to Malott, "From Grocer's Clerk to Millionaire." Sweeny told the same story to Walter L. Nichols, who related it to the author. No record that Sweeny owned waterfront property was found in the Multnomah County deed indexes. If Sweeny's story of putting eighteen thousand dollars into property is accurate, the amount represents approximately 36 percent of the Merchants' Exchange capital, and seems to be the best evidence to support Sweeny's assertion that he organized the Exchange and thus held a major share in it. The twenty acres, recorded in Multnomah County deeds, book 59, p. 317, lie approximately two and one-half miles from water.

Sweeny also told Malott that he organized the Hibernia Bank in Portland about 1879. No indication of this could be found in the articles of incorporation of various Hibernia banks or associations in Multnomah County records. Professor O. K. Burrell, an authority on early Oregon banking, wrote me on August 31, 1961, that he had found no record of Sweeny's participation in establishing a bank or similar enterprise in Portland.

10. J. Orin Oliphant, ed., "The Early History of Spokane, Washington, as Told by Contemporaries" (typescript from newspaper stories, Eastern Washington State College, 1927), pp. 215–20. In the same work (pp. 190–91) I. C. Libby recalls that "in the dead of the coldest night of that winter —1882–83—the Moore & Cutter store building caught fire. The water supply—then drawn on four wheels by two horses—was frozen solid, and there was nothing for it but to form a bucket line from the river."

11. The quotation was combined from two sources: one letter is quoted by Nelson W. Durham, *Spokane and the Inland Empire*, I, 383, and the

other by Robert Wayne Smith, "A History of Placer and Quartz Gold Mining in the Coeur d'Alene District" (Master's thesis, University of Idaho, 1932), p. 104. Durham doubts the authenticity of the letter he prints, but its spirit and language are typical of Prichard. Smith offers his letter as genuine. The adherents of the cult were called "Liberals," and their periodical, *The Truthseeker.*

12. *Spokane Falls Review,* November 10, 1883.

13. The papers of Waldo E. Rosebush in the Eastern Washington State Historical Society collection, Spokane, contain a letter from Garrett B. Hunt to George W. Fuller, July 17, 1917, describing the failure of the water company and its rescue by an association of businessmen. Other documents relating to the water company are in this file, including its articles of incorporation and order for equipment.

14. Sale to Sweeny with reference to original claim, Shoshone County, Idaho, deeds, book F, p. 365.

15. From the *Coeur d'Alene Nugget,* March 15, 1884. The *Nugget* apparently published at least nine issues, the first four printed on the presses of the *Spokane Falls Review.* It preceded the *Eagle* by a month. The *Eagle* began publication in April, 1884.

16. Shoshone County, Idaho, civil case 24, called to the author's attention by Richard G. Magnuson of Wallace, Idaho. The suit against Prichard is also discussed in Chapter VIII.

An unflattering contemporary impression of Sweeny appears in the diary of Warren Hussey, pioneer banker, for Saturday, June 28, 1884: "Sweeny's men object to our sawing their house off—down in evening to settle the dispute—obstinate, ugly set—but got away with them." The incident refers to Hussey's branch bank building at Eagle City. Hussey's papers, 1880–1905, are in the Bancroft Library, Berkeley, Calif., microfilm P-B214, and are quoted by permission of Mrs. William Howe, Spokane.

17. Sales to Loewenberg are recorded in Shoshone County deeds, book G, p. 202, and to O'Neil, book G, p. 212. Sales of the Spokane Falls and Eagle City stores also reported in *Spokane Falls Review,* September 13 and 15, 1884. Sweeny's frequent mining deals seem too numerous to cite individually; they were discovered by combing the indexes to deeds in the Shoshone County courthouse at Wallace, Idaho, where the deeds are on file. The O'Neils do not appear to have been prosperous. Apparently Jeremiah raised money by mortgaging four parcels of San Francisco property. A letter in the Heyburn papers (UI) from a San Francisco attorney, E. L. Campbell, to Heyburn, October 5, 1897, reports the land had been continuously mortgaged since 1861 with occasional new mortgages to satisfy the old.

18. *Wallace Free Press,* March 24, 1888 (UI), and *Spokane Falls Re-*

*view*, April 16, 1884. This seems to have been a change of ownership that was not recorded in deed books. Such transactions often varied from formal to informal depending on the faith one party had in the other.

## II. "AT THE MERCY OF F. LEWIS CLARK"

1. The staking of the Last Chance and nearby claims is described by Divine, 108 Fed. 189, and by Carlin in the brief, Tyler v. Last Chance, Ninth Circuit Court of Appeals, 1893 (Asarco).

The Emma probably was named for the famed Emma silver mine discovered in 1865 south of Salt Lake City, and subsequently sold to London buyers due to President U. S. Grant's personal interest in it. A general description of the Wardner mines can be found in William S. Shiach et al., *An Illustrated History of North Idaho*, pp. 1034–38, and geological theories of the time in Joseph B. Umpleby and E. L. Jones, Jr., "Geology and Ore Deposits of Shoshone County, Idaho," Bulletin 732, U.S. Geological Survey, 1923. Many of the lawsuits involved conflicting notions of the district's geology, so that decisions were made on the evidence of an engineer or geologist whose theories would later be proved erroneous. There is no single source that provides a background for the events described in this chapter; the information was derived from raw files.

2. Moore's various reorganizations have been simplified here because Moore's method of operation is relevant while many details are tedious. Perhaps a single example will indicate what is involved in tracing his activities: The recorded changes in control of the Emma and Last Chance appear in Shoshone County deeds, books X, p. 29, and V, p. 292, and in the *Wallace Free Press*, July 2, 1887 (which is, by the way, No. 1 of Vol. I). Changes in the name or holdings come from articles of incorporation, Spokane County, miscellaneous book B, p. 291, and Shoshone County deeds, book O, pp. 429, 431, and 568, and Q, p. 209. To identify Stout and Mason, newspaper articles of the period were consulted. In tracing frequent changes of corporate structure, it is not unusual to read the name of a company (or find its letterhead) which cannot be discovered in official records—the Emma and Last Chance Consolidated, for example, which appears in newspaper discussions that seem accurate, but does not seem to have been incorporated in Washington, Idaho, or Oregon. Moreover, newspapers occasionally guessed at names or initials. Moore appears as Frank R. Monroe in the *Wallace Free Press* cited, and R. K. Neill as W. Richard O'Neil. To complicate inquiry even further, James C. Hoban, who has a wide acquaintance with the district, says (personal communication) that his inquiry indicates that agreements involving more than five hundred dollars were often recorded as transactions of one dollar.

3. Sale recorded in Shoshone County deeds, book R, p. 370. One of the

striking factors in mining corporations' operations is the frequency with which one company sells property or rights to another company made up of the same men.

4. The description is of Wardner in 1892, written by Flora Cloman, *I'd Live It Over*, p. 60. Mrs. Cloman was the widow of Victor Clement, manager of the Bunker Hill and Sullivan.

5. *Wallace Press*, January 3, 1891 (UI). This article illustrates another difficulty of reconstructing mining history. The newspapers got their information from mine managers, who were willing to plant stories for their own purposes. The prospect of the Last Chance is more carefully reported in a letter from F. R. Culbertson to the comptroller, May 16, 1897 (NA), which describes the mine's ore as occurring in pockets that play out abruptly.

6. Detailed in a letter from Burns and Chapman to F. L. Clark, January 6, 1896 (NA).

7. *Wallace Press*, July 4, 1891 (UI). The figure for lead content is quoted correctly from the newspaper article but readers familiar with ores will be quick to note that galena contains a maximum of 86.6 percent lead. That the Last Chance production was less than this glowing report says, is evident from a letter from F. L. Clark to the comptroller, February, 1897 (NA), reporting poor output.

8. Tyler v. Sweeny, 54 Fed. 284. The Idaho Mining Company articles of incorporation appear in Spokane County, book A, p. 243, and some details of the dispute in the *Spokane Review*, April 1, 1891. Further details can be elicited from Shoshone County deeds and agreements, book A, p. 170, showing that Sweeny, Fuller, and Linden paid five hundred dollars down on the Tyler (but did not take up their bond). Other elements appear in Sweeny's testimony before the Ninth Circuit Court of Appeals, Tyler v. Sweeny, October, 1892 (Asarco), and 39 Law Ed. 859. For a summary of the Tyler and Last Chance contests from 1891 to 1898, see 90 Fed. 15. See also discussion in Chapter VIII.

9. The amount spent on the Last Chance is based on Sweeny's testimony before the circuit court in 1892 (see note 8 above). Bear in mind that Sweeny may have given this figure for its significance to the court and that few men could dispute its accuracy. Record-keeping was both secret and haphazard, so that the common means of disputing an estimate of value or cost was to find another expert with a different opinion.

10. 61 Fed. 557.

11. The First National opened its doors on December 5, 1882, as the second bank in Spokane Falls, and built a six-story brick and granite building in 1890 at one corner of Howard and Riverside. All during the first six months of 1893 there had been heavy withdrawals, diminishing the deposits from approximately $603,000 in December, 1892, to $263,000 on

the day of failure. When the bank closed at two o'clock on the afternoon of July 26, 1893, its president, James N. Glover, explained that continual withdrawals for fifty days, and the bank's inability to realize on securities on short notice, were the proximate reasons for suspending. When the government of the City of Spokane proposed to withdraw its $34,000, hope ended for the First National.

The bank could not liquidate its assets because "about $200,000 was loaned to practically one person," F. L. Clark wrote the comptroller on December 29, 1893 (NA). Although the loans seemed within statutory limits, "upon the books this loan appears to be made to a number of different persons but the real security in the matter was F. R. Moore and the Last Chance Mine," Clark continued. The National Bank Act of 1864 permitted any five or more persons to form a national banking association with routine formalities if they provided a capital of not less than $50,000 (in cities of fewer than six thousand population). Under the act, banks were not authorized to lend on the security of real estate or to lend amounts greater than 10 percent of capital stock to an individual borrower. These statutes applied to the First National.

12. Judge C. H. Hanford, Eastern Washington District Court Journal No. 1, pp. 318–25 (April 3, 1895), in the federal clerk's files, Federal Building, Spokane.

13. These debts are listed in part in Moore's will, Spokane County probate 1032, in the court journal mentioned in note 12 above, and in a letter from F. L. Clark to the comptroller, September 26, 1895 (NA).

14. James Parkes to A. D. Benjamin, January 8, 1898 (NA).

15. On December 17, 1892, Sweeny paid James Bell thirteen thousand dollars for Havermale Island property encumbered by an eight-thousand-dollar mortgage, which Sweeny assumed. See Spokane County deeds, book 50, p. 577.

16. From April 13 to the end of May, 1894, the *Spokesman-Review* printed items nearly every day on the Coxey movement which provided general information for this discussion. Sweeny is mentioned in the newspaper on May 18 and 20, 1894.

17. Pinkham to Attorney General, February 23, 1895. This and other letters relating to Sweeny's service as a deputy marshal are from the Accounts for Protecting Property in the Hands of United States Courts, Department of Justice file 4017–1894, Record Group 60 (NA). These files also contain explanations of Pinkham's property accounts, a roster of deputies employed and amounts paid them, interdepartmental memorandums, telegrams, and other letters.

18. Beatty to Attorney General, February 22, 1895 (NA).

19. Pinkham to Attorney General, February 23, 1895 (NA).

20. F. L. Clark to Comptroller, October 6, 1894 (NA).

21. 15 Sup. Ct. 733. Aspects of the case appear in 79 Fed. 277, and reports in the *Spokesman-Review,* April 16, 1895, and October 8, 1897.

22. Outlined in a letter from F. L. Clark to Comptroller, September 26, 1895 (NA).

23. Heyburn's plea, Last Chance v. Bunker Hill & Sullivan, Ninth Circuit Court of Appeals, 1892 (Asarco). Details of the Shoshone Company's formation and the reasons for it appear in a letter from F. L. Clark to the comptroller, September 26, 1895 (NA). The Shoshone overlapped the Ibex, also an underground location, as well as the Wardner and the Kirby. The Ibex was bounded by the Stemwinder on the east, the Last Chance on the north, and the Shoshone on the west. The ground was strategically important, therefore, in this and later suits, which are investigated in some detail in Chapter VIII.

24. 87 Fed. 801. See *Spokesman-Review,* June 1, 1897. Apparently Rutter and Bradley discovered the Kirby's strategic value belatedly. A letter from William L. Spalding to Clayton Miller, April 9, 1897, in the Heyburn papers (UI) describes Spalding's attempt to buy the Kirby, indicating the transfer was not made simply because Spalding could not find one of the owners to sign a sale contract. Incidentally, Heyburn's papers show that he also represented the Bunker Hill on occasion during this period although not in their suits against Sweeny.

25. Agreement, November 23, 1895, document No. 283 in file of First National Bank (Insolvent) (NA).

26. F. L. Clark to Comptroller, December 14, 1895 (NA).

27. F. L. Clark to Comptroller, January 13, 1896 (NA).

28. The supplemental agreement, December 13, 1895, and letter, F. L. Clark to Stephens, January 11, 1896, are with the bank records (NA). The *Spokesman-Review,* February 17, 1896, lists the company officers after Moore's death. Obituaries for Moore, *Spokesman-Review,* November 22, 1895, and Sarah F. Moore, *Spokesman-Review,* October 20, 1941.


## III. AFFAIRS OF A MOST PECULIAR NATURE

1. Sweeny to O'Connor, November 27, 1895 (NA). This chapter, like the preceding one, has been drawn from raw files.

2. The quotations and statements about the mine were taken from letters, Clark to Comptroller, June 29, 1896 (NA), Culbertson to Comptroller, May 16, 1897 (NA), and Miller's report of operations for July and August, 1896, among Last Chance Mining Company records (Asarco). Among the Heyburn papers (UI) is a letter from Clark to State Senator S. P. Donnelly, January 27, 1897, quoted below in full:

"I would respectfully call your attention to the fact that the Last Chance mine paid taxes for the last four years as follows:

| For 1893 | $793.18 |
|---|---|
| 1894 | 793.66 |
| 1895 | 680.63 |
| 1896 | 831.67 |

"I am Treasurer of the Last Chance Mining Company having come into that position as representative of the creditors of the Company. The inability of the Last Chance Mining Company to pay its debts has already caused the failure of three banks, the First National Bank and the Spokane Savings Bank of Spokane, Washington, and the banking house of J. A. Prickett & Son, Edwardsville, Indiana [sic]. The property has been operated in the hope that there might be some slight recovery in the price of lead which would enable it to make a profit. During the past year it has made no profit and if any tax is levied or if anything is done to increase its operating expense or diminish the net value of its ore it will very likely close the property entirely. The Company at present gives employment to one hundred men directly and a good many more indirectly, and helps to support through this employment the town of Wardner from the property in which the State of Idaho derives considerable income.

"The lead properties of Wardner are of such low grade that I earnestly hope no steps will be taken to make it more difficult to continue operations in that locality."

In evaluating correspondence by Clark purporting to convey conditions in various mines, it must be remembered that Clark's information generally came from others. In 1900 when he and Sweeny ended their business partnership, Clark was to confess that he had never visited some of their mines.

3. Clark to O'Connor, December 29, 1896 (NA).

4. Culbertson to Comptroller, May 16, 1897 (NA).

5. Clark to Comptroller, December 14, 1895 (NA).

6. See Prickett v. Clark and Sweeny, Spokane County civil case 19061. The suit was in court until June, 1909, when Sweeny's demand that the Pricketts produce certain records went unanswered and resulted in dismissal. Arthur J. Shaw, the third receiver for the First National Bank of Spokane, made his complaint in a letter to the comptroller, August 6, 1903 (NA), to which he attached some of Sweeny's personal letters to O'Connor. These letters had been given Shaw for the purpose of bringing a charge of fraud against Clark and Sweeny. Note 14, Chapter VII, suggests that Clark and Sweeny used mining stock as collateral for loans to their partnership. A letter from Clark to Heyburn, July 16, 1897, in the Heyburn papers (UI) asks Heyburn to "draw an instrument for our execution pledging to the Exchange National Bank for monies advanced or to be advanced to the [Last Chance] company the claims against the Tyler company and

bondsmen in accordance with the directors' resolutions which you dictated recently." This indicates that funds for continued operation of the mine were obtained from the Exchange National Bank in Spokane after the failure of the First National. Clark and Sweeny were to purchase a substantial interest in the Exchange two years later. See Chapter 11.

7. A letter in the Heyburn papers (UI) from Clark to Heyburn, February 6, 1897, asks Heyburn to ascertain whether "the law in British Columbia would allow us to make an underground location" to follow a vein that appeared to dip from the Red Mountain into the adjoining Cliff claim. Obviously the location of the Shoshone as an underground claim in the Coeur d'Alenes had led Clark to hope that a similar underground exploration could be successful in British Columbia. Heyburn's reply is not among his papers but subsequent events indicate that no attempt was made to extend beyond the Red Mountain's legitimate boundaries.

For information about the Rossland Red Mountain, see the *Report of the Minister of Mines, 1896* (Victoria, B.C.), p. 560. Sweeny received his patent for this claim, Lot 1000, G, Trail Creek district, on September 28, 1896, and a report of the company organization appears in the *Spokesman-Review*, July 4, 1896. The incorporators included Sweeny; Clark; Willis E. Goodspeed, their bookkeeper; Jacob Hoover, president of the Exchange National Bank of Spokane; Maurice McMicken, a Seattle attorney and banker who represented O'Connor there; and J. Couch Flanders and Charles E. Benn of Portland, Ore. The company was capitalized for one million dollars. Sweeny's offer of stock to O'Connor to act as eastern sales representative is in his letter of June 16, 1896 (NA). O'Connor's New York activities are described in his obituary in the *Elmira Star-Gazette*, November 29, 1913. For a discussion of Rossland promotions, see Harold A. Innis, *Settlement and the Mining Frontier*, p. 291.

8. John Spencer Church, "Mining Companies in the West Kootenay and Boundary Regions of British Columbia, 1890–1900: Capital Formation and Financial Operations" (Master's thesis, University of British Columbia, 1961), lists the Silverene (also spelled "Silverine" in some records) Gold Mining Company as organized October 30, 1895, registered under the British Columbia Companies Act, 1897 (p. 292); re-registered January 3, 1898, with no further information submitted (p. 383). Shares were sold in December, 1896, at eleven cents, the following September at four cents, and from November, 1898, to July, 1905, at six cents (p. 486). See also the *Rossland Miner*, July 8, 1897. Sales of stock are detailed in Sweeny's letters to O'Connor, December 2, 1896, and February 24, 1897 (NA).

9. Indenture, Last Chance Mining Company to Spokane and Eastern, January 2, 1896 (NA), and letter, A. D. Lynch to Comptroller, December 2, 1896 (NA).

10. Clark's receipts, November 7, 1895 (NA) ; letter, Clark to Sarah F. Moore, January 14, 1897, in Spokane County probate 1032.

11. Clark to Comptroller, January 13, 1896 (NA).

12. Braden to Comptroller, February 2, 1897 (NA). The report of a second investigation by L. R. Fry, supporting Braden's conclusions, was attached by Braden to his own.

13. Culbertson's selection is described in a 19-page letter from Frank T. Post to the comptroller, February 22, 1906 (NA) ; Culbertson's report with its supplementary report and Anderson's letter, May 16, 1897 (NA). Post's letter is designed to explain why he cannot represent the comptroller in a possible suit against Clark and Sweeny, and reviews the events from the failure of the bank until Clark and Sweeny acquired the Last Chance. Generally, Post represents Clark and Sweeny as having acted in the best interests of the bank's creditors and the mining company.

14. Sweeny to O'Connor, August 6, 1896 (NA). A second letter, Sweeny to O'Connor, November 1, 1896 (NA), is the basis of the next paragraph in the text. For O'Connor's version of his relationships with Sweeny, see Chemung County, New York, Court Records, XXV, 144.

15. Articles of incorporation, Spokane County, book E, p. 220. The articles were not filed until September 28, 1897, after O'Connor had broken off his relationship with Clark and Sweeny. Hanley apparently was brought into the company with some reluctance because he was involved in a dispute with O'Connor over money, according to a letter from Clark to Heyburn, March 30, 1897, in the Heyburn papers (UI), which says in part, "We desire to have Mr. O'Connor vest title in the Carriboo [sic] but we do not want to ask him to do anything that will injure his position towards Hanley as he feels that Hanley owes him money while Hanley takes the position that O'Connor owes him money. O'Connor is afraid that if he should deed away his interest that would stop him from denying that he had accepted the property and therefore owed Hanley." Hanley entered the Chemung, consequently, contending with one of its directors and before long was fighting Sweeny and Clark, as well, as will be discussed in the text.

16. A letter, Clark to O'Connor, March 6, 1897, shows that O'Connor held 48,333 shares and Father O'Dwyer, 26,667. This letter is contained in Prickett v. Clark and Sweeny, Spokane County civil case 19061.

17. Articles of incorporation, Spokane County, book D, p. 524. Sweeny's offer is advanced and expanded in letters to O'Connor dated March 30 and April 8, 1897 (NA). According to a memorandum in the Sweeny papers dated June 1, 1899, Clark held 331,799 shares and Sweeny 331,797, of 1,000,000. The *Report of the Minister of Mines, 1899* (British Columbia), pp. 688 and 843, says the company shipped 106 tons of ore in 1899 and added to its properties the Dump Fraction and Silver Bell No. 2 claims. The Sweeny papers also contain an ore receipt from the Puget

Sound Reduction Company at Everett, Wash., dated November 11, 1899, reporting the value of one carload of ore.

Clark and Sweeny also organized a fourth Canadian company, the Caledonia Consolidated Mining and Smelting Company, which apparently was not operated. Neither mentions it in letters available to me. It is named among their holdings in a letter from Clark to Heyburn, June 13, 1898, in the Heyburn papers (UI), inquiring about licensing the partners' Canadian companies.

18. Sweeny acted on Heyburn's advice in paying interest on the bonds. Clark asks Heyburn in a letter, April 13, 1897, in the Heyburn papers (UI), whether paying the interest will affect his petition to the comptroller for permission to sell the Last Chance. Clark's last sentence in this letter reads, "Is there any way in which I would be authorized and the Last Chance Company able to pay its interest with bonds so long as it has any, either directly or in a round-about way?" Heyburn apparently recommended that an individual, rather than the Company itself, appear to pay the interest.

19. Sweeny to O'Connor, April 8, 1897 (NA).

20. Sweeny's receipt of, and refusal to return, his stock is reported in a letter, Lynch to Comptroller, May 18, 1897 (NA), and in Post to Comptroller, February 22, 1906 (NA), mentioned in note 13 above.

21. Clark to Comptroller, April 19, 1897 (NA). Later events, including a direct offer by a second receiver to sell the Last Chance to Bradley, suggest that the Bunker Hill had no intention of buying but did what it could to embarrass Sweeny. Post tells about Bradley's attitude toward a possible purchase.

22. The dispute was reported in the *Spokesman-Review*, July 20, 21, and 23, 1897. Among the newspaper items are creditors' accusations that the pool was broken and that Clark was not truthful, and Happy's explanation of his sale.

23. Lynch to Comptroller, May 18, 1897 (NA). Lynch is careful not to join in the accusations against Clark and Sweeny but mentions these charges in various letters to the comptroller, now among the records of the First National Bank of Spokane (Insolvent) (NA).

24. Lynch to Comptroller, February 20, 1906 (NA). Lynch writes his impressions and his actions in detail, including his formation of the creditors' committee to determine the best course for the trust. Post also gives detail of the committee's deliberations.

25. Sweeny to O'Connor, April 24, 1897 (NA).

26. In addition to letters previously cited (Lynch to Comptroller, February 20, 1906, and Post to Comptroller, February 22, 1906) the order for sale of the mine, dated September 24, 1897, is among the exhibits in Shaw v. Clark and Sweeny, Spokane County civil case 10516. Judge Prather's

court journals are in a tower storeroom in the Spokane County courthouse.

27. Agreement, November 6, 1897, between Clark, as one party, and Lynch and Grinnell, as the other party (Asarco). Spokane County civil case 10516 contains as exhibits copies of two court orders, dated January 19, 1898, and November 14, 1898, authorizing the sale. Another exhibit is Shaw's petition for the sale, November 14, 1898. (Shaw was appointed receiver of the bank on September 13, 1898.) The contract for sale, dated July 14, 1898, is also in this case file, as is Clark's request for a discount and its approval, November 15, 1898.

28. The assets of the First National and Spokane Savings banks were offered for sale on November 22, 1899, by Receiver Shaw. These assets were mainly small notes, judgments, and real estate. During his receivership, Clark had settled some claims by authority of the district court (see Eastern Washington district court journal No. 1, pp. 318–25, dated April 3, 1895, in clerk's file, Federal Building, Spokane). The First National creditors received forty-four cents on the dollar, according to a letter, Shaw to Comptroller, August 6, 1903 (NA). The Last Chance mortgage was foreclosed in 1902 by the Empire State–Idaho, a Sweeny company.

29. Clark's and Sweeny's arrangements with O'Connor, their demands for money, the formation of two short-lived companies, and O'Connor's reasons for breaking with Clark and Sweeny are detailed in the complaint of O'Connor v. F. L. Clark and one, Equity 235½ C.C., U.S. District Court, Western District of New York, Buffalo. Exhibit A in this case is the contract for O'Connor and Company. These records were obtained through the courtesy of Dorothy E. Moulton, clerk of the district court, Eastern District of Washington. In view of the various arguments about the value of the Last Chance Mine, the reader may be interested in a summarized Statement of Profit and Loss by Companies Acquired by Federal Mining and Smelting Company (Asarco). Under an entry, "Net profit of Last Chance Mine" appears the statement, "Ledger entries from January 1–May 31, 1898, show an apparent loss of $8,817." A table for the Last Chance, titled "Profit by years ending April 30," shows:

| | |
|---|---|
| 1903 | $354,062.76 |
| 1902 | 384,540.79 |
| 1901 | 438,921.74 |
| 1900 | 436,546.66 |
| 1899 | 270,585.73 |

30. This contract, outlined in a memo agreement dated November 2, 1897, and two other agreements, both dated November 30, 1897, are among the First National Bank records (NA).

31. Parkes to Benjamin, January 8, 1898 (NA). Compare Parkes's assessment with a letter in the Heyburn papers (UI) from Clark to the

Spokane County Assessor, April 8, 1899, which says in part: "On the first of March, 1898, Messrs. Clark and Sweeny had on deposit the sum of $3324.29, but they owed the [First National] Bank more than this amount."

32. Circumstances of the company's formation were drawn from a letter, Clark to Benjamin, May 26, 1898 (NA); the Bill of Complaint, Hanley v. Sweeny, Clark, et al., Idaho district court, November 20, 1901 (Asarco); and the certificate of incorporation, May 9, 1898, New York State, book 41, p. 760, filed at Albany. The Heyburn papers (UI) contain several letters from Clark and Sweeny written between January and August, 1899, pointing out that the Empire State–Idaho had no central office and asking Heyburn which of the states offered the most attractive corporate and tax laws. For further discussion of the Hanley affair, see pp. 153–57.

33. Early financing and operations of the Empire State–Idaho were educed from the company's minute books (Asarco); its holdings from Shoshone County, leases, book B, p. 149; and reports from Clark to Benjamin, May 28, 1898, Clendening to Benjamin, April 26, 1898, and May 16, 1898, and Sweeny and Presley to Benjamin, May 25, 1898 (NA). A prospectus for the Empire State–Idaho Mining and Developing Company, Stokes Building, 45 Cedar Street, New York City, circa 1898, is among the company's records (Asarco).

34. Committee report to Empire State–Idaho directors, September 2, 1898 (Asarco).

35. Clark to Benjamin, September 9, 1898 (NA).

36. Benjamin to Clark and Sweeny, October 17, 1898 (NA). The stock increase is recorded in the minutes of the Empire State–Idaho, September 2, 1898 (Asarco); a certificate of increase, filed with New York State on September 3, 1898, is among the incorporation records (see note 32 above).

37. Based on Sweeny's deposition, Philip Foster v. Sweeny, Spokane County civil case 15242. According to the Spokane and Eastern Trust Company's financial committee log book (Washington State University archives) entry of February 10, 1899, Clark and Sweeny also sold Empire State–Idaho stock worth fifty thousand dollars to an unnamed banker in Montreal. Parkes, incidentally, became Clark and Sweeny's office manager briefly, according to a letter, Clark to Heyburn, October 21, 1899, in the Heyburn papers (UI). Parkes's own office was No. 1, Wolverton Block, Spokane.

38. Packard's report to stockholders, May 10, 1899 (Asarco). It does not agree with the profit statement cited in Note 29 above.

39. Empire State–Idaho minutes, May 3, 1900 (Asarco). Clark's letter to the company, August 26, 1898 (Asarco), assigns his title to the Last Chance Mining Company stock and lists the claims held by the Last Chance

and Shoshone companies. (As a minor point of interest, Clark's cherry-wood rolltop desk, polished and well maintained, stood in the office of managing editors of the *Spokesman-Review* for some years. When it was replaced by newer furniture in 1958, the old Clark desk still had two cardboard labels on pigeonholes in Clark's handwriting, one reading, "Last Chance Mine.")

40. Sweeny's proposed contract with the Omaha & Grant was described in his deposition of December 12, 1913, in Sidney Norman et al., v. Federal Mining & Smelting (Asarco). The production limits from American Mining & Smelting were outlined in two letters from H. Lyne, secretary of the ore purchasing committee, A.S. & R. Co., to Clark and Sweeny, December 28, 1899, and January 12, 1900 (Asarco).

41. Empire State–Idaho minutes, January 14, 1901 (Asarco), and F. L. Clark's testimony, Patrick Clark v. Buffalo Hump Mining Co., Idaho district court, January 7, 1902 (Asarco). Clark and Sweeny used their prospect of buying the American Exchange holdings as security for a thirty-thousand-dollar loan from the Spokane and Eastern Trust Co., according to the Trust's log entry of January 14, 1898 (Washington State University archives).

42. In Asarco files.


## IV. DISSENT AND DYNAMITE

1. This date and those referring to other union organizing come from Thomas O'Brien's deposition in Idaho District Court civil case 7, Coeur d'Alene Mining and Concentrating Co. v. Wardner Miners' Union (now 7-N, Federal Records Center, Seattle). See also a statement by John W. Sweeny, president of the Wardner union, in the *Spokane Review*, March 31, 1892. The most useful general guides to the labor conflict will be found in William S. Shiach et al., *An Illustrated History of North Idaho*, and in two congressional documents: *Report of the Industrial Commission on the Relations of Capital and Labor Employed in the Mining Industry*, House Document 181, Fifty-seventh Congress, First Session (1901), and the *Report of the House Committee on Military Affairs*, House Report 1999, Fifty-sixth Congress, First session (1900).

Vernon H. Jensen, *Heritage of Conflict*, devotes his chapters 4 and 7 to the Coeur d'Alene events of 1892 and 1899, relying chiefly on congressional reports, union publications, and semifictional accounts.

The discussion in this chapter deviates from the story of Charles Sweeny. The treatment of the labor conflict seems necessary for an understanding of Sweeny's role, and of conditions in the district, 1903–10. The chapter is too short, nonetheless, for a broad investigation of the labor situation in the Coeur d'Alenes. Anyone who makes his own inquiry into the labor wars there will find that the bitterness of conflict has not been entirely dispelled with the passing of years.

2. Letters exchanged between Gompers and Edward Boyce, president of the Western Federation of Miners, who was in the Coeur d'Alenes in person, are quoted in Senate Document 42, Fifty-sixth Congress, First Session (Serial 3846), and in Philip S. Foner, *History of the Labor Movement in the United States*, II, 379–80, whose bias is obvious. Gompers' letters are also available in his letterbooks, 1883–1924, which comprise thirty-five letterpress volumes in the manuscript division of the Library of Congress. When Boyce wrote Gompers in 1897 that "no two men in the labor movement differ so widely" as he and Gompers, Gompers replied that the A.F. of L. was as impressed as Boyce with "the necessity of effective political action and proper use of the ballot by labor," but "as for your suggestion that the resort must be to the sword, I prefer not to discuss it" (letterbooks, XIX, 313.) An objective statement can be found in Philip Taft, *A.F. of L. in the Time of Gompers*, pp. 150–58, which traces the defection of the Western Federation of Miners from the A.F. of L. under Boyce's leadership. Throughout the mining war in the Coeur d'Alenes, the American Federation of Labor regarded its contribution as publicizing the unions' treatment by management. Lloyd G. Reynolds, *Labor Economics and Labor Relations* (New York: Prentice-Hall, 1949), pp. 253–56, follows evolving employer attitudes toward unionism in the United States, noting that until the 1930's public control of labor relations resided almost entirely in the courts, necessarily a conservative force. In this connection, the personal letters of Federal Judge James H. Beatty afford an interesting sidelight. Some can be found in Department of Justice file 6899/99, "Wardner Strikes" (NA). For example, Beatty wrote the attorney general on May 2, 1899, "The law-abiding people of Idaho greatly appreciate the President's prompt action [in sending troops] and his readiness to assist us in trying to bring to justice these most lawless men." Beatty had enjoined union men from interfering with operations of the mining companies.

3. These quotations are from a letter, Sweeny to O'Connor, April 20, 1896 (NA), and Rev. Charles Mackin, S.J., "Wanderings," II, 28, a manuscript in the Gonzaga University archives. Catholic and Protestant clergy alike had attacked the Knights of Labor for the secret elements of its organization. In 1881 the secret rituals were abandoned, but religious antipathy lingered. When craft unions began eroding the Knights' strength, the Knights' appeal as a national organization was weakened despite the miners' preference for the direct action in labor-management relations that the Knights advocated.

4. For the unions' attitude on the drills, see May A. Hutton, *Coeur d'Alenes*, p. 57, and Job Harriman, *Class War in Idaho*, p. 4. Electrification

of the mining district is treated more fully in Chapter 6 of this book. The widow-maker drilled upward, showering dust on its operator.

5. This is the version presented by Robert Wayne Smith, "Idaho Antecedents of the Western Federation of Miners, 1890 to 1893" (Ph.D. dissertation, University of California, 1937), pp. 50–54. See also the *Spokane Review*, August 12, 1891.

6. The point that costs of closing are higher than profitless operation is made at some length by Fred Burbidge, acting manager of the Bunker Hill and Sullivan, in his statement reproduced in House Document 181 (see note 1 above), p. 441.

7. See *Spokesman-Review*, November 25, 1894. The Bunker Hill and Sullivan policies are stated under oath in House Document 181.

8. See John Fahey, "Coeur d'Alene Confederacy," *Idaho Yesterdays*, XII, No. 1 (1968), 2–7, tracing the development of the association. Clement's letter to S. G. Reed, dated November 23, 1889, is in the Reed collection at Reed College, and was called to my attention by Dr. Merle Wells, archivist, Idaho Historical Society. Formation of the Mine Owners Association was announced in the *Wallace Press*, February 21, 1891 (UI), and recorded in Shiach et al., *Illustrated History of North Idaho*, p. 1000. Roberts' report to the Empire State–Idaho directors, April 30, 1904, is among the Asarco papers. Discussions of the MOA also appear in legal reports: McCarthy v. Bunker Hill and Sullivan, 147 Fed. 981 and 984; 164 Fed. 927; and in Curtis H. Lindley, *Treatise on the American Law Relating to Mines and Mineral Lands*, III, 2080–81. After the labor wars, the MOA devoted its attention primarily to controlling land for waste disposal, and to defending itself against suits based on alleged water contamination. Usually the MOA spoke through one man; its views are expressed at various times by Charles Sweeny, John A. Finch, W. Clayton Miller, and Stanly Easton, among others. So far as I know, there was no minute book for the organization, but Thomas O'Brien (see note 1 above) listed original member companies or mines as Sierra Nevada, Custer, Stemwinder, Emma and Last Chance, Bunker Hill and Sullivan, Milwaukee Mining Co. (operators of the Gem), Helena and Frisco, Galena, Mammoth, Union Group, Tiger, Poorman, and Morning (while controlled by Warren Hussey). In a letter to Sweeny, November 30, 1900 (Asarco), Clayton Miller mentions levies of four and one-half mills per ton for the Tiger and three mills for the Empire State–Idaho imposed by the MOA. Other letters in Empire State–Idaho letterbooks (Asarco) mention MOA activities; when seven companies joined in a single smelting contract with American Smelting and Refining on September 1, 1902, the MOA negotiated its terms.

9. The Hunter and Sierra Nevada mines were exempted from closure because they shipped to smelters without concentrating their ores; conse-

quently they were not affected by changes in the rate on concentrates which was the owners' principal complaint. Some sources indicate that the closure date was January 15 rather than January 19, as given in the text.

10. Quoted in Shiach et al., *Illustrated History of North Idaho*, p. 1005.

11. Charles A. Siringo, *Cowboy Detective*, pp. 135–40; Flora Cloman, *I'd Live It Over*, p. 84. See also William T. Stoll, *Silver Strike*, pp. 194–96. All three accounts contain elements of fiction.

12. Margaret Dundon, Carnegie Public Library, Ishpeming, Mich., supplied quotations from *Iron Ore*. Copies of *Iron Ore* for July 25, 1891; May 14, 1892; and 1897–99 (less some missing issues) are also in the library of the Michigan College of Mining and Technology, Houghton, Mich. The warning published in *Iron Ore* appeared April 23, 1892. For a statement on the costs and conditions of transportation, see the deposition of John Drenig as typical, in Idaho District Court civil case 7 (see note 1 above.)

13. From Sweeny's deposition in Idaho District Court civil case 7. This account of Sweeny's service as director of the armed guards is from his deposition and others in the same file, checked with newspaper accounts of the time to verify dates and places. Sweeny's deposition includes his cost bill, dated May 31, 1895, which shows that he traveled one thousand miles at five cents a mile to attend the trial, was present five days at $1.50 a day, and received a total payment in witness and travel fees of $57.50.

14. In this connection, see Paul Frederick Brissenden, *I.W.W.: A Study of American Syndicalism*, p. 42. Brissenden points out that the support of management by state governments generally provided socialists with one convincing argument in favor of union political action. He writes, "The western miners were forced by the obvious connivance between the state and city governments and the mine operators, by the use of the militia for the suppression of strikes and by the abuse of the injunction, to consider the possibilities of political action along socialistic lines." Robert W. Smith, *Coeur d'Alene Mining War of 1892*, p. 50, calls Heyburn "the master technician of this campaign of pressure" to achieve and continue martial law in the district. The various reports of military men and congressional investigators do not indicate unusual influence on official activities by Heyburn. Neither do the Heyburn papers (UI), although Heyburn was doubtless among the principal spokesmen for the mine owners. The *Anaconda Standard*, May 11, 1892, estimated that a million dollars in wages were lost from January to June in the Coeur d'Alene district.

15. Warren's affidavit is in Idaho District Court civil case 7. A typical guard's affidavit is that of William Forsyth, on which this account is partly based. For a first-hand impression of Warren, see the article by Jay Kalez, "Lawman Joel Warren," in the *Spokesman-Review* magazine, November 14, 1965, p. 9. Warren became Seattle police chief in 1917.

16. Accounts of the number of scabs vary. Sweeny said, "I brought these

men from Helena myself and consequently I should know something about it. When the train left St. Paul it had seventy-eight miners on board. When I took charge of it in Helena there were seventy-four and all of them I delivered to the Union Mine. . . . The miners are receiving $3.50 and the laborers $3.00 a day and all are in possession of a written contract for one year's work at these wages" (quoted in *Spokane Review*, May 19, 1892). Many of the miners signed affidavits with their marks in Idaho District Court civil case 7, indicating that they could not read or write English.

17. Cloman, *I'd Live It Over*, p. 84.

18. *Spokane Review*, May 19, 1892. Sweeny's statement illustrates the usual management viewpoint during the period 1880–1930, a time when injunctions were granted not only to prevent possible property damage but to protect an employer's expectation of profit. In the following paragraphs of the text, counts of nonunion workmen have been taken from contemporary reports in the *Spokane Review, Coeur d'Alene Miner, Wallace Press,* and *Anaconda Standard.* The *Review,* in general, reflects the views of the Mine Owners Association, and the *Standard* reports, if not condones, those of the union.

19. Sweeny's deposition, Idaho District Court civil case 7.

20. *Spokane Review*, June 14, 1892. Adam Aulbach asserted that the MOA fined its members five thousand dollars for defection but offers no instance of the penalty being imposed.

21. George Edgar French, "Coeur d'Alene Riots of 1892," *Overland Monthly,* XXVI (1895), 39. Union sympathizers persist to this day in believing that the Negro troops were sent out of malice, but in fact these units were among the closest. They were stationed at Fort Missoula in 1892, and at Fort Wright, Spokane, in 1899. Clement himself delayed the arrival of white soldiers by his demand for trains to evacuate his nonunion employees.

22. See Pettibone et al. v. United States, 148 U.S. 197, and Fremont Wood, *Introductory Chapter to the History of the Trials of Moyer, Haywood, and Pettibone, and Harry Orchard,* pp. 6–7. Wood was U.S. District Attorney for Idaho in 1892. The A.F. of L. contributed five hundred dollars to the miners' legal defense, according to a letter from Gompers to Peter Breen, January 13, 1893, in Gompers letterbooks, VIII, 299.

23. Brissenden, *The I.W.W.,* pp. 40–43 and 104–5; Smith, "Idaho Antecedents of the Western Federation of Miners," pp. 236–38.

24. Activities of the unions against imported labor, and the various company policies, are detailed in Steunenberg's testimony, House Report 1999, pp. 17–24; and in Burbidge's testimony, based in part on the *Coeur d'Alene Miner,* in House Document 181, pp. 444–49. A fairly detailed account may also be found in Shiach et al., *Illustrated History of North Idaho,* p. 1009.

25. *Spokane Daily Chronicle,* August 10, 1895. The union spread the report that the Bunker Hill and Sullivan was controlled by the Standard Oil Company with the apparent intention of playing on public antipathy for trusts. There seems to be no evidence to support the accusation that Standard Oil controlled the Bunker Hill.

26. A series of tables of prices, among the records of the Federal Mining and Smelting Company (Asarco), shows that the prices of silver and lead continued to fall after 1893, and that lead reached its lowest average price in 1896 of $2.98 per one hundred pounds. Silver by 1896 had begun apparent recovery from its low point of $63 an ounce in 1894, but fell again in 1897 to $59.79, and in 1898 stood at $58.26.

27. Harriman, *Class War,* p. 12. It should be remembered, in this connection, that Charles Sweeny was both a Catholic and a member of the Mine Owners Association. The general bitterness is demonstrated by the fact that Butte, Montana, had a riot on July 4, 1894, when union men attacked two saloons displaying the APA orange colors. The fight climaxed with a gun battle during a wild thunderstorm.

28. See note 26 above. During this period, most of the mines in the Coeur d'Alenes relied on silver for profit, rather than lead.

29. The estimate of Sweeny's involvement in MOA activities is based upon letters between Clayton Miller and Sweeny in Empire State–Idaho letterbooks. That Sweeny was not entirely inactive in the association is evident, however, from letters written by John Finch to the Empire State–Idaho company. On November 22, 1901, Finch advised the company of an increased assessment of six mills on each dollar of gross sales to make up a shortage in association funds. In a second letter, December 4, 1901, he challenged Sweeny's billing of six hundred dollars to the association for travel expenses incurred in its behalf. Finch pointed out that the association had voluntarily observed a two-hundred-dollar limit per trip, and that his Standard company had been carrying the MOA financially for the past year (Asarco).

30. Estimate by A. B. Campbell, quoted in the *Spokesman-Review,* July 31, 1897.

31. House Document 181, p. 493.

32. See Burbidge, House Document 181, p. 439. In April, 1899, the Bunker Hill and Sullivan paid a twenty-one-thousand-dollar dividend, and Burbidge estimated its total dividends to that time at approximately six hundred thousand dollars.

33. For reports of the events leading immediately to April 29, 1899, see the *Spokesman-Review,* April 25, 28, and 29, 1899. Quotations in the text dealing with the events immediately surrounding April 29 are mainly from newspaper stories. Those after April 29 are from the *Spokesman-Review, Spokane Daily Chronicle,* House Document 181, and House Report 1999.

The reader who wishes a more detailed account should peruse contemporary newspapers day by day.

34. Anticipation of higher wages when a new compressor was installed at the Last Chance seems to have been one of the chief reasons that the union allowed its men to return to the Last Chance at this time.

35. House Document 181, pp. 564–65. James Sovereign, editor of the *Idaho State Tribune,* is quoted in House Report 1999, pp. 6–7, as writing of white identification bands, men experienced with dynamite, and the organized character of the movement, including a prearranged meeting with the Mullan contingent at Wallace. These statements by the editor of the union's newspaper indicate that the train ride was neither unplanned nor spontaneous.

36. Harry Orchard, a professional dynamiter who later killed Steunenberg, confessed his presence at the Bunker Hill explosion, and witnesses identified Edward Boyce among the mob's leaders. The *Spokane Daily Chronicle,* April 29, 1899, printed a detailed report of the dynamiting. As the mob's intent became apparent, the Oregon Railway and Navigation Company ordered its tracks cleared along the route to be followed by the captured train.

37. A report of Thiel Detective Service Company Operator 38 to the Mine Owners Association, August 22, 1907, now in files of the prosecuting attorney, Shoshone County.

38. Empire State–Idaho letterbooks, April 29, 1899 (Asarco). Strathy was general manager of the Traders Bank (now defunct) of Toronto from 1885 to 1907.

39. Wood, *Trials of Moyer, Haywood, Pettibone, and Orchard,* pp. 11–12.

40. Hutton, *Coeur d'Alenes,* p. 127, makes this accusation. Mrs. Hutton thinly disguises Sweeny in her book as a character called "Coxey Charlie," and asserts that he met the governor in Wallace on May 1 to ask if there was not sufficient reason to declare martial law. Coxey Charlie then went with the governor to Spokane, wined and dined him, and offered him fifty thousand dollars in campaign expenses to run for the Senate if he would declare martial law. Charlie was allowed virtually unlimited expenses by the MOA as fighting funds. In Mrs. Hutton's book, Charlie wired the MOA on May 3, "Everything is okay," and martial law was declared May 4. As a matter of fact, Governor Steunenberg was hospitalized in Boise during the period that Mrs. Hutton depicts him visiting the mining district. She later attempted to buy up the copies of her book to put it out of circulation— after she and her husband had become mine owners themselves.

41. House Document 181, pp. cv, 413–16. The commissioners were Populists. Sinclair replaced them with Silver Republicans and Democrats,

leading many citizens to conclude that he was motivated by political considerations.

42. Empire State–Idaho letterbooks (Asarco). Some telegrams were addressed to Emeline and some to Charles Sweeny. The difficulty of keeping men, once they reached the district, can be educed from a letter, W. H. North to Empire State–Idaho, June 29, 1899 (Asarco), listing twenty-two men supplied by O'Neil, of whom seventeen are recorded as "left" or "no work." North was manager for Sweeny at the time.

43. Empire State–Idaho letterbooks (Asarco) contain letters from Sweeny to Bennett, April 28, 1899, demanding quick delivery of the compressor; and from Rand Drill Co. to Clark and Sweeny, April 27, 1899, on the size of the new plant. A later letter cancels the Rand order. Bennett was one of the builders of the 50.6-mile Fairhaven and Southern Railway in western Washington, and later a contractor for the Post Falls dam of the Washington Water Power Co.

44. See Sinclair's statement, House Document 181, pp. 543–64.

45. *Engineering and Mining Journal*, February 25, 1904, p. 331, mentions the MOA employment bureau as "keeping the lawless element out of camp." The permit was judged at the time to be in violation of an Idaho state act of March 6, 1893, but the U.S. Supreme Court later declared this act invalid. Idaho's governor ordered the permit system discontinued January 11, 1901, according to Nelson W. Durham, *Spokane and the Inland Empire*, I, 506. Nevertheless, screening of applicants continued through an employment bureau until after the First World War. Copies of 1899 permits appear in House Document 181, p. 391.

46. Dr. France's report is in an expanding cardboard file marked "Labor" in Asarco files. House Document 181, in its minority report, estimates that 1,100 men were in the bullpen at various times. General Merriam, in Senate Document 24, Fifty-sixth Congress, First Session (Serial 3846), p. 13, estimates the total number of arrests at approximately 700 but says men were "instantly released on investigation," so that those held long enough for a statistical report numbered 528. He gives the following tabulation of national origins among the bullpen prisoners: Americans 132; Swedes 99; Italians 63; Finns 47; Irish 43; and other foreign 144. John A. Finch, quoted in House Document 181, pp. 489–94, says the MOA recruited workers in the California, Colorado, Lake Superior, and Missouri mines.

47. For a concise summary, see *Engineering and Mining Journal*, November 15, 1899, p. 602. The A.F. of L. again contributed five hundred dollars for miners' legal defense, according to a letter from Gompers to James Maher, October 21, 1899, in Gompers letterbooks, XXX, 327–28. Gompers declined, however, to accede to Boyce's demand for a special

labor convention to protest martial law. See Gompers to Boyce, June 20, 1899, in letterbooks, XXVIII, 670. Acknowledging that the five hundred dollars was a pittance, Gompers regarded it as symbolic.

48. A report by Dr. France, "The Permit System" (Asarco).

49. *Engineering and Mining Journal,* January 7, 1904, p. 13. It may be useful to students of the conflict to know that the files of the Department of Justice labeled "Wardner Strike," 6899/99 in the National Archives, do not shed new light. The bulk of the correspondence in these files concerns the costs of maintaining troops and prisoners. The U.S. Marshal in Idaho paid for housing and feeding the prisoners, the War Department for military personnel, and the State of Idaho for lumber and construction of buildings at Camp Osborne occupied by troops. A letter from the marshal, F. C. Ramsey, to the U.S. Attorney General, July 6, 1901, listing quarterly costs for prisoners indicates some were held as late as March, 1901. The files also contain letters written in 1916 listing men indicted in 1899 who had not been apprehended in the intervening seventeen years, and a request (J. L. McClear, U.S. Attorney, to the U.S. Attorney General, October 31, 1916) for dismissal of the charges against these men. A letter from "One Who Loves Justice," written at Burke, to President McKinley, May 15, 1899, suggests the attitude of the district's residents: "Even for those who are guilty of destroying the mill, I will say this: They were animated by the same spirit that caused our forefathers to take a stand against British tyranny. . . . The bullpen was on a par with Andersonville . . . [and prisoners] were informed they would have to remain there until they could identify some of the men who went on the train [to destroy the mill]." The file also hints at the high level of influence brought to bear. Secretary of War Elihu Root wrote the attorney general, October 12, 1899, that he was "exceedingly reluctant to permit federal troops to remain as guards over civil prisoners."

## V. TEN-FOOT HOLES AT BUFFALO HUMP

1. *Idaho County Free Press* (Grangeville), June 9, 1897, in the collection of the University of Idaho, Moscow. Except for geological studies, there does not seem to exist a unified story of the Buffalo Hump mining camp. Pertinent material can be found in annual reports of the Idaho Inspector of Mines, and in S. P. Jellum, *Some Central Idaho Gold Districts,* and Robert G. Bailey, *River of No Return.* It should be noted that Jellum's account was published by Sidney Norman, who was inimical to Charles Sweeny.

2. The status of gold-recovery processes at the time is apparent from the design of the Huntington mill, a patented crushing machine that used a series of weights revolving around an iron drum to crush the ore. The

ore was then washed by water over tables of canvas, burlap, discarded blanket, animal hide, or carpeting, to catch the fine particles of gold. Some more advanced mills washed the crushed ore over copper plates faced with a teaspoon of mercury that formed a heavy amalgam with the gold, which could then be extracted by heat. The mercury would be recovered for reuse. The mills ran with whatever power was available—water, steam, mule, or man. Historical discussions of gold-recovery processes can be found in a number of mining textbooks, but for specific reference to the Buffalo Hump, see *Report of the Idaho Inspector of Mines,* for 1906, pp. 85–86, and for 1913, p. 176. Descriptions of amalgamation and cyaniding appear in W. W. Staley, *Elementary Methods of Placer Mining,* Idaho Bureau of Mines and Geology, Pamphlet 35, pp. 12–14.

3. *Idaho County Free Press,* March 10, 1899.

4. Spokane County articles of incorporation, book E, p. 160. Some confusion may arise from Sweeny's formation of three companies to promote the Buffalo Hump in the East and in Idaho. The Buffalo Hump Development Company was for local exploitation, as was the Buffalo Hump Syndicate, formed March 25, 1899 (see Spokane County articles of incorporation, book F, p. 453), to extend stock sales into Canada. The Buffalo Hump Mining Company, organized March 2, 1899, as a New York corporation, was used both as a stock promotion in the East and as a holding company for various Sweeny interests in the Buffalo Hump and Coeur d'Alene districts (see New York State articles of incorporation, book 47, p. 68).

The companies were loosely organized, as demonstrated in a letter from Clark to Heyburn, September 12, 1899, in the Heyburn papers (UI), asking for articles for a new company "as general as the Buffalo Hump Syndicate," with nominal capital, able to do business of every kind except banking, and which would "afford every convenience of the corporation and every security to the individual." Clark encloses a copy of the Buffalo Hump syndicate articles as a guide to Heyburn. Sweeny's testimony in court, reported in the *Spokesman-Review,* October 3, 1901, is interesting because he was unable to recall under oath which directors belonged to which companies. The Buffalo Hump Syndicate was stricken from the records of Washington State on August 23, 1909, and its claims sold at public auction in Spokane on January 15, 1932 (notice of sale among Sweeny papers). Its holdings in 1931 are listed in Abstract No. 12812, Inland Abstract Co. (Grangeville), August 5, 1931 (Sweeny).

5. Walter Hovey Hill is authority for this version, printed in the *Lewiston Tribune* (Idaho), August 9, 1942, and in Bailey's *River of No Return,* p. 179. For a discussion of De Lamar, see G. W. Barrett, "When Big Money Came to Owyhee," *Idaho Yesterdays,* XIII, No. 1 (spring, 1969), 2–9, 22–29.

6. *Idaho County Free Press,* January 13, 1899. Silverman later sued

Sweeny for his share of the claims, but the records of Silverman v. Sweeny, Idaho County civil case 538, supposed to be deposited as NC-207 in the Federal Records Center, Seattle, cannot be located, according to Ed M. Bryan, clerk, U.S. District Court, Boise.

7. *Oregonian* (Portland), March 2, 1899.

8. Miller's report to the Sweeny Investment Company, July 15, 1932, recalling his conclusions after an investigation in the winter of 1898–99 (Sweeny).

9. Gilliam's report was printed in the *Grangeville Standard* April 19, 1899 (UI).

10. Sister M. Alfreda Elsensohn, O.S.B., *Pioneer Days in Idaho County*, II, 212.

11. *Grangeville Standard*, April 19, 1899, and *Idaho County Free Press*, September 8, 1899. The *Spokesman-Review*, June 2, 1899, reported that mining men were wagering high stakes on whether Clark and Sweeny would make their next payment on the Big Buffalo group claims.

12. *Idaho County Free Press*, April 21, 1899.

13. Roberts' recollection (personal communication), corroborated by the *Idaho County Free Press*, August 18, 1899. Roberts was new to mine management in 1899, and seems to have formed no conclusion then about the real value of the Buffalo Hump. Later he came to regard the Hump as largely a promotional venture, and recalled that Sweeny wanted to abandon his claims there, but could not because eastern shareholders, who knew nothing of the mines but what they had read in the prospectus, would not hear of selling or closing down.

14. De Lashmutt's story, *Spokesman-Review*, October 8, 1900 (see also discussion of the legal battle with Patrick Clark in Chapter 8). A deed dated April 6, 1900 (Sweeny), indicates that De Lashmutt received one-fourth of the stock in the Buffalo Hump Syndicate for his services. See the *Spokesman-Review*, November 6, 1901, for Albert Allen's testimony in a suit by Patrick Clark against Clark and Sweeny to recover the Tiger-Poorman. The Empire State–Idaho general manager's report, April 30, 1901 (Asarco), describes the condition of the Tiger-Poorman when it was acquired, indicating confidence in the mines but picturing the property as run down and shabbily managed. The Asarco papers contain a memo of agreement, February 2, 1900, between De Lashmutt and John F. Forbis et al., stockholders of the Consolidated Tiger-Poorman, stipulating that all the stock deposited with W. A. Clark & Brother, Butte, by February 12, would be bought (by Sweeny) at forty-nine cents a share, and agreeing that as a consequence, all suits would be dropped.

15. These amounts are quoted by De Lashmutt, *Spokesman-Review*, October 8, 1900. The Buffalo Hump Mining Company had obtained a loan of

$153,200 at 8 percent from the Spokane and Eastern Trust Company, Spokane, on October 5, 1899, giving 612,800 shares of Consolidated Tiger-Poorman stock as security. (Trust Company financial committee log book, Washington State University archives.) This money could have been used to settle the dispute with Tiger-Poorman stockholders, or to pay for the Buffalo Hump claims. Unfortunately the Trust Company records do not indicate how Sweeny proposed to use his loan. The date of the loan, however, suggests that Sweeny anticipated one or both of the settlements negotiated by De Lashmutt.

16. Clendening to Sweeny, November 30, 1900 (Asarco).

17. The proposal and the deeds to water rights are among the Sweeny papers.

18. Letter from Miller to Sweeny, December 26, 1900 (Asarco), which says in part, "It is apparently costing fully forty dollars a day for wood. From this distance, this seems to be twice too much."

19. For elements of this account, see Arthur L. Flagg, "Buffalo Hump Mining District, Idaho," *Mining and Engineering World*, XXXVIII (1913), 814, and Elsensohn, *Pioneer Days in Idaho County*, II, 205 and 214.

20. Letter, March 16, 1901 (Asarco).

21. Attempts to use various processes are reported by Staley and the Idaho Inspector of Mines at the places cited in note 2 above.

22. Flagg, "Buffalo Hump Mining District," p. 814; Jellum, *Central Idaho Gold Districts*, pp. 68–69; *Report of the Idaho Inspector of Mines for 1906*.

23. *Spokesman-Review*, December 17, 1903.

24. In this connection, it is relevant to note a statement of profit and loss for companies acquired by the Federal Mining and Smelting Co. (Asarco), which includes the account of the Buffalo Hump Mining Company for the eighteen months ending April 30, 1901. The company reported an income of $196,131.81 against which were charged construction and development costs of $251,758.89.

25. Contracts with Hughes, dated December 31, 1902, and Prader, dated October 19, 1908, are among the Sweeny papers.

26. Radcliffe H. Beckwith, "The Geology and Ore Deposits of the Buffalo Hump District," *New York Academy of Science Annals*, XXX (October, 1928), 292–93.

27. Jellum, *Central Idaho Gold Districts*, p. 62. Miller's report to the Sweeny Investment Company, July 15, 1932 (Sweeny), suggests that Bunker Hill investigators concluded that gold lay at deep levels of the old mines, but that transportation and the economic circumstances of mining at the time precluded its extraction at a profit. As late as 1908, Mike

Sweeny was reported to have bought the Crackerjack mine for sixty thousand dollars for Charles Sweeny. See *Daily Missoulian* (Missoula, Mont.), April 4, 1908.

In many cases, the local historian relies on contemporary newspaper accounts. The animosity toward Sweeny of the editor of the *Grangeville Standard* seems evident in his published observations quoted in this chapter. But the personal interest of A. F. Parker, the editor of Grangeville's other newspaper, the *Idaho County Free Press*, comes to the surface more clearly in a letter to Heyburn, November 25, 1899 (UI), which says in part:

"Mr. Bartlett [Grangeville attorney assisting Heyburn] advises me that he is having difficulty in getting the application for patents in the Hump published in my paper—the *Free Press*. Now I have always intended taking a block of stock in the Buffalo Hump Tunnel Co., and if you care to use your influence to secure these publications for me, I am willing to have you cut me stock in said Tunnel Co. to the full amount of such publications. . . .

"Incidentally, I may state that I have published a good deal of matter relative to the Tunnel Co., having confidence in it, and on the principle that one good turn deserves another, venture to ask you to secure me these publications in the above terms—payment in Tunnel stock at the least rate you can give.

"Yours truly, A. F. Parker"

## VI. LONG COPPER WIRES

1. John B. Fisken, "How Electricity Came to the Mines," *Northwest Mining Truth* (Spokane), May 18, 1925, p. 15. Supporting sources include a letter, Frank Culbertson to the Comptroller of the U.S., May 16, 1897 (NA), and the *Coeur d'Alene Miner*, December 17, 1892 (UI). No general discussion of this subject has been published.

2. *Coeur d'Alene Miner*, April 4 and 11, 1891; *Spokesman-Review*, April 7, 1891.

3. *Wallace Press*, April 4, 1891. See *Spokesman-Review*, January 8 and December 8, 1891.

4. Electricity had been used in Colorado mines as early as 1888, and at Bodie, California, in 1893. For the Silver Lake mines near Silverton, Colorado, a 150-kilowatt system with a transmission line three miles long was built in 1895. This electrical installation used a three-wire alternating current to replace direct current, which had proved both expensive and limited in its capacity. The three-wire alternating system was developed by Thomas A. Edison and patented in 1883. Among the advantages claimed for it

were a saving of 60 percent of the wire required for transmitting direct current of comparable voltage, and adaptability to high voltages over long distances. Thus the Silverton plant signaled a new era in mining electricity. In his article Fisken attempts to trace the development of electricity in mining throughout the world, and suggests that electricity was perhaps first used to ignite blasting charges, later to sound bell signals, and in 1882 to run locomotives in Saxony mines. He puts the first use in the United States as 1888 in Pennsylvania.

5. *Spokesman-Review,* October 3, 1901.

6. Contract forms, and engineering reports on Post Falls, are in Asarco files.

7. Richards to W. A. White, December 17, 1900, in letterbooks of the Washington Water Power Co.

8. Neill's purchases are recorded in Kootenai County, Idaho, deeds, book U, pp. 164 and 166, and book 1, p. 9, in the courthouse at Coeur d'Alene. A good study of Post Falls' potential usefulness both as power site and reservoir can be found in R. W. Davenport, *Coeur d'Alene Lake, Idaho, and the Overflow Lands,* U.S. Geological Service, Water Supply Paper 500 (1921). It should be noted that Neill, Finch, Campbell, and Norman were not without experience in generating systems. In 1895 these four, with Patrick Clark, Frank Campbell, and two Rossland men, had organized the Rossland Light and Power Company in British Columbia. They rigged an Edison bipolar generator, turned by a reconditioned sawmill steam engine, to light some seven hundred bulbs on Rossland streets and in homes beginning in January, 1896. The demand for current soon outstripped their tiny plant, and after buying power from the British-financed West Kootenay Power and Light Company for a short time, they sold their Rossland plant to the town of Rossland. It is of interest, too, that the West Kootenay company stretched a thirty-two-mile transmission line from Bonnington to Trail and Rossland, to deliver 20,100 volts to substations which stepped down the current for residences and mining operations. The West Kootenay line was among the longest attempted in its time, and afforded the Coeur d'Alene mine owners a model close to home for their own scheme.

9. Riblet's report, undated, to Coeur d'Alene Transmission Company (Asarco). There is no record in Spokane, Shoshone, or Kootenai counties of incorporation of the transmission company. Many mine owners openly favored Thompson Falls, Montana, as a power site. For descriptions of the Post Falls surface area, power rights, and similar details, see Kootenai County deeds, book W, p. 166; book 9, pp. 460 and 464; and book 1, p. 9. Post Falls, originally called Upper or Little Falls, had been part of the Coeur d'Alene Indian Reservation created in 1873. The northern part of the reservation, including much of Coeur d'Alene Lake in which the Spo-

kane River rises, was ceded to the United States by treaty in September, 1889, and opened to homesteading in 1891. Post had chosen a mill site in 1871 on the north bank of the Spokane River at the falls, and on June 1, 1871, had purchased from Andrew Seltice (Saltese), a chief of the Coeur d'Alenes, the entire falls, rights to the power capable of generation, and land enough on both sides of the river to develop power and industrial sites. The contract between Post and the chief was painted on rocks near the falls. Post's deed was patented under the Homestead Act of March 3, 1891. At Post Falls the river divided into three channels separated by rocky islands. Post dammed all three channels, raising the natural forty-foot fall about four feet with log barriers. He sold 200 horsepower to the Dart brothers who assigned it to the Cable Milling Company; 100 h.p. to one of his five daughters, Mrs. Alice L. Martin; and 200 to Charles M. Patterson and Hugh L. Strathern to run their sawmill. Of the 4,000 potential horsepower Post had leashed with his modest dams, this left him 3,500. He sold 2,000 of this to the Post Falls Water Company. Post's remaining right and that of the water company were sold to R. K. Neill. Northeast of the cataract, Post promoted the town of Post Falls, which in 1901 consisted of perhaps twenty-five buildings and scattered cottages, overshadowed by a twenty-five-thousand-dollar three-story wooden hotel (fifty-four rooms, with an observatory on top) built by Post in the hope that steamers from the lake would come downriver to his landing. A woolen mill, erected in 1895, lay idle; it had spun not a thread. The Spokane Falls and Idaho branch of the Northern Pacific served Post Falls but its few passengers were bound for the mines. Post's dream of establishing an important town languished.

10. Roberts to Sweeny, May 8, 1901 (Asarco).

11. White to Richards, January 24, 1901, in letterbooks of the Washington Water Power Co.

12. White to Richards, December 11, 1900, in letterbooks of the Washington Water Power Co.

13. Personal interview with Roberts. In this connection, the Washington Water Power Company's Statement A to the Federal Power Commission, May 11, 1937 (in WWP files), remarks that Coeur d'Alene mining interests approached the power company to take the Post Falls power site.

14. White to Comptroller, December 11, 1897 (NA). See also *Washington Water Power Company*, which states that WWP issued 5 percent collateral bonds in 1899 due July 1, 1929. As WWP teetered close to bankruptcy, White arranged an agreement in June, 1897, between the stockholders and investors who had bought the company's bonds. "The substance of said plan is that the stockholders agree to make a contribution to the [financial rescue] committee of either ten percent in cash, or forty percent in stock, and the bondholders agree to make a reduction in the rate of interest on their bonds from six to four and one-half percent, and the

committee agrees to sell a certain amount of the securities coming into their hands and discharge the floating debt," was White's explanation of the financial rescue of the company in his letter to the comptroller, December 11, 1897. White's plan worked. In July, 1899, WWP was able to issue its 5 percent collateral trust bonds for further financial support. White himself was the senior member of a Wall Street brokerage house established by his father in 1837, a collector of rare books, and a pragmatic businessman. See his obituary, *New York Times,* May 7, 1927.

15. Huntington to editor, *Poor's Manual of Railroads,* April 30, 1901, in letterbooks of the Washington Water Power Company. It is relevant to note that on December 13, 1900, WWP had paid $375,000 in capital stock for the so-called upper falls of the Spokane River (within the city limits— not to be confused with Post Falls). The site, bought from the Amsterdamsch Trustees Kantoor, a Holland corporation, represented one-third of the water power potential inside the city; WWP already owned the other two-thirds at Monroe Street. WWP had limited experience with high-tension lines. In early 1901, it had completed a 6,600-volt system to serve homes and the Great Northern Railway shops at Hillyard, northeast of Spokane—then a suburb, now a part of the city.

16. See *Electrical World and Engineer,* December 12, 1901, p. 583, for a description of the Bay Counties' lines. An impression has grown in Spokane that Washington Water Power's line to the mines was the longest in the world at the time, but the company itself has not fostered this version. Huntington's letters to various companies, including Bay Counties and Tellerude, demonstrate his knowledge of the other lines and search for useful information on long-distance transmission. (These are in the WWP letterbooks.) The Bay Counties line was 142 miles long, designed for 60,000 volts, to carry electrical current from the North Yuba River to Oakland and other eastern communities on San Francisco Bay, and then by a branch connection, to the Standard Electric Company of California in San Jose, 184 miles from the North Yuba station. It went into service April 27, 1901.

17. The minutes are in Asarco files.

18. Kootenai County deeds, book 1, p. 11, and book U, p. 166. The acquisition of Post Falls is also detailed in A. M. Philleo, "Cost Data, Post Falls Development, Post Falls, Idaho," MS dated November 7, 1925, in WWP files.

19. Fisken, quoted in the *Spokesman-Review,* June 23, 1931. The line's route is also described in a letter, Richards to White, May 6, 1902, in WWP letterbooks.

20. See C. S. McCalla, "The Post Falls Development of the Washington Water Power Company," *Electrical World,* May 23–30, 1908; and *Spokesman-Review,* April 22, 1903.

21. Interviews with the late William Dittmer of Washington Water Power, who drove wagons for such crews, and O. M. Fahey, the author's father, a member of the crew that installed cable to Post Falls. Labor rates from Philleo, "Post Falls Development," Exhibit B.

22. Roberts to Packard, October 10, 1902 (Asarco).

23. The contract for construction of the Post Falls station was awarded January 24, 1904, to Nelson Bennett and Charles Bihler of Tacoma. They built a concrete dam seventy-eight feet long in the south channel, with six-by-thirteen-foot Puget Sound fir gates to control the water level, dammed the north and middle channels, and installed an 11,250-kilowatt power station. The contractors did not complete the work on schedule, and WWP finished it after dismissing them. (The contract and related documents are in WWP files.) Coeur d'Alene No. 2 was strung in 1907 along the general route that Huntington had inspected and rejected for the first line. The Post Falls decision was pivotal in development of the power company. From this time, it began to exploit power sites outside the City of Spokane in eastern Washington and northern Idaho. The company's correspondence files show that until Post Falls, the Company had inclined toward confining its generation sites to those inside the city on the Spokane River.

## VII. DIGRESSIONS: POLITICS AND REAL ESTATE

1. *Spokesman-Review*, July 2, 1902. There does not seem to be a breadth of intimate material on Sweeny's political and real estate diversions. The story has been reconstructed from newspaper files unless otherwise indicated. The Spokane County Republican Committee does not hold records or documents from the period and regarded contributions and alliances as private rather than matters of record. Washington State did not provide for care of archival materials until 1909. Personal letters, of the kind cited in other chapters, came from lawsuits or mining company files; letters, if any, regarding political or property ventures were retained by individuals and presumably destroyed. The account relies chiefly on the *Seattle Times* for political, and the *Oregonian* and *Spokesman-Review* for real estate information. Another useful source was the file of deeds held by the Sweeny Investment Company, and the deed indexes and files of Spokane and Multnomah counties.

2. *Spokesman-Review*, January 17, 1904. Sweeny's manager, Hopkins, was widely known throughout eastern Washington as a consequence of his ownership of the *Palouse Gazette* during 1877–83, the *Spokane Chronicle* in 1883, and his organization in 1889 of the first telephone company in Spokane Falls, the Inland Telephone Company, which he managed for some years. See his obituary, *Spokesman-Review*, February 5, 1920. Hop-

kins' son, Charles, married a daughter of John P. Vollmer, an influential merchant-banker of eastern Washington and northern Idaho.

3. *Seattle Times,* May 7–12, 1904.

4. The author is indebted to Hazel E. Millett, Washington State Library, for information about the Horr mansion. In a later legislative session, the house was to be the headquarters for May Arkwright Hutton in her campaign to obtain suffrage for women in Washington State.

5. *Spokesman-Review,* January 20, 1905.

6. Sweeny's story is from the *Spokesman-Review,* January 30, 1905, and is supported by a personal interview by the author with the late Walter L. Nichols.

7. Rev. Charles Mackin, S.J., "Wanderings" (manuscript memoirs, Gonzaga University, n.d.) II, 27.

8. Contents of this agreement were published in the *Seattle Times,* January 27, and the *Spokesman-Review,* January 28, 1905. Piles kept his word. He did not run for re-election in 1910 but resumed his law practice in Seattle. For a time in his later life he served as United States Minister to Colombia. He died in Los Angeles in 1940, aged eighty-one.

The extent of Sweeny's support is clear from the names and counties of legislators who voted for him on the last ballot as reported in the Journal of the House, January 26, 1905: Adams-Franklin-Walla Walla—Hutson; Franklin County—Allen; Garfield —Long; Klickitat—Coate; Klickitat-Skamania—Baker; Lewis—Ulsh, Veness; Lincoln—Reiter; Spokane—Bowers, Bratt, C. G. Brown, Crane, Doolittle, Fancher, Henry, Hoch, Huxtable, J. B. Lindsley, N. E. Lindsley, Ratcliffe, Scott, Stansell; Skamania—Stevenson; Stevens County—Kellogg; Walla Walla—Pauly, Rudio, Weber; Whitman—McGregor.

9. *Spokesman-Review,* January 30, 1905.

10. Spokane County deeds, book 50, p. 577; also cited in note 15, Chapter II.

11. Activities of the Dutch in the Inland Empire are an aspect of the economic history of the region that has not been carefully investigated. Consequently the extent and significance of the Dutch investments is not known. The Northwestern and Pacific Mortgage Company was incorporated July 15, 1885, in Washington, Idaho, and Montana "to loan money on real estate security." On November 24, 1886, the company amended Article III of its incorporation to add Oregon to its areas of interest. (See Spokane County articles of incorporation, book B miscellaneous, pp. 149 and 222.) Mary Burnham, "Who Were the Major Netherlands Investors and Investment Firms Influencing the Development of the Inland Empire?" (graduate paper, Eastern Washington State College, 1962, now in files of the Eastern Washington State Historical Society), p. 13, asserts that the company established itself in 1883 in Olympia. The articles of incorpora-

tion on file in Spokane County show 1885 as the date of incorporation in Washington Territory. In 1896 its name was changed to Northwestern and Pacific Hypotheekbank. Among others, Miss Margaret Bean, writing in the *Spokesman-Review*, June 9, 1957, perpetuates the traditional story of the company's activities in Spokane; however, there appears to be no study of the Dutch's widespread dealings in farm lands. Certain of the Washington Water Power Company lands, notably the upper falls of the Spokane River within the city, were purchased from the Dutch who apparently acquired them by foreclosure. The 12 to 15 percent interest charged by the Hollanders was not an unusual rate for farm real estate, 1890–1900. The scant published evidence suggests that, in sum, the Dutch were a stabilizing influence on the region's economy during the last years of the nineteenth century and the first of the twentieth. Their Spokane managers were respected, and moved in the city's best society.

12. Sweeny to O'Connor, July 5, 1896, in exhibits of Spokane County civil case 19,061 (Jules Prickett v. Clark and Sweeny). For a description of the old frame building at Lincoln and Riverside, see *Spokesman-Review*, January 7, 1897. Sweeny tried to persuade several erstwhile eastern associates to invest in Spokane. Some of his letters to Packard (Asarco) include suggestions for joint investments in Spokane land. Packard formed the Spokane Suburban Company with the Spokane real estate man, Frederic E. Elmendorf, to deal in property but did not join in Sweeny's acquisitions. See Spokane County articles of incorporation, book G, p. 467.

13. Spokane County deeds, book 96, p. 259. One not familiar with Spokane's early history may be confused by the designation "Resurvey and Addition" to J. N. Glover's original pre-emption entry, patented on authority of President Rutherford B. Hayes on April 5, 1878. The Glover pre-emption was resurveyed in August, 1880, by G. F. Wright who found the 1878 boundaries in error, and when Glover, A. M. Cannon, and J. J. Browne filed a plat and dedication on September 2, 1880, the central part of the town as defined by Wright was designated "Resurvey and Addition to Spokane Falls." Thus, early titles are described as lying within the Resurvey and Addition, rather than in their relation to an original townsite. Any abstract of title to property within the Resurvey and Addition will provide this information.

14. Spokane County deeds, book 96, p. 259. The *Spokesman-Review*, April 13, 1899, put the purchase price at $45,000. The inconsistency between Clark's and Sweeny's tight financial situation and their ability to invest heavily in real estate may be partially explained by a series of notations in the log book of the financial committee of the Spokane and Eastern Trust Company, Spokane, now in the archives of Washington State University. An entry dated January 14, 1898, shows the Trust Company loaned Clark and Sweeny $30,000 against the Last Chance bonds, and

accepted the Last Chance judgment against the Tyler as security. On February 10, 1899, the Trust Company granted a new note of $50,000 "to take up all other obligations of the firm [Clark and Sweeny]," which the partners expected to meet with the sale of Empire State–Idaho stock in Montreal. On October 3, 1899, the Buffalo Hump Mining Company received a credit of $150,000 from the Trust, and on October 5, 1899, the company received a loan of $153,200 at 8 percent, secured by 612,800 shares of Consolidated Tiger-Poorman stock. These notations, intended as private advices to members of the Trust Company's financial committee, suggest strongly that Clark and Sweeny used the stock of mining companies as collateral for loans to buy real estate. From the Trust records, however, there is no way to be sure how the loans were used.

15. Spokane County deeds, book 99, p. 155.

16. Spokane County deeds, book 98, p. 521.

17. Spokane County deeds, book 102, pp. 166, 173; book 104, p. 471.

18. See Spokane County deeds, book 103, p. 368, and book 80, p. 588; both entries dated March 27, 1900. The important real estate properties held by the partnership of Clark and Sweeny were administered, after the separation, by a new firm, the Consolidated Improvement Company, organized May 31, 1902, by Clark and Arthur D. Jones. (See Spokane County articles of incorporation 65717.)

19. Spokane County deeds, book 104, p. 325. The Spokane and Eastern Trust Company financial committee, according to a notation in its log book February 19, 1899, advised Sweeny of Bravinder's financial difficulties and agreed to take a mortgage on the property until Sweeny could acquire it.

20. This is the Rookery Building today. See Spokane County deeds, book 156, p. 333 (N&P Hypotheekbank); book 150, p. 310 (Hams); and book 162, p. 452 (Turner).

21. *Spokesman-Review*, November 4, 1904. The newspaper reported the sale price as $360,000, as did the *Spokane Daily Chronicle*, November 3, 1904. Both papers called this the largest real estate transaction in the history of Spokane to that time.

22. Reed to Sweeny Investment Company, *circa* 1933 (Sweeny).

23. The transactions are recorded in Multnomah County, Oregon, deeds, book 324, p. 197; book 322, p. 472; and in an agreement drawn August 2, 1904, at Portland outlining the stock and repurchase stipulations (Sweeny).

24. *Oregonian*, July 27, 1904.

25. Plans described in stories in the *Oregonian*, November 6, 1904; June 2, 1906; and April 2, 1910. Cordray managed the Washington Theater in Spokane for a short time.

26. Multnomah County deeds, book 343, p. 263 (Seventh and Morri-

son); book 340, p. 450 (Washington Block); and book 339, p. 387 (Church). Comment from *Oregonian*, June 25, 1905.

27. Multnomah County deeds, book 373, p. 263. Sweeny assumed an $85,000 mortgage on the property. Comment from the *Oregonian*, October 4, 1906. The *Spokane Daily Chronicle*, November 17, 1904, reported the Seventh and Morrison purchase as involving $91,125.20 and said Sweeny planned an eight-story brick and steel building there for Tull & Gibbs.

28. Spokane County articles of incorporation 121,475. Minutes in possession of Sweeny Investment Company, Spokane.

29. In the legends of Spokane real estate men, the event that swung the city's retail traffic westward from Washington and Riverside was the location of the Culbertson-Grote-Rankin department store at Main and Wall in 1914. It is said that Frank R. Culbertson, located with Grote-Rankin on Riverside east of Washington, intended to build a new store one block south of Riverside between Sprague and First on the west side of Washington Street, but that the property he wanted was held at too high a price by the Greenough Investment Co., a firm comprised of Thomas L. Greenough, Missoula, and W. J. C. Wakefield and D. W. Twohy, Spokane. The Crescent had always been located west of Washington, and when it was joined by Culbertson's, these two, as Spokane's leading department stores, swung the retail shopping center away from the million-dollar intersection. (When the Culbertson store declared bankruptcy in 1929, one of the stockholders wiped out was R. K. Neill, promoter of the Post Falls power site.) This legend gains credence from news items such as the one published May 10, 1906, in the *Spokane Daily Chronicle*, reporting that major department store owners were negotiating for the Greenough property. I have investigated the evolution of downtown polarization more fully in, "The Million-Dollar Corner: Spokane's Downtown Development, 1890–1920," *Pacific Northwest Quarterly*, Vol. LXII (April, 1971).

As a final observation, attention is called to Sweeny's reliance on the Spokane and Eastern Trust Company in his real estate operations. Not only did he obtain loans that totaled $430,000 at one time (Trust Company log book, November 15, 1904), but Mose Oppenheimer, an influential stockholder in the Trust, represented Sweeny in his acquisition of properties at Howard and Riverside, noted previously. Sweeny's cordial relationships with members of the Spokane and Eastern financial committee continued after he had purchased the Exchange National Bank. The committee's minutes (Washington State University archives) for August 15, 1907, report, "Mr. Sweeny was present and the general policy of the bank was discussed and it was decided that every effort should be made to reduce loans, decline new business involving additional loans, and build up the reserve." Sweeny evidently was regarded as a reliable advisor on economic conditions.

## VIII. PROSPECTING BY PRECEDENT

1. Shoshone County civil case 24, of which the University of Idaho holds photocopies. Also cited in note 16, Chapter I. It must be remembered that some of Sweeny's lawsuits were intended to obscure his activities. I ignore, in this discussion, a number of Sweeny's lawsuits, or elements of suits, in the hope of providing an uncomplicated overall impression of Sweeny's use of the courts. Much of the direction for this chapter resulted from interviews with the late E. J. Roberts, who treated Sweeny's legal endeavors with evident scepticism, regarding them as threads in a promotional fabric.

2. During his twenty-five-year sway in the Coeur d'Alenes, Sweeny was abetted and beset by many of the renowned barristers of western mining. One, Curtis H. Lindley, wrote a standard legal treatise on mining, using Sweeny cases among those he cited as shaping and illustrating mining law. These pioneer lawyers merit mention, for they have been pictured as a special class of citizen, heavy-eating, hard-drinking, Bible-quoting orators who lived by their wits and regarded themselves as the learned leaders of the community. See Benjamin H. Kizer, "The Pioneer Lawyer," *Pacific Northwesterner*, VI (Winter, 1962), 1–8.

Among the attorneys of northern Idaho, the prototype was a master of eloquent invective, Frank Ganahl, of medium height and huge girth, born in the state of Georgia, the son of an Austrian court attaché. Ganahl was educated at the state university and Harvard, and was a world traveler before he established his practice in California at twenty-three. He had moved to Idaho in 1866 and was famed on the Pacific Coast as a criminal lawyer when he defended mine union leaders in 1892.

Another whose notoriety preceded him to the Coeur d'Alenes was Albert H. Hagan, a former Confederate colonel who had counseled Brigham Young's twenty-seventh wife in her divorce action against Young. Hagan married a daughter of Young and Lucy Bigelow, Dora, who turned Roman Catholic and bore widower Hagan four children.

Many attorneys without degrees from recognized law schools learned their trade "reading" in law offices, wrote documents in longhand, and copied them on tissue paper with waterpress, until about 1890 when colleges and typewriters together worked their revolution on office procedures. In the days before typewriters, legal documents were usually briefer. Despite a tradition for bombast, many solicitors in the Coeur d'Alenes were able legal minds; a number of them were unregenerated rebels who came

West after the Civil War and wafted the soft accents of the South through the frame courthouses.

Heyburn, three years younger than Sweeny, was a short, stout, stubborn Pennsylvanian, vehement in denouncing the Confederate cause. In 1910, for example, as U.S. Senator, Heyburn almost alone opposed the loan of army tents to Confederate veterans for their annual encampment, and by implication attacked the selection of a statue of Robert E. Lee for the U.S. Hall of Fame. He was once characterized by the *New York Tribune* as "uncomfortably inflexible" on the rebel cause "as on all other subjects." A graduate of the University of Pennsylvania, Heyburn reached the Coeur d'Alene mines late in 1883. He spent his first three days in the district, wearing his best clothes, struggling in the muddy tailrace as a common workman at the old Last Chance gold claim. Soon after his arrival, he plunged into Republican politics, took on Sweeny as a lifetime client, and began to impress his shrewd arguments on American mining law. See R. G. Cook, "Pioneer Portraits: Weldon Brinton Heyburn," *Idaho Yesterdays*, X (Spring, 1966), 22–26.

Heyburn's constant opponent was John R. McBride, a native of Missouri whose family had migrated to Oregon by ox-cart. At twenty-four, McBride was the youngest member of Oregon's constitutional convention, a congressman at thirty-seven, chief justice of Idaho Territory at forty. He established his practice in Spokane Falls in 1890 and almost immediately embarked on a career of disputing Heyburn.

One of the most respected barristers of the mining region was stumpy Albert Allen, a graduate of the University of Wisconsin, who reached the Coeur d'Alenes on foot pulling a toboggan through the snows of 1884. He acquired a share in the Bunker Hill for advising its early owners, and was a careful, hard-working attorney—who nonetheless joined in the roistering tradition of winner-buy-the-drinks after the jury came in.

Doubtless Sweeny's most famous counselor was the former carpetbagger, George W. Turner. Born in Missouri in 1850, one of the nine children of a cabinet maker and itinerant preacher whom he seldom mentioned in later life, Turner had the barest formal education. He served in the Civil War with the military telegraph corps at the age of eleven, rising within a year to telegraph operator. During Reconstruction, Turner headed the Republican Party in Alabama, at twenty-six was appointed marshal for the state's middle and southern districts, and after leading the Alabama delegation to the national Republican conventions of 1876 and 1880, resigned his federal appointment. As a result of his support of Chester A. Arthur for president, Turner was appointed a justice of the Washington territorial supreme court, and came West in 1884 bringing several Alabamans whom he placed as court clerks. During four years on the bench, Turner proved a candid independent and a foe of railroads. He retired in

1888 to enter private practice with his older brother, W. W. D. Turner, and George M. Forster, and between 1888 and 1897 acquired a comfortable fortune from law and mining investments. He was elected by the Washington Legislature to the U.S. Senate in 1897, winning through a fusion of unpledged votes with the Populists after his own party abandoned his candidacy as hopeless. When he was escorted to the rostrum to accept, Turner declared, "I never expect, as long as God permits me to live, to cast another Republican ballot." After his election, Turner's friends felt obliged to deny that he had bribed his way into Congress, saying that he had done nothing that the times would regard as dishonorable. In 1903 the Legislature passed him over for a "safe" Republican, and he was defeated by William Randolph Hearst in 1905 for nomination as a vice-presidential candidate. Turner served on the Alaska Boundary Dispute Commission in 1903, and as counsel for the United States in northeast fisheries arbitration at The Hague in 1906, withdrawing from the latter post to make room for Elihu Root. Turner's interests were varied; in addition to those mentioned in this book, he was also an incorporator of a company to promote a railroad into Yellowstone Park. After Frank Moore died, Turner bought his home, which was later torn down to make room for Pioneer Park, an extension of the grounds of the D. C. Corbin home.

Sweeny's best-known opponent was Lindley, the scholarly San Francisco attorney. Born in Marysville, California, Lindley grew up among the mines, attended Santa Clara and the University of California, and then by coincidence was apprenticed as a machinist to the Union Iron Works in San Francisco during 1866–68, the same years that Sweeny was an apprentice bookkeeper there. Lindley was admitted to the bar in 1872, achieved recognition as a teacher of mining law, and served on the faculties of California and Stanford universities.

William T. Stoll won Cooper and Peck their shares of the Bunker Hill claim and was Patrick Clark's attorney in the Ella suit against Sweeny. Frank T. Post, who was to become president of the Washington Water Power Company, once attempted to overturn a breach of contract verdict against Charles and Emeline Sweeny with the assertion that the plaintiff had failed to offer evidence they were married, a plea the judge dismissed as "frivolous." (See Foster v. Sweeny, Spokane County civil case 15242.) A beginner who entered Heyburn's office in 1901, John P. Gray, was to head the legal staff of William A. Clark of Butte and to become one of the select attorneys who also were members of the American Institute of Mining and Metallurgical Engineers. The Heyburn papers (UI) indicate that Gray handled most of Sweeny's legal affairs in Idaho after Heyburn went to the Senate.

This is an incomplete list of the lawyers celebrated in Sweeny's cases. Most of them were also politicians. From the attorney of this period springs the classic caricature of a senator with flowing hair and huge belly, arm upraised in valedictory. Heyburn died in the Senate, as did William E. Borah, who fought Sweeny for the Day family, operators of the Hercules; Turner had been a senator when he joined Sweeny. It was a brief age of knighthood in the courtroom that ended soon with a platoon of youngsters from law schools who ignored the custom that the victor bought the vanquished his dinner and his drinks.

3. It is difficult to suggest a nontechnical discussion of the development of mining laws, but the reader may wish to see a series of articles by William E. Colby in the *California Law Review*, 1916–17. Owen Cochran Coy, *Gold Days* (Los Angeles: Powell Publishing Co., 1929) discusses the evolution of California law in gold camps but does not annotate. Edith James, "Claims Law and Miners' Courts of the Montana Gold Camps" (Master's thesis, University of Chicago, 1949), attempts to trace the migration of miners' law from California and Colorado to the Pacific Northwest but does not specifically discuss Idaho. In most of this chapter, the author follows Curtis H. Lindley, *A Treatise on the American Law Relating to Mines and Mineral Lands*.

4. *Weekly Eagle* (Eagle City, Idaho), July 11, 1884 (UI).

5. This notion of pursuit has been variously attributed to German, Welsh, and Spanish customs, but its injection into American law lies in California miners' codes, written with the conviction that the lode was the miner's principal possession. This concept is fundamental in the federal regulations of 1866 and 1872 (see Lindley, *American Law Relating to Mines*, I, 77–78). The *Northwest Mining Truth* (Spokane), February 16, 1920, p. 4, follows Colby in saying that pursuit was first expressed in article 3 of the Code of Saunders Ledge Mining District, Nevada County, California, in 1851, providing that "one hundred feet on the ledge, with the dips, spurs, and angles, shall constitute a claim." Long before Sweeny's lawyers were to argue his last case, most nations of the world had abandoned the apex concept as unworkable. Lindley believed the apex law "responsible for nine-tenths of the expensive litigation arising in the conduct of quartz or vein mining" (*American Law Relating to Mines*, III, 2161).

6. 54 Fed. 284.

7. The description of the Tyler litigation 1887–95 is mainly from 54 Fed. 284. In a different context, this lawsuit is also treated briefly in Chapter II.

8. 15 Sup. Ct. 733.

9. Heyburn's brief, including testimony by Tyler, Carlin, and Sweeny, is filed with the records of the Last Chance Mining Company (Asarco). See also 79 Fed. 277 and 90 Fed. 15. The Last Chance won from the Tyler, but the Tyler won from the Idaho and Republican Mining Company. The

distinction seems too involved to mention in the text and is of minor importance to subsequent litigation.

10. Heyburn's brief, Last Chance v. Bunker Hill and Sullivan (1903) in files of Empire State–Idaho (Asarco). See 109 Fed. 504.

11. 87 Fed. 801; 109 Fed. 504; 20 Sup. Ct. 726; 44 Law Ed. 864. Descriptions and quotations in the text are from these sources.

12. W. C. Miller statement in complaint of Kennedy Hanley to the circuit court, northern division of Idaho, March, 1899 (Asarco).

13. Quoted in Hanley's complaint (see note 12 above). Hanley acquired one-eighth of the Skookum on August 1, 1897, from W. N. Morphy for $700. See 53 Pac. Rep. 451; 77 Pac. Rep. 226; 126 Fed. 97; and 112 Pac. Rep. 1055. This episode is treated briefly in Chapter 3.

14. 56 Pac. Rep. 85. See also *Spokesman-Review,* September 13, 1902. Sweeny never admitted switching the deed, but the court decided that he had.

15. Hanley complaint to the district court, 1900 (Asarco). Although in reconstruction, the opponents involved in these suits appear to have been secretive, there actually was a good deal of conversation about them out of court among the participants. For example, in a letter to Heyburn, undated but written in April or May, 1898, Sweeny says: "Look up pretty carefully if there is any way that Hanley can get into court again on that interest if we win it in the State Supreme Court. He says that it is only the first round if we win there, and McBride has led him to believe that he can then come back in the U.S. Court and try it over. We want to know about it for sure before we conclude any trade with him" (Heyburn papers, UI).

16. Miller to Roberts, April 1, 1902 (Asarco), gives a typical month's report: milling ore from outside the Skookum, 38.7 percent; inside, 61.3 percent.

17. 126 Fed. 97.

18. Roberts to Heyburn, June 11, 1902 (Asarco).

19. Empire State–Idaho letterbooks (Asarco). Heyburn was perhaps clearing the way for his appointment to the Senate in 1903. Roberts' letters in ES-I letterbooks indicate frequent threats from Heyburn to resign, which Roberts considered simply as bids for a higher retainer. Roberts makes this observation in letters to Sweeny, June 12, 1901, and to Packard, July 30, 1901, in the ES-I letterbooks. See also note 31 below.

20. Based on letters, A. J. Shaw to U.S. Attorney General, January 30, 1906, and F. L. Clark to Comptroller, February 5, 1906 (both in National Archives with First National Bank records). *The Outburst* somehow acquired and published Shaw's letter to the Spokane County commissioners urging prosecution of F. L. Clark. Clark's letter to the comptroller calls

these efforts "made not by people who honestly wanted to get something for the creditors of the First National Bank, but who wanted to get even with Mr. Sweeny and myself or bring odium on us." The National Archives also contain wires from W. H. Cowles, publisher of the *Spokesman-Review,* attempting to learn whether federal prosecution was contemplated. It was Cowles who alleged that Hanley paid *The Outburst* to attack Clark and Sweeny.

21. Clendening to American Bonding Company, March 29, 1904, in files of Federal (Asarco).

22. 112 Pac. Rep. 1055.

23. The general manager's report, April 30, 1901, to directors of the Empire State–Idaho (Asarco) asserts that the Consolidated Tiger-Poorman Mining Company, "owing to the loss of their surface improvements by fire in 1896 . . . had been allowed to get behind in development work in the mine, and the property, in a general way, was in bad shape." The report says the Buffalo Hump Mining Company spent $400,000 improving the property. (See Chap. V for discussion of Van DeLashmutt's settlement of a renegotiated sale.) The Empire State–Idaho acquired the Tiger-Poorman from the Buffalo Hump Mining Company in January, 1901, for $2,100,000 in ES-I stock, which was authorized at a special meeting of the directors on January 14, 1901 (minute books in Asarco files). The directors also approved an increase in the capital stock of ES-I from one million to six million dollars, of which two million was distributed among stockholders on the basis of two shares for one.

24. 122 Fed. 243, and 24 Sup. Ct. 843. See also MacDonald's statement in the *Spokesman-Review,* November 18, 1901. F. L. Clark and Patrick Clark were not related. In a transcript of F. L. Clark's testimony on January 7, 1902 (Asarco), it is said Culbertson paid five hundred dollars for his share of the Ella.

25. Clark's complaint quoted in *Spokesman-Review,* June 12, 1901.

26. In records of the First National Bank of Spokane (NA). That all the maneuvering did not take place in courtrooms is evident from Miller's letter to Heyburn, August 27, 1899, in the Heyburn papers (UI), reporting that the Bunker Hill laid track at night between the Stemwinder and the Tyler, and that Miller thereupon re-laid an old rail line to the Last Chance No. 2 dump to block the Bunker Hill "and sent a man up to prevent them from crossing our dump."

27. Cases involving Sweeny and the Bunker Hill discussed in this chapter can be found in: 108 Fed. 189; 109 Fed. 538; 114 Fed. 417; 131 Fed. 579; and 131 Fed. 591.

28. Miller to Sweeny, January 25, 1901 (Asarco).

29. 131 Fed. 591. This was in 1904 when Frank Post had succeeded

Heyburn as Sweeny's principal attorney. In appellate court, however, Post was assisted by George Turner and Heyburn.

30. 108 Fed. 189.

31. Roberts to Sweeny, June 5, 1901 (Asarco). Heyburn chose this moment of apparent victory to renew his threats to quit Sweeny unless his ten-thousand-dollar annual retainer was increased substantially.

32. Sweeny to Burbidge, July 20, 1901 (Asarco).

33. Heyburn to Empire State–Idaho, August 29, 1901 (Asarco).

34. Easton affidavit, July 30, 1903, Bunker Hill and Sullivan v. Last Chance, Idaho district court, p. 232 (Asarco). T. A. Rickard, *The Bunker Hill Enterprise,* p. 80, sees these suits as a Guggenheim plot. The author has not been able to verify a connection between Sweeny and the Guggenheims before 1903, but the apex litigation had begun some years earlier.

35. Personal interview with Roberts.

36. Lindley, *American Law Relating to Mines,* II, 1411.

37. Miller to Sweeny, October 21, 1908 (Asarco).

38. See Robert N. Bell, *Nineteenth Annual Report of the Idaho Inspector of Mines,* p. 26. According to the *Spokane Daily Chronicle,* October 3, 1907, the Last Chance tailings were reworked during 1908 by contract to the Shoshone Concentrating Company, which built a three-hundred-ton mill. The company's directors were M. C. Murphy, Julius Zittel, and William A. Bradley, all of Spokane.

## IX. MERGING THE MINES

1. Mrs. H. L. Day to Eleanor Boyce, July 16, 1901, in the Day files. For a general discussion of the Coeur d'Alenes in 1902, see J. R. Finlay, "Mining Industry of the Coeur d'Alenes, Idaho," *Transactions of the American Institute of Mining Engineers,* XXXIII (1903), 235–51. Finlay begins: "The Coeur d'Alene silver-lead mining district . . . is probably best-known to the general public as a seat of labor troubles. . . . Little has been written and little is known about its geology and resources."

Statistical information can be found in Walter Renton Ingalls, *Lead and Zinc in the United States.* The New York Public Library has a run of the annual reports of the Federal Mining and Smelting Company from 1918–48, with some gaps; its earlier holdings, 1906–16, are "missing." Asarco's files appear to contain the Federal's reports from 1903 until its dissolution, although these are not collected in one shelf.

The direction of this chapter was influenced chiefly by interviews with Edward Roberts and Walter Nichols, and the deposition of Charles Sweeny, December 19, 1913, in the case of Sidney Norman et al., v. Federal Mining and Smelting Co. et al., before the New York Supreme Court (Asarco).

A valuable guide is William J. Hall's typewritten "Organization and History of the Federal Mining and Smelting Company," dated May 1, 1913, in file Z 11–2 (Asarco), a chronology of acquisition and disposition of mining properties by Federal, prepared in memorandum form for the company's officers.

2. Sweeny deposition, Norman v. Federal, p. 9.

3. For a general discussion of the trust's position in lead smelting, see T. A. Rickard, *History of American Mining*, pp. 126–27.

4. Sweeny deposition, Norman v. Federal, p. 14. The possibility of legal action to secure accurate price quotations is raised in a letter from F. Lewis Clark to Heyburn, January 11, 1897, in the Heyburn papers (UI), which reads in full: "I submit herewith some correspondence on the subject of Western Union quotations. Mr. Happy has already read them over. While it is probably true the smelters take somewhat into consideration the fact that they can manipulate the price quoted in New York, yet during the last two weeks the difference between the real price and the so called 'brokers' price of lead has been excessive and if we admit their right to have a fictitious price sent out I cannot see what is going to limit the difference between the real price and the quotation, other than their own sweet will. Mr. Sweeny is about to go East again. If you think it worth while to go to law about this it would be [a] desirable and opportune time for Mr. Sweeny to get evidence in New York. As we produced seven thousand tons in 1896, the difference of ten cents per hundred weight would amount to a very considerable sum."

5. Ingalls, *Lead and Zinc*, pp. 203, 205.

6. Finlay, "Mining Industry of the Coeur d'Alenes," p. 235.

7. Empire State–Idaho minutes containing this notice are in Asarco files at Wallace Mills.

8. Empire State–Idaho minutes (Asarco). Of this contract, Sweeny said in his deposition, Norman v. Federal, pp. 13–15, that "all companies in the Coeur d'Alenes that were doing business with the American company— that was about all, I do not know of any other smelting company that was doing any business with the Coeur d'Alenes in those days . . .—agreed that in consideration of the stability of price [that] might be arranged by the American Smelting company handling all of the product [they would sign the contract]." The Bunker Hill and Hercules did not join the seven-companies contract. Sweeny agreed with a cross examiner (p. 16) that "the seven companies contract is practically the Mine Owners Association contract." E. J. Roberts was incensed by Hyman's later successful demand for a royalty of thirty cents a ton for arranging the contract (Roberts to Packard, November 6, 1902 Asarco). Hyman had represented the Mine Owners Association in its bargaining with American before this meeting.

A letter from A. B. Campbell to Hyman, March 6, 1902, asks Hyman on behalf of the MOA "to ascertain the view of Asarco about its sales and exports with a view to a new contract for smelting." The letter is in the Campbell letterbook for 1901–2 in the collection of the Eastern Washington State Historical Society, Spokane.

9. It should be noted that, apparently unknown to Sweeny, Fred Burbidge and Fred Bradley were attempting to arrange a consolidation of Coeur d'Alenes mines in the interest of American Smelting and Refining Company. Their activities are mentioned in three letters from F. H. Brownell to Burbidge, April 18, May 1, and May 18, 1916, extracted in a memorandum in Asarco files. A letter, Bradley to Albert Burch, November 17, 1902 (Asarco), mentions that Hyman and Burbidge are working for Asarco to line up a consolidation to be called Federal. Asarco dropped out of this plan, as the text will observe. It is obvious from these reports why many persons concluded Sweeny, too, must be working for Asarco.

The efficacy of merger was generally accepted among owners, as demonstrated in a letter from A. B. Campbell to P. J. Hennessey of Chicago, January 20, 1902, referring to an unspecified proposition: "I am satisfied . . . that the Mine Owners Association would never get together on any proposition of this kind. The only way in which anything could be brought about would be first to consolidate all the properties in the Coeur d'Alene country" (Campbell letterbook, Eastern Washington State Historical Society).

10. Roberts joined Sweeny on February 22, 1901, according to an announcement to employees by Sweeny (Asarco), but he had been looking over the Sweeny properties for some time before this, trying to decide whether to accept Sweeny's overtures to come to work for the Empire State–Idaho. His own role in Sweeny's plan to merge the mines was described to me in interviews in 1948. Roberts' activities as a railway builder, before and after his services with Sweeny, are described in John Fahey, *Inland Empire: D. C. Corbin and Spokane.* Roberts' general attitude toward Sweeny seemed cautious, and he apparently did not join in Sweeny's promotions. Roberts' estimate of their relationship was that he followed orders as an employee but was not a confidant.

11. Sweeny to Roberts, December 3, 1901 (Roberts). Roberts' report as general manager to the Empire State–Idaho directors, April 30, 1903 (Asarco), affirms that he produced the dividends Sweeny demanded.

12. Sweeny's encounter with Gates was told to me in substantially the same detail in separate interviews with the late Walter Nichols in 1952 and E. J. Roberts in 1948. Both obviously had heard the story from Sweeny himself. Gates's son, Russell, checked his father's manuscript autobiography without finding references to the Coeur d'Alenes, Sweeny, or Federal (personal communication, April 4, 1962). According to Joseph W.

Ernst, archivist, Rockefeller Brothers (personal communication, April 25, 1962), "The correspondence files of John D. Rockefeller relating to the Federal Mining and Smelting Company have been destroyed."

13. Information about the smelter in 1892–93 was supplied by Mrs. Edith Jennings, reference librarian, Everett Public library, who checked newspaper files and local histories.

14. Information about Rockefeller was drawn generally from: Allan Nevins, *Study in Power, John D. Rockefeller, Industrialist and Philanthropist*, II, 204–9; Raymond B. Fosdick, *John D. Rockefeller, Jr., A Portrait*, p. 86; John D. Rockefeller, *Random Reminiscences of Men and Events*, pp. 115–19; and *Mines and Minerals*, XXI (1900), 69.

15. Charles R. Stark, "Hercules and the Day Family," *Pacific Northwesterner* (Spokane), IV (Winter, 1960), 4.

16. Sweeny to Roberts, May 19, 1901 (Roberts).

17. In First National Bank records (NA).

18. In Roberts letterbooks.

19. From *Northwest Mining News*, April 13, 1940, in files of the Northwest Mining Association, Spokane. A great deal of the Bunker Hill's trouble resulted from its containment in unprofitable ground by Sweeny's attorneys. This is clearly stated in an affidavit filed by Stanly Easton on July 30, 1903, before the Idaho district court (Asarco) and an affidavit by F. W. Bradley, August 8, 1903, to the same court (Asarco) in the case of the Last Chance v. Bunker Hill and Sullivan. It should be recalled that Sweeny blocked exploration via the Kellogg Tunnel for approximately four years.

20. Personal interview with Roberts.

21. Charles R. Stark, *Stanly A. Easton, Eighty-Four Years in Mining* (privately printed, 1956), p. 14.

22. In Roberts letterbooks.

23. Roberts to Sweeny, February 2, 1901 (Roberts). Harry Day asserted, in a letter to A. J. Ralston, president of the Selby smelting company, March 28, 1904, that Hammond "has thrown all his influence in the Bunker Hill company . . . to effect a sale of the property to his present employers [Guggenheims], or to Mr. Sweeny as a second choice." Thus Miller's report appears to have reached Hammond.

24. Bernard M. Baruch, *My Own Story*, pp. 196–99, and a letter, Roberts to Sweeny, January 29, 1903 (Roberts), in which Roberts reports his conversation on the train with Rust. The letter contains detailed estimates of the Tacoma smelter's production, to demonstrate to Sweeny that "if you should buy the Bunker Hill and Sullivan mine without assuming the contract with the Tacoma smelter, it would be badly crippled until it could get another contract." Rust told Roberts that Darius O. Mills had telegraphed the information to him that the Bunker Hill had given its option

to prospective buyers who also offered $500,000 for the Tacoma smelter. Rust said he answered Mills opposing sale of the smelter because, although it had been losing money, its contracts now promised a profit.

25. Hall, "Federal Mining and Smelting Company," details options on lesser properties, which, he says, lapsed. The Kerns and Olympia groups were in litigation, prompting Federal to drop its option several years after it was taken.

26. Ibid. The fact that Burbidge and Hyman, who openly represented the Guggenheims, had proposed calling a consolidation of the Coeur d'Alene mining the "Federal company" suggests strongly that the Rockefeller and Guggenheim interests were conferring at a level higher than Sweeny. Subsequent events indicate that the Rockefellers simply organized the company for the profit they would make in selling it to the Guggenheims, as the text will observe.

27. Memorandum of Federal Mining and Smelting Company property purchases and stock issue, Federal voucher 67, September 1, 1903 (Asarco), and *Spokesman-Review*, August 20, 25, and 26, 1903.

28. Sweeny's holdings are listed in the memorandum cited in note 27 above. E. J. Barney also invested in Spokane business property.

## X. SWEENY AS PRESIDENT OF FEDERAL

1. *Overland*, LII(1908), 407–18. This chapter is based in part on the deposition of Charles Sweeny, December 19, 1913, in the case of Sidney Norman et al. v. Federal Mining and Smelting Co. et al., before the New York supreme court (Asarco); on the memorandum by William J. Hall, "Organization and History of the Federal Mining and Smelting Company," May 1, 1913, file Z 11–2 (Asarco); and on contemporary accounts in *Engineering and Mining Journal* and the *Spokesman-Review*. R. Worth Vaughan, vice chairman of the board, American Smelting and Refining Company, provided extracts from the minutebooks of Federal in the New York offices of the company.

2. Sweeny deposition, Norman v. Federal, p. 34.

3. Roberts to Sweeny, December 4, 1903 (Asarco).

4. See *Engineering and Mining Journal*, LXXVI (1903), 865, and LXXVII (1904), 147. Sweeny's correspondence does not verify these reports, but the correspondence files are incomplete.

5. Sweeny to Roberts, January 22, 1902 (Roberts).

6. Sweeny deposition, Norman v. Federal, and a report by George D. Potter, Spokane, December 12, 1902, of a "careful but somewhat hasty examination" of all mining camps near Spokane for a supply of dry ore and fluxes (Asarco). Sweeny apparently made his decision on the basis of this report.

7. Sweeny deposition, Norman v. Federal, pp. 19–20.

8. Ibid.

9. Based on Hall, "Federal Mining and Smelting Company."

10. Roberts to R. W. Phelps, Rochester, Minnesota, April 13, 1904 (Roberts).

11. The market quotations were taken from the *New York Times* for the dates mentioned.

12. Bernard M. Baruch, *My Own Story*, pp. 196–99. Baruch confuses the Everett and Tacoma smelters in his account. The negotiations he describes occurred during purchase of the Tacoma plant.

13. *Spokesman-Review*, March 29, 1905.

14. Roberts to Sweeny, September 27, 1904 (Roberts).

15. Sweeny to Roberts, March 7, 1905 (Roberts). For a brief exposition of F. Augustus Heinze's relationship to Amalgamated, a holding company, see Ernest F. Richter, "Amalgamated Copper Company: A Closed Chapter in Corporation Finance," *Quarterly Journal of Economics*, XXX (1915–16), 387–407. No evidence has been found, other than the letter quoted, that Sweeny was considered for Amalgamated's presidency.

16. Sweeny deposition, Norman v. Federal, p. 20. Apparent agreement between Federal and the Guggenheims had become obvious to a number of watchful mine operators. The attorney and mine owner, John H. Wourms, wrote Harry L. Day on March 23, 1905, that he had been following the stock manipulation of Federal and believed "the Trust and Federal have come to the conclusion that it would be better for them to join hands and hold up the dear public than go into a battle which must necessarily be very wasteful to both." The news of Federal's purchase was not yet general knowledge.

17. Details of the transfer to Daniel Guggenheim are recounted by R. Worth Vaughan, (personal communication, July 10, 1962), quoting Federal minute books; in the Sweeny deposition, Norman v. Federal, pp. 3–4; and in Isaac F. Marcosson, *Metal Magic*, pp. 77–78.

18. Quoted in 167 N.Y. Supp. 795.

19. *Spokesman-Review*, May 12, 1905. Sweeny says in his deposition that he sold 8,450 shares of common at $120, which is the figure given in the Federal minutes for March 20, 1905.

20. 167 N.Y. Supp. 795. The Asarco files contain a copy of a lengthy argument by William J. Hall supporting a long smelting contract, apparently prepared for guidance of the attorneys in this trial.

21. In Asarco files.

22. In Asarco files. That Sweeny had been exerting competitive pressure on the Hecla for some time is evident in a letter from A. B. Campbell to W. G. Pearce, second vice-president of the Northern Pacific Railroad, July 11, 1901, in which Campbell asks whether the railroad will cooperate

in constructing a line to the Hecla. Campbell writes: "Sweeny would not give us right of way, so that we have been tied up and are at an expense of over $300 every month, at the Hecla mine, in getting coal up to our boilers and timber" (Campbell letterbook, Eastern Washington State Historical Society). Denial of access was a favorite Sweeny ploy, as demonstrated by his relations with the Hercules mine (see note 26 following) and the Bunker Hill.

23. Sweeny deposition, Norman v. Federal, pp. 65–66; Federal minutes for July 20, October 16, and October 21, 1905; 167 N.Y. Supp. 795. A story was told in the Coeur d'Alenes that Sweeny got five hundred thousand dollars as his commission.

24. Applications, on a form supplied by the Exchange, in Asarco files.

25. There were a number of lesser claims involved in the purchase. A letter, Miller to Sweeny, May 26, 1905 (Asarco), describes an inspection of the Morning by Miller and Roberts, indicating that good ore could be expected at the 1,800-foot level and lower, and detailing the condition of the Morning and the You Like. The letter remarks that "the boarding house shows a profit on full operation of the mine of about $2,500 per month," and suggests that $35,000 profit a month is possible from the mines with efficient operation. The purchase, observes Miller, "will make Federal dominant in the Mullan camp." Located in 1887, the Morning had been purchased from its discoverers for $12,600 by Charles Hussey, a banker, and his partner, Charles L. Dahler, Helena, Montana, and Salt Lake City. After two years of development, when the Morning had risen in value to $70,000, Hussey added nearby claims, including the Evening, and bought out Dahler. In 1890 Hussey's banks in Spokane and Idaho failed, and several attempted negotiations to liquidate his mining properties proved fruitless. One offer was reputed to approach $900,000. A Milwaukee, Wisconsin, syndicate eventually bought the Morning group, enabling Hussey to satisfy most of his banks' creditors, but in August, 1897, the Wisconsin combine, discouraged by persisting low lead prices, sold the Morning and its associated claims to the lessors, Larson and Greenough.

26. Letter, June 12, 1905, lent by Charles R. Stark. This was the same Borah who later won world attention as a champion of disarmament while serving as U.S. Senator from Idaho.

27. Walter Renton Ingalls, "Lead," *Engineering and Mining Journal,* LXXXV (1908), 12, discusses the relationship of silver to lead content in ores produced by Federal and other Coeur d'Alene mining companies. It should be noted that the mining companies openly fought a proposed eight-hour day for laborers in Idaho.

28. Miller to Burbidge, December 13, 1908 (Asarco). Under Sweeny's management, no sinking fund was established.

29. See Ingalls, "Lead." *Engineering and Mining Journal,* LXXXV (July 18, 1908), 140, compares the profits of Coeur d'Alene companies for 1906–7. *Mines Handbook* (1918), p. 765, lists Federal dividends during 1903–14. The *Spokesman-Review* published the annual statements of net income filed with the Shoshone County auditor. In addition, Asarco files contain the following: a printed listing of lead and silver prices at New York from 1893 through 1913; a statement of Federal stock issued and dividends paid, 1904–13, for each year ending August 31; a statement of lead and silver product of Federal, 1904–13; and a statement of average metal content of lead and silver product and the average prices received, 1904–13.

30. Sweeny deposition, Norman v. Federal, p. 62.

31. Miller to Sweeny, March 31, 1908 (Asarco).

32. 147 Fed. 981.

33. October 26, 1907, p. 803.

34. *Engineering and Mining Journal,* LXXXV (November 21, 1908), 1024.

35. Ibid., LXXXVI (January 9, 1909), 63, 115, ascribes the closing of the Tiger-Poorman (and the declining profits of other companies) to a "lack of market" and the low price for lead.

36. Federal minutes, January 29, 1909.

37. Compiled from Federal's annual reports, and from a statement of Federal stock issued and dividends paid, 1904–13 (Asarco).

38. The valuations are those given by Hall, "Federal Mining and Smelting Company."

39. Annual report, Federal Mining and Smelting Company, 1910 (Asarco).

40. Table of earnings by years, annual report, Federal Mining and Smelting Company, 1947, p. 13.

41. 167 N.Y. Supp. 795.

## XI. LAST DAYS

1. On the discovery and history of the Sullivan Group, see Walter C. Burchett's story by A. C. White in the *Spokesman-Review,* May 13, 20, and 27, 1928. The Sullivan Group story is too complex to be discussed at length in the text. The function of this chapter, as denouement, precludes referring to a single background source.

2. The Sullivan Group organization can be found in Spokane County articles of incorporation, book D, 338. These articles are amended by Spokane County articles of incorporation 56338, recording an increase of capital stock at the same time as the bond issue. A stock bonus was given

as an incentive to buy the bond issue, according to two letters from Roberts to Sweeny, both dated December 8, 1903 (Roberts).

3. *Spokesman-Review,* July 19, August 17, and September 28, 1902. Apparently Sweeny paid personally for materials to reconstruct this smelter. The Spokane and Eastern Trust financial committee log book shows that on November 15, 1904, Clendening asked the Trust to advance Sweeny "personally and temporarily the sum necessary to finish paying for brick blocks bought by him in the sum of $175,000 with no security." The request was disapproved. (Trust records in Washington State University archives.)

4. Miller's undated report, circa November, 1903 (Asarco), estimates that $532,000 would settle the company's obligations, and predicts a profit in sight of $1,800,000. Roberts, in one of his letters to Sweeny, December 8, 1903 (Roberts), remarks that "this proposition seems to me to be a most attractive one as the tonnage said to be in sight is so much greater than any developed mine in this country. . . . It would be well for us to investigate this property and take it up ourselves rather than let a mine which can produce such a quantity of lead fall into the hands of the A.S. & R." It appears that both Miller and Roberts based their appraisals of the Sullivan Group at this time on what Turner had told them. Gates's opposition is recounted in a letter, Packard to Roberts, May 26, 1904 (Asarco).

5. Based on a personal interview with Roberts. See also the *Report of the Minister of Mines, 1909,* British Columbia, pp. K95–96.

Although Sweeny opposed Federal's abandonment of the Sullivan Group, he divested himself of his personal interest in mid-1907, when he was reported to have sold 250,000 shares to Mose Oppenheimer. No evidence of this transaction was found in the company's records, but Oppenheimer's purchase appears to be connected with George Turner's attempt to regain control of the Sullivan. The *Spokane Daily Chronicle,* June 22, 1907, reports that Finucane resigned as treasurer, and Clendening as a director of the Sullivan, demonstrating that Sweeny had withdrawn. The newspaper also observes that Sweeny had recently been hypothecating his Portland real estate. Probably Sweeny was trying to raise money for stock-market purchases. He is known to have invested heavily during a market revival that followed a minor recession in March, as the text will show.

6. A bitter letter, Sweeny to Miller, July 21, 1908 (Asarco), says, in part, "Turner should not have allowed the Federal money to go in until the titles were right." Turner had forgotten to turn in stock in the original company when Sweeny formed a new one, and Sweeny regarded this oversight as an unnecessary complication if not a double-cross. A letter, E. L. Nash to Brownell, March 26, 1909 (Asarco), details the decision of Federal to jettison the Sullivan Group.

7. Brownell to Edward Brush, vice president of Asarco, June 20, 1909 (Asarco). See also *Cranbrook Herald*, June 3 and July 22, 1919.

8. Perhaps best related in R. W. Diamond, *A Detailed Account of the Development of the Treatment by Flotation of the Ore of the Sullivan Mine, Kimberley, B.C., 1917–1923*, pp. 7–27. F. M. Ethridge, superviser of libraries for Cominco, called this account and others to my attention. See also *Cominco Story*, pp. 4–5.

9. Information supplied by the New York Steamship Historical Society.

10. For an informal history of the house, see *Spokesman-Review*, December 2, 1956. It still stands as offices and meeting hall of the Unitarian Church of Spokane at West 321 Eighth Avenue.

11. Spokane County deeds, book 155, p. 160. Deed to adjoining property, Spokane County, book 156, p. 57. See *Spokane Daily Chronicle*, July 30, 1904.

12. Although the Sweenys moved from Spokane, they paid their pew rent (on pew E-9) at Our Lady of Lourdes cathedral through the first nine months of 1909, according to the parish ledgers. Sweeny rented seats only for Emeline and himself, unlike Patrick Clark, who rented eight seats for his whole family.

13. Sweeny deposition, December 29, 1913, in the case of Sidney Norman et al. v. Federal Mining and Smelting et al., pp. 47–48 (Asarco). Walter Nichols (personal interview) said that Sweeny had related to him the story about Rockefeller's warning. Nichols believed that after the crash, Sweeny mortgaged the Rookery Building in Spokane, but no record appears of such a mortgage.

14. *Spokesman-Review*, December 31, 1909.

15. Annual reports of the Globe Exploration Company, filed in Dover, Delaware. The company filed application for Consent to Dissolution on April 15, 1916.

16. Information supplied by the New York Steamship Historical Society. According to the U.S. Treasury Department, this vessel was sold in 1913 to Robert Graves of New York, who sold it in 1918 to the U.S. Navy for ninety thousand dollars.

17. The trust agreement is among the papers held by the Sweeny Investment Company. The records of the company speak, from this time, of property held separately by Emeline, including "a large sum, realized for the sale of Empire State stock and Federal Mining Company stock [sic] which was owned by her," mentioned in a letter from Charles Sweeny to the secretary, Sweeny Investment Company, January 12, 1906 (Sweeny). No matter what the record showed the stock distribution to be, the company's resources apparently were at Sweeny's personal disposal. The investment company files show that between 1907 and 1911, Sweeny borrowed in varying amounts at various times a total of $2,500,000 from the com-

pany. The largest borrowing was $360,000 in 1911. The company's records do not disclose the purposes for which these funds were used or indicate whether the money was repaid. My interpretation of these facts is that Sweeny legally transferred his assets to Emeline long before his death, and then continued to use their money as his own.

18. Records of Fairmont Cemetery, Spokane, showing removal of remains from other cemeteries to the Sweeny crypt. After the death of their daughter, Emeline, the Sweenys gave the name to another daughter.

19. See Spokane County civil cases 92,976 and 99,973. Packard's will, probated in Somerset County, New Jersey, includes a sworn statement on his stocks by his executor.

20. Rev. Charles Mackin, S.J., "Wanderings," (Manuscript memoirs, Gonzaga University, n.d.), II, 27. Called to my attention by Father Wilfred Schoenberg, S.J.

21. *Spokesman-Review,* October 20, 1940. A search of the records of the dioceses of Spokane and Seattle did not uncover statements of Sweeny's gifts to Catholic parishes or organizations.

22. These transactions are detailed in the accounts of Raymond, Pynchon and Company filed with Sweeny's will in Multnomah County, Oregon, probate 13,603.

23. Emeline's will, Spokane County probate 12,990. Her will and taxes are summarized in a letter and its attachment from Gearin to Frank Sweeny, November 18, 1919 (Sweeny), and in a letter from Gearin to the Commissioner of Internal Revenue, February 28, 1920 (Sweeny).

# BIBLIOGRAPHY

*T*HIS listing includes published and unpublished material that has a bearing on Charles Sweeny and his times. It has not been swelled by background reading, general reference works, directories, manuals, state guides, or the reports of public and private agencies. Relevant collections of personal or company papers have been described briefly in the explanation of the notes.

## BOOKS

*An Analysis of the Position, History and Outlook of the Bunker Hill and Sullivan Mining Company.* San Francisco: Leib, Keyston and Co., 1936.

Bailey, Robert G. *River of No Return.* Lewiston, Idaho: R. G. Bailey Printing Co., 1935–47.

Bancroft, Hubert Howe. *California, 1860–1890.* (Vol. XXIV of *Works*) San Francisco: The History Co., 1890.

———. *History of Washington, Idaho, and Montana, 1845–1889.* (Vol. XXXI of *Works*) San Francisco: The History Co., 1890.

Baruch, Bernard. *My Own Story.* New York: Henry Holt and Co., 1957.

Beal, Merrill D., and Merle W. Wells. *History of Idaho.* 3 vols. New York: Lewis Historical Publishing Co., 1959.

Boughton, Jennie. *Spokane from Memory*. Spokane: Privately printed, 1941.

Brissenden, Paul Frederick. *The I.W.W.: A Study of American Syndicalism.* New York: Columbia University, 1920.

Burt, William P. (ed.). *Fifty Years of Progress.* (A special edition of the *Wallace Miner.*) Wallace, Idaho: Miner Publishing Co., 1937.

272

Carey, Charles Henry. *History of Oregon.* Chicago: Pioneer Historical Publishing Co., 1922.

Cloman, Flora. *I'd Live It Over.* New York: Farrar and Rinehart, 1941.

*Cominco Story.* Trail, B.C.: Consolidated Mining and Smelting Co. of Canada, *circa* 1960.

Crosby, Edward J. *Story of the Washington Water Power Company.* Spokane: Washington Water Power Co., 1931.

DeQuille, Dan. *See* Wright, William.

Diamond, R. W. *Detailed Account of the Development of the Treatment by Flotation of the Ore of the Sullivan Mine, Kimberley, B.C., 1917–1923.* Trail, B.C.: Hall Printing Co., 1961.

Durham, Nelson W. *Spokane and the Inland Empire.* 3 vols. Chicago: S. J. Clarke Publishing Co., 1912.

Edwards, Rev. Jonathan. *Illustrated History of Spokane County.* Spokane: W. H. Lever, 1900.

Elsensohn, Sister M. Alfreda, O.S.B. *Pioneer Days in Idaho County.* 2 vols. Caldwell, Idaho: Caxton Printers, 1947.

Fahey, John. *Inland Empire: D. C. Corbin and Spokane.* Seattle: University of Washington Press, 1965.

Foner, Philip S. *History of the Labor Movement in the United States.* 3 vols. New York: International Publishers Co., 1955.

Fosdick, Raymond B. *John D. Rockefeller, Jr., A Portrait.* New York: Harper and Brothers, 1956.

Fuller, George W. *History of the Pacific Northwest.* New York: Alfred A. Knopf, 1931.

————. *Inland Empire.* 4 vols. Spokane and Denver: H. G. Linderman, 1928.

Glover, James N. *History of Spokane.* Spokane: *Spokane Daily Chronicle,* 1917. Newspaper recollections gathered into book form.

Greenough, W. Earl. *Coeur d'Alene Mining Region, 1849–1946.* Mullan, Idaho: W. Earl Greenough, 1947.

Hammond, John Hays. *Autobiography.* 2 vols. New York: Farrar and Rinehart, 1935.

Harper, Franklin (ed.). *Who's Who on the Pacific Coast.* Los Angeles: Harper Publishing Co., 1913.

Harriman, Job. *Class War in Idaho.* New York: Volks-Zeitung Library, 1900.

Hines, Rev. H. K. *Illustrated History of the State of Washington.* Chicago: Lewis Publishing Co., 1893.

Hook, Harry H., and Francis J. McGuire. *History of the Early Settlement and the Spokane Falls of Today.* Minneapolis: Frank L. Thresher Co., 1889.

Hutton, May Arkwright. *Coeur d'Alenes.* Denver: Privately printed, 1900.

Ingalls, Walter Renton. *Lead and Zinc in the United States.* New York: Hill Publishing Co., 1908.

Innis, Harold A. *Settlement and the Mining Frontier.* Toronto: Macmillan Co. of Canada, 1936.

Jellum, S. P. *Some Central Idaho Gold Districts.* Spokane: *Northwest Mining News,* 1909.

Lindley, Curtis H. *A Treatise on the American Law Relating to Mines and Mineral Lands.* (3rd ed.) 3 vols. San Francisco: Bancroft-Whitney Co., 1914.

Maddux, Percy. *City on the Willamette: the Story of Portland, Oregon.* Portland: Binfords and Mort, 1952.

Magnuson, Richard G. *Coeur d'Alene Diary.* Portland: Metropolitan Press, 1968.

Marcosson, Isaac F. *Metal Magic.* New York: Farrar, Straus and Co., 1949.

Nevins, Allan. *Study in Power: John D. Rockefeller, Industrialist and Philanthropist.* 2 vols. New York: Charles Scribner's Sons, 1953.

O'Connor, Harvey. *Guggenheims.* New York: Covici-Friede, 1937.

Onderdonk, James L. *Idaho.* San Francisco: A. L. Bancroft and Co., 1885.

*Oregonian's Handbook of the Pacific Northwest.* Portland: *Oregonian* Publishing Co., 1894.

*Oregonian Souvenier.* Portland: Lewis and Dryden Printing Co., 1892.

Paul, Rodman W. *Mining Frontiers of the Far West, 1848–1880.* New York: Holt, Rinehart and Winston, 1963.

Reavis, John R. *City of Spokane.* Spokane: Clough and Graves, 1891.

Rickard, T. A. *The Bunker Hill Enterprise.* San Francisco: Mining and Scientific Press, 1921.

——. *History of American Mining.* New York: McGraw-Hill Book Co., 1932.

Rockefeller, John D. *Random Reminiscences of Men and Events.* New York: Doubleday, Doran and Co., 1933.

*Rossland . . . A Residential City.* Rossland, B.C.: Board of Trade, 1951.

Ruffner, W. H. *Report on Washington Territory.* New York: Seattle, Lake Shore and Eastern Railway, 1889.

Sanders, Wilbur E. (ed.). *Mine Timbering.* New York: Hill Publishing Co., 1907.

Schoenberg, Rev. Wilfred P., S.J. *Chronicle of Catholic History of the Pacific Northwest, 1743–1960.* Spokane: Gonzaga Preparatory School, 1962.

Shiach, William S., John M. Henderson, and Harry B. Averill. *Illustrated History of North Idaho.* Chicago: Western Historical Publishing Co., 1903.

Siringo, Charles A. *Cowboy Detective.* Chicago: W. B. Conkey Co., 1912.

————. *Riata and Spurs*. Boston and New York: Houghton Mifflin Co., 1927.

Smith, Grant H. *History of the Comstock Lode, 1850–1920*. Reno: University of Nevada, 1943.

Smith, Robert Wayne. *Coeur d'Alene Mining War of 1892*. Corvallis, Ore.: Oregon State College, 1961.

Smyth, Fred J. *Tales of the Kootenays*. Cranbrook, B. C.: *The Courier*, 1942.

Stark, Charles R. *Stanly A. Easton, 84 Years in Mining*. Spokane: Privately printed, 1956.

Stoll, William T., as told to H. W. Whicker. *Silver Strike*. Boston: Little, Brown and Co., 1932.

Storms, William H. *Timbering and Mining*. New York: McGraw-Hill Book Co., 1909.

Taft, Philip. *A.F. of L. in the Time of Gompers*. New York: Harper and Brothers, 1957.

Wardner, James F. *Jim Wardner of Wardner, Idaho*. New York: Anglo-American Publishing Co., 1900.

*War of the Rebellion*. 70 vols. (Series I, Vols. I–LIII, reports of operations.) Washington, D.C.: Government Printing Office, 1880–1902.

*Washington Water Power Company*. New York: American Bank Note Co., 1910.

Wheeler, Olin D. *Wonderland '99: Description of the Region Tributary to the Northern Pacific Railway*. St. Paul: Northern Pacific Railway, 1899.

Whitfield, William (ed.). *History of Snohomish County*. Chicago: Pioneer Historical Publishing Co., 1926.

Whittaker, Lance H. *Rossland, the Golden City*. Rossland, B.C.: Rossland Miner, 1949.

Wood, Fremont. *Introductory Chapter to the History of the Trials of Moyer, Haywood, and Pettibone, and Harry Orchard*. Caldwell, Idaho: Caxton Printers, 1931.

Wright, William [Dan DeQuille]. *History of the Big Bonanza*. Hartford, Conn.: American Publishing Co., 1877.


ARTICLES AND MANUSCRIPTS

Affleck, Edward Lloyd. "Sternwheelers, Sandbars, and Switchbacks: A Chronicle of Steam Transportation in Southeastern British Columbia." Mimeographed. Vancouver, B.C., 1958.

Allison, Theodore Francis. "History of the Northwest Mining Unions through 1920." Master's thesis, Washington State University, 1943.

Baily, Joe. "The Dramatic Story of the Steunenberg Murder," *Spokesman-Review Magazine,* January 1, 1956.

Beckwith, Radcliffe H. "Quartz-veins of the Buffalo Hump," *The Pan-American Geologist,* XLVI (September, 1926), 111–20.

———. "Ore Deposition at the Buffalo Hump," *The Pan-American Geologist,* XLVIII (October, 1927), 191–95.

———. "Geology and Ore Deposits of the Buffalo Hump District," *Annals of the New York Academy of Science,* XXX (October, 1928), 263–96.

Church, John Spencer. "Mining Companies in the West Kootenay and Boundary Regions of British Columbia, 1890–1900: Capital Formation and Financial Operations." Master's thesis, University of British Columbia, 1961.

Cook, R. G. "Pioneer Portraits: Weldon Brinton Heyburn," *Idaho Yesterdays,* X (Spring, 1966), 22–26.

Cottingham, Mollie E. "History of the West Kootenay District in British Columbia." Master's thesis, University of British Columbia, 1947.

"Cominco, A Canadian Enterprise," *Canadian Mining Journal,* May, 1954, pp. 1–50.

Deutsch, Herman J. "Geographic Setting for the Recent History of the Inland Empire," *Pacific Northwest Quarterly,* XLIX (October, 1958), 150–61, and L (January, 1959), 14–25.

Doubleday, D. G. "Buffalo Hump, Idaho," *Mines and Minerals,* XXI (February, 1901), 296–98.

Dunnigan, Loretta. "History of Coeur d'Alene, Idaho, to 1910." Master's thesis, Gonzaga University, 1956.

Easton, Stanly A. "Coeur d'Alene in 1905," *Engineering and Mining Journal,* LXXXI (January, 1906), 11.

Fahey, John. "Coeur d'Alene Confederacy," *Idaho Yesterdays,* XII (1968), 2–7.

———. "Million Dollar Corner," *Pacific Northwest Quarterly,* Vol. LXII (April, 1971).

Finlay, J. R. "Mining Industry of the Coeur d'Alenes, Idaho," *Transactions of the American Institute of Mining Engineers,* XXXIII (1903), 235–71.

Fisken, John B. "Growth of the Washington Water Power Company." Unpublished manuscript, Washington Water Power Co., 1927.

———. "How Electricity Came to the Mines," *Northwest Mining Truth* (Spokane), May 18, 1925, p. 4.

Flagg, Arthur L. "Buffalo Hump Mining District, Idaho," *Mining and Engineering World,* XXXVIII (1913), 813–14.

Flucke, A. F. "History of Mining in British Columbia." Manuscript, British Columbia Provincial Archives, *circa* 1954.

Fowler, S. S. "Early Smelters in British Columbia," *British Columbia Historical Quarterly*, III (1939), 183–201.

French, George Edgar. "Coeur d'Alene Riots of 1892," *Overland Monthly*, XXVI (1895), 32–49.

Gates, Frederick T. "Man Who Gave Away Rockefeller's Millions," *American Heritage*, VI (1955), 65–86. Autobiographical excerpt with introduction and postscript by Allan Nevins.

Greene, Fred T. "Application of the Apex Law at Wardner, Idaho," *Transactions of the American Institute of Mining Engineers*, LII (1916), 555–62.

Howard, William W. "Spokane Falls and Its Exhibition," *Harper's Weekly*, XXXIV (1890), 689–706.

James, Edith. "Claims Law and Miners' Courts of the Montana Gold Camps." Master's thesis, University of Chicago, 1949.

Johnson, Claudius O. "George Turner of the Supreme Court of Washington Territory," *Oregon Historical Quarterly*, XLIV (1943), 370–85.

———. "George Turner, " *Pacific Northwest Quarterly*, XXXIV (1943), 243–71.

Jones, Fred O. "Valuation Study of the Mineral Resources of the Lands Ceded by the Coeur d'Alene Tribe of Indians on March 3, 1891." Manuscript, Spokane Public Library, 1956.

Livingston-Little, Dallas E. "Bunker Hill and Sullivan," *Idaho Yesterdays*, VII (1963), 34–43.

Lomax, Alfred L. "Pioneer Woolen Mills in Oregon," *Oregon Historical Quarterly*, XXX (1929), 238–58.

Lindgren, Waldemar. "Gold and Silver Veins of Silver City, De Lamar, and Other Mining Districts in Idaho," Twentieth Annual Report (1898–99), United States Geological Survey, Part 3, pp. 65–256.

Mackin, Rev. Charles, S.J. "Wanderings." Unpublished memoirs, 2 parts, Gonzaga University, n.d.

Malott, Conner. "From Grocer's Clerk to Millionaire Mining Man, Charles Sweeny's Career Reads Like a Fable," *Spokesman-Review*, July 23, 1916.

McCalla, C. S. "Post Falls Development of the Washington Water Power Company," *Electrical World*, May 23 and 30, 1908.

Oliphant, J. Orin (ed.). "Early History of Spokane, Washington, Told by Contemporaries." Typescript of newspaper interviews, Eastern Washington State College, 1927.

Philleo, A. M., and J. T. Freitag. "Cost Data, Post Falls Development, Post Falls, Idaho." Unpublished report, Washington Water Power Co., March 7, 1925.

Phipps, T. E. (comp.). "Report of the Chief Engineer to the Public Service Commission of Washington on the Appraisal of the Washington Water Power Company." 3 vols. Unpublished report, Washington Water Power Co., December 31, 1916.

Slade, Lou M. "Heyburn Has Sylvan Beauty," *Spokesman-Review Magazine,* July 22, 1962, p. 7.

Smith, Robert Wayne. "History of Placer and Quartz Gold Mining in the Coeur d'Alene District." Master's thesis, University of Idaho, 1932.

———. "Idaho Antecedents of the Western Federation of Miners, 1890 to 1893." Doctoral thesis, University of California, 1937. Published, with little revision, as *Coeur d'Alene Mining War of 1892.*

Stark, Charles R. "Hercules and the Day Family," *Pacific Northwesterner* (Spokane), Vol. IV, Winter, 1960.

Stearns, Clement. "General History of the Washington Water Power Company." Press information, Washington Water Power Co., 1949.

Thrupp, Sylvia L. "History of the Cranbrook District in East Kootenay." Master's thesis, University of British Columbia, 1929.

Turnbull, Elsie G. "Rossland Camp," *Pacific Northwesterner,* Vol. VI, Winter, 1962.

Whittle, C. H. "Buffalo Hump Mining Camp," *Engineering and Mining Journal,* LXVIII (1899), 215–16.

## OFFICIAL DOCUMENTS

Carlyle, William A. *Report on the Trail Creek Mining District.* Bulletin 2, Provincial Bureau of Mines, British Columbia, 1896.

Davenport, R. W. *Coeur d'Alene Lake, Idaho, and the Overflow Lands.* Water Supply Paper 500, United States Geological Survey, 1921.

Reed, John C. *Early and Recent Mining Activity in North Central Idaho.* Press Bulletin 18, University of Idaho, May, 1936.

Ross, Clyde P. *Graphic History of Metal Mining in Idaho.* Bulletin 821, United States Geological Survey, 1930.

Staley, W. W. *Elementary Methods of Placer Mining.* Pamphlet 35, Idaho Bureau of Mines and Geology, June, 1932.

———. *Gold in Idaho.* Pamphlet 68, Idaho Bureau of Mines and Geology, 1946.

Umpleby, Joseph B., and E. L. Jones, Jr. *Geology and Ore Deposits of Shoshone County, Idaho.* Bulletin 732, United States Geological Survey, 1923.

U.S. Congress, House Committee on Military Affairs. *Coeur d'Alene Labor Troubles.* House Report 1999 (1900), 56th Cong., 1st Sess.

———. *Report of the Industrial Commission on the Relations of Capital and Labor Employed in the Mining Industry.* House Document 181 (1901), 57th Cong., 1st Sess.

———. *Report of Brigadier General H. C. Merriam on Miners' Riots in the State of Idaho.* Senate Document 24 (1899), 56th Cong., 1st Sess. (Serial 3846).

———. *Edward Boyce, President, Western Federation of Miners: Crime of the Century.* Senate Document 25 (1899), 56th Cong., 1st Sess. (Serial 3846).

———. *Reply by John L. Kennedy, Member of the Industrial Commission Which Visited Idaho.* Senate Document 42 (1899), 56th Cong., 1st Sess. (Serial 3846). Kennedy's reply to Boyce's assertions in Senate Document 25.

*Washington Water Power Company, Statement A, Outline of Origin and Development.* Statement to the Federal Power Commission, May, 1937.


## NEWSPAPERS AND PERIODICALS

*Anaconda Standard* (Anaconda, Montana)
*Bonners Ferry Herald* (Bonners Ferry, Idaho)
*California Law Review*
*Canadian Mining Journal*
*Coeur d'Alene Miner* (Wallace, Idaho)
*Coeur d'Alene Nugget* (Eagle City, Idaho)
*Coeur d'Alene Sun* (Murray, Idaho)
*Cranbrook Herald* (Cranbrook, B.C.)
*Daily Alta California*
*Electrical World*
*Elmira Star-Gazette* (Elmira, N.Y.)
*Engineering and Mining Journal*
*Everett News* (Everett, Washington)
*Grangeville Standard* (Grangeville, Idaho)
*Idaho County Free Press* (Grangeville)
*Idaho Press* (Wallace)
*Idaho Sun* (Murray)
*Irish World* (New York)
*Iron Ore* (Ishpeming, Michigan)
*Kootenai Courier* (Rathdrum, Idaho)
*Kootenai Tribune* (Rathdrum, Idaho)
*Lewiston Evening Teller* (Lewiston, Idaho)
*Lewiston Tribune* (Lewiston, Idaho)
*Mining and Engineering World*
*Mullan Mirror* (Mullan, Idaho)

*New York Herald*
*New York Sun*
*New York Times*
*New York Daily Tribune*
*Northwest Mining Truth* (Spokane)
*Nelson News* (Nelson, B.C.)
*Oakland Daily News* (Oakland, Calif.)
*Oregonian* (Portland)
*Overland Monthly*
*Rossland Miner* (Rossland, B.C.)
*Rossland News* (Rossland, B.C.)
*San Francisco Daily Examiner*
*San Francisco Daily Morning Call*
*San Francisco Evening Bulletin*
*Spokane Daily Chronicle*
*Spokane Falls Review*
*Spokesman-Review* (Spokane)
*Tacoma Forum* (Tacoma, Washington)
*Territorial Enterprise* (Virginia City, Nevada)
*Toronto Globe*
*Transactions of the American Society of Mining Engineers*
*Wallace Free Press*
*Wallace Press*
*Wardner News* (Kellogg, Idaho)
*Weekly Eagle* (Eagle City, Idaho)
*Winston's Weekly* (Spokane)
*The World* (New York)

# INDEX